Studies of the New Testament and Its World

Edited by
JOHN BARCLAY
JOEL MARCUS
and
JOHN RICHES

'Into the Name of the Lord Jesus'
Baptism in the Early Church

Lars Hartman

T&T CLARK
EDINBURGH

T&T CLARK LTD
59 GEORGE STREET
EDINBURGH EH2 2LQ
SCOTLAND

First published 1997

ISBN 0 567 08589 9

British Library Cataloguing-in-Publication Data
A catalogue record for this book is available from the British Library

Typeset by Fakenham Photosetting Limited, Fakenham, Norfolk
Printed and bound in Great Britain by Bookcraft Ltd, Avon

Contents

Preface

This book has a prehistory, some features of which ought to be mentioned here. After producing a few articles on some problems and issues concerning baptism in the New Testament writings, I wrote a long, still unpublished article on the topic for *Aufstieg und Niedergang der römischen Welt*. The German version of the present book, *Auf den Namen des Herrn Jesus* (Stuttgarter Bibel-Studien 148, 1992) was based on this *ANRW* article, but was not simply a revision of it. Thus, as compared with the article, the book spent considerably more space on the exegesis of individual texts, whereas footnotes contained fewer references to the contributions of other exegetes. All in all, the book was about twice as long as the article.

The reader of this book, both the biblical scholar and the ordinary Bible reader, will often find that I have left aside several of the problems and aspects of the passages I have treated. But succinctness was necessary and I hope that the presentation is not too concise to be understandable by specialist and non-specialist alike.

I have abstained from discussing any consequences of the investigation to the baptismal thought and practice of the church. But as a member of an established church, a so-called *Volkskirche*, and also a professional exegete, I have found it useful once more to scrutinise the oldest traditions on the matter. In one way or another, they are still authoritative. I trust others may be of the same opinion as to the usefulness of an investigation such as this.

For the English version of this book, the German text has been revised. The revision also includes some new references in the footnotes, particularly to recent literature; this, however, has not been done in any systematic and thorough way. Furthermore, a new chapter has been added, viz. an article of mine on baptism in the *Didache* and the *Shepherd of Hermas*. It was published after the appearance of the German book and has now been modified so as to fit its new context.

Translations of passages from the Bible and other texts are my own, unless otherwise stated. Often, however, my translations from the Bible are inspired by the RSV.

Lars Hartman

Abbreviations

Pseudepigraphical and Early Patristic Books

1 En.	First (or Ethiopic) Enoch
2 Bar.	Second (or Syriac) Baruch
OTP	Old Testament Pseudepigrapha
Ps. Sol.	Psalms of Solomon
Test. Job	Testament of Job
Did.	Didache
Hermas, Mand.	Hermas, Mandate(s)
Hermas, Sim.	Hermas, Similitude(s)
Hermas, Vis.	Hermas, Vision(s)

Qumran Texts

CD	Damascus Document
1QM	War Scroll
1QS	Manual of Discipline
1Q22	Manuscript no 22 from cave 1

Rabbinic Works

b.	Babylonian Talmud
j.	Jerusalem Talmud
m.	Mishna
t.	Tosephta
Ab.	Abot
Ab.Z.	Aboda Zara
Eduy.	Eduyyot
Ḥul.	Ḥullin
Ker.	Keritot
Nid.	Niddah

Pes.	Pesaḥim
Sanh.	Sanhedrin
Shab.	Shabbat
Taan.	Ta'anit
Yeb.	Yebamot
Zeb.	Zebaḥim
Mekh. Exod.	Mekhilta to Exodus
S.Num	Siphre to Numbers

Introduction

1. An early text

About twenty-five years after the death of Jesus, Paul wrote to the Christians in Galatia:

> In Christ Jesus you are all sons of God, through faith, for as many of you as were baptised into Christ have put on Christ. There is neither Jew nor Greek, there is neither slave nor free, there is neither male nor female; for you are all one in Christ Jesus. But if you are Christ's, then you are Abraham's seed, heirs according to the promise. (Gal 3.26–29)

This is one of the oldest texts of the New Testament which deals with baptism.[1] Later on we shall study the passage in more detail, but here it can indicate various questions and perspectives which will recur in what follows.

First, the bare fact of the baptismal rite: Paul takes it for granted, and its existence seems somehow to be self-evident to him. Other New Testament authors regard the matter in the same way. But how does this rite compare with other rites, and how did the first Christians come to practise it?

Furthermore, Paul writes that the Galatians are baptised 'into (εἰς) Christ'. Modern readers may be so accustomed to biblical writers' somewhat odd use of prepositions (e.g. 'in the Spirit') that they are hardly confused by the phrase. But the secular meaning of the Greek word for 'baptise' (βαπτίζειν) is 'to dip', 'to plunge', or 'to drench'; thus one may 'dip' something 'into' something, e.g. into the sea.[2] But 'baptise into Christ' = 'dip into Christ' would surely have sounded strange to a Greek ear.

The next remark on the Galatians passage concerns its contents. Paul

---

[1] Possibly 1 Corinthians – with 1.13ff. – is a couple of months older and maybe also 2 Corinthians. But in any case the three letters bring us to a time c. 55 CE.

[2] E.g. Plutarch, *Moralia (De superstitione)* 166A; Josephus, *Antiquities* 9.212: 'The ship was about to sink' (μέλλοντος βαπτίζεσθαι τοῦ σκάφους).

1

seems to imply that baptism effected a particular relationship between Christ and the baptised person; he expresses this by using the image of donning Christ like a garment. Consequently, because of their baptism the baptised persons somehow belong to Christ, or are his property. What manner of religious thinking is the basis for a rite understood in such a way?

The verses above may also seem somewhat astonishing with regard to the way in which baptism is introduced into the argument. Anyone who thinks of Paul as particularly the apostle of faith feels at home with the first sentence of the quotation: 'In Christ Jesus you are all sons of God, through faith'. But what follows may appear peculiar, for Paul goes on to explain: 'For as many of you as were baptised into Christ put on Christ'. An attribute of baptism is thus the reason why, through faith, the Galatians are God's sons! Such a combination calls for an explanation.

The lines from Galatians 3 belong to an argument, and a complicated one at that, in which Paul demonstrates that the era of Old Testament law had ended. One consequence is that the Galatian Christians, who were Gentiles, were not obliged to undergo circumcision. Otherwise this law required that all males of God's people were to be circumcised (Gen 17.10–14; Lev 12.3). But from baptism Paul draws the conclusion that 'there is neither Jew nor Greek . . . for you are all one in Christ Jesus'. Thus baptism also brings the person who submits to it into a larger group, which is 'one in Christ Jesus', where social and religious differences are invalidated. This may be called an 'ecclesiastical' aspect of baptism. Other texts will later invite us to reflect upon similar features.

Finally, we should note at which stage of the argument of Galatians Paul introduces baptism. He will demonstrate that the promises to Abraham also concern the Galatians and that this is so because a new epoch has begun with Christ. The previous conditions are described in this manner: 'The law was our custodian until Christ came' (3.24). But now the situation has changed: 'We are no longer under a custodian' (3.25). The reason why 'we' are under these new conditions is stated in the verses cited above: 'You are all sons of God – because you were baptised. . .' Thus according to the Apostle, a new age, indeed, the expected new age, has dawned, and baptism has a given place in this turn of the ages. In other words, baptism is regarded in an eschatological perspective.

A number of the New Testament baptismal texts mention the gift of the remission of sins (e.g. Rom 6.11; 1 Cor 1.13; 6.11); indeed this gift is also among those expected at the time of salvation according to several Jewish and Christian texts.[3] In our passage from Galatians this is not explicit, but it is implied. Thus according to the context, it was typical of the old epoch, the one under the custodian, that Old Testament law could not give life or righteousness (3.21), but 'Scripture confined everything under sin' (3.22). When Paul claims that the conditions of the new epoch are different, this implies that now forgiveness prevails instead.

These ideas and the perspectives which we thus encounter in one of the oldest New Testament baptismal texts also raise such questions as: How do these motifs relate to each other? And to what extent can they be understood against the background of the prehistory of baptism as we can reconstruct it? In order to answer these questions we shall consider the perception of baptism in the time before Galatians and before Paul. Then we shall return to Paul, and go on to other New Testament texts on baptism.

Already now, however, it may be appropriate to recall that nowhere in the New Testament do we find a text to which could be assigned the title 'On baptism' or the like. Certainly baptism is mentioned occasionally, and in a few cases the author dwells on it for a while. But baptism is taken for granted and apparently writers need not instruct their readers about it. This circumstance, however, enables our authors to adduce baptism, or, rather, ideas concerning its meaning, when they discuss other matters. Actually, as we have surmised, this is also the case in the passage from Galatians just quoted.

2. Baptism as a rite

Early Christianity was no lonely island in the sea of the religions of antiquity, nor was its Jewish mother-religion. It was a common feature of several contemporary religions that they contained rites in which water was sprinkled on something or somebody, or that something or somebody was washed or immersed. This holds true of both Judaism and other, 'pagan' religions.[4]

Normally such rites mean that the object or person washed is cleansed of dirt in some religious sense.[5] Such 'dirt' may be sin, as e.g. in the baptism of John the Baptist, which was 'a baptism of repentance unto the remission of sins'. The 'dirt' may also be something forbidden or otherwise

---

[3] Jer 31.34; 33.8; Ezek 16.63; *1 En.* 1.5; 5.6; Rom 4.4ff; Matt 1.21.
[4] Leipoldt 1928; Thomas 1935; Stommel 1959; Rudolph 1981.
[5] Stommel 1959, 5ff; Ratschow 1962.

defiling, e.g. because one has touched an unclean animal (Lev 11) or is smitten with leprosy (Lev 13f.). The 'dirt' is not always something forbidden or threatening. Thus a woman who has given birth must be cleansed (Lev 12), and when a priest is to perform an act of worship, he must cleanse himself, leaving the ordinary, profane world behind (e.g., Lev 16.4); but he must also cleanse himself in order, so to speak, to leave behind in the holy place the 'contamination' of holiness with which he has been 'infected' during the service (Lev 16.24).

The examples in the preceding paragraph all have their origin in the Bible. It was self-evident to Jews of New Testament times that the biblical rules concerning washing, bathing etc. were to be observed, and the scribes carefully discussed how they should be applied. A whole group of treatises in the Mishnah[6] deals with the problem. The Qumran community also adhered to the biblical rulings; indeed they did so with more care than most others, and also enjoined other cleansings for their members.[7] Josephus describes the Essenes of his day in this manner in *Jewish War* 2.129–150.[8]

> (129) When they have worked diligently until the fifth hour, they assemble in one place, and, after girding their loins with linen cloths, wash their bodies in cold water ... (149) Although the discharge of excrements is natural, it is their custom to wash afterwards as if they had been defiled ... (150) The junior members are so much inferior to the seniors that if the latter happen to touch them, they bathe as if they had touched a foreigner.

Josephus himself was not an Essene, but he reports in his autobiography how as a young man he spent three years with a certain Bannus, who led a strict ascetic life in the desert and 'often for the sake of purity bathed himself in cold water, day and night'.[9] This Bannus may be reckoned as a distant spiritual relative of John the Baptist – to whom we shall return later on. But although the evidence is sparse, it seems that in those days there were other baptist movements in the area too.[10] Probably we can also

---

[6] Among the treatises in the group are such as *Kelim* (Vessels), *Negaim* (Leprosy signs), *Taharoth* (Cleannesses), *Niddah* (Menstruant).

[7] CD 10.10–13; 1QM 14.2–3; 1QS 3.4–5; 5.13. See Thiering 1979/80 and 1980/81.

[8] I need not enter the discussion of how far these Essenes are identical with the Qumran community. But scholarship tends to regard the Qumran community as Essene and to find various explanations of the differences between the texts of Josephus (and of Philo and Pliny) on the one hand and of the Qumran texts on the other. See Stegemann 1993, 184–226.

[9] *Life* 11.

[10] Thomas 1935.

glimpse features of such a phenomenon in the following lines from the Sibylline Oracles:

> Ah, wretched mortals, change these things, and do not
> lead the great God to all sorts of anger, but abandon
> daggers and groanings, murders and outrages,
> and wash your whole bodies in perennial rivers.
> Stretch your hands to heaven and ask forgiveness
> for your previous deeds and make propitiation
> for bitter impiety with words of praise: God will grant repentance
> and will not destroy. He will stop his wrath again if you all
> practise honourable piety in your hearts.[11]

John the Baptist and his followers were probably of considerable importance for Mandaeism, the adherents of which certainly belong to a later time, but who often refer to the Baptist. Within this movement too ritual bathing played an major role;[12] this is further evidence of the sort of baptismal movement of which we have encountered a few other examples.

Lastly, proselyte baptism should be mentioned among the Jewish water rites. It belonged to those ceremonies which were performed at the transition from paganism to Judaism: ritual immersion and a sacrifice and, for male converts, circumcision.[13] As some scholars have been of the opinion that this baptism was taken up and reinterpreted by John the Baptist as well as by the early Christians,[14] it deserves a somewhat closer description. It may have become an established rite already during the first century CE, but the date is a matter of dispute.[15] It is not mentioned either by Philo, Josephus or the New Testament,[16] although in the case of Josephus it would have been very natural for him to mention it in his description of how King Izates of Adiabene (reigned 30–54 CE) became a

---

[11] *Oracula Sibyllina* 4.162–67 (trans. J. J. Collins in Charlesworth, *OTP*). The text is from around 80 CE. Reitzenstein, 1929, 235ff understands it in the same way as I do above. In Schürer 1973–87, 3.1, 174 it is taken as referring to proselyte baptism.

[12] See Widengren 1982.

[13] b.Ker 9a, b.Yeb 46a. After the Temple had been destroyed, the rule concerning the sacrifice could not be upheld (taking into account the possibility that the rite was not introduced until after 70, the ruling about sacrifice might also be a sheer construct in the rabbinic deliberations; see footnote 17, below).

[14] Cullmann 1958, 6f; Jeremias 1958, 28ff; Böcher 1988, 172.

[15] Kuhn-Stegemann 1963; Schürer 1973–87, 3.1, 173f.

[16] Nor is it mentioned in *Joseph and Aseneth*, a main theme of which is Aseneth's conversion to Judaism. The dating of the book is, however, a matter of debate.

proselyte, not least because he refers at length to the discussions concerning the king's circumcision (*Antiquities* 20.34–48).[17]

As it belonged to the entrance into a new religious community, proselyte baptism was performed only once in a person's life. In this respect it was different from many other water rituals which one could undergo repeatedly. According to the Babylonian Talmud (Yebamoth 47ab)[18] the proselyte-to-be immerses himself or herself and two witnesses who are learned in the Law present some easy and some difficult commandments that are to be observed by every Jew.[19] Then, 'when he comes up from the bath, he is as an Israelite in every respect'.

In the case of proselyte baptism, as in other Jewish immersions, the rite signifies cleansing, viz., of the pagan who is regarded as unclean from a religious point of view.

But water rites were also practised in other religions in the area around the Mediterranean Sea. When e.g. Apuleius was to be initiated into the Isis mysteries, he reports that, *inter alia*, the following happened:

> The priest brought me to the next baths, surrounded by the pious troop, and after I had had an ordinary bath, he prayed for the grace of the gods and cleansed me completely, sprinkling me with water from all sides.[20]

The passage describes an element of an initiation which signifies a transition from one phase in a person's life to another. Apuleius takes the step into the flock of the Isis adherents. Such rites are often called *rites de passage*,[21] and are performed at transitions in life, as when young people become adults, on marriage, on acceptance into a community or a group,

---

[17] The rabbinic passage which is often taken as the earliest reference to proselyte baptism is m.Pes 8.8 (see also m.Eduy 5.2); so Kuhn 1959, 738f., and Schürer 1973–87, 3.1, 173f. Cohen's understanding (1990, 194) is that the passage gives no support for the idea that proselyte baptism was practised in the first century. Meier follows him, as it seems with good reasons (1994, 51, 53, 93f): the statement (by R. Eliezer ben Jacob) that the proselyte had to bring a sacrifice (m.Ker 2.1) cannot support a pre-70 date of the immersion, since the passage only deals with sacrifices. Legasse (1993, 93–101) has a balanced discussion concerning the dating of proselyte baptism, concluding that the results cannot affirm a pre-Christian date of the rite (101). Billerbeck 1922–28 1, 102–111, however, dates its beginning to pre-Christian times.

[18] See further the material in Billerbeck 1922–28 1, 110–112, Cohen 1990, and Legasse 1993, 89–93. All of them also quote the 'extra-canonical' treatise Gerim 1.

[19] If the convert was a woman, the Torah-interpreters gave their instructions from outside the locale.

[20] *Metamorphoses* 11.23.1. For other mysteries, see Cumont 1911, 144; Reitzenstein 1927, 20, 41, 143f; Graf 1974, 115, 127.

[21] The term was coined by Gennep (1909, 71ff).

e.g. among the adherents of a religion.[22] The transition is often connected with negative descriptions of that which is left behind: it can be characterised as death, chaos, darkness, dirt, or misery, while the new status is described in such terms as new birth, life, light, cleanness, salvation.[23]

Like other ceremonies, water rites and cleansings have their particular meanings determined by the context, not least their ritual context. When the ceremony is a transition or initiation, this context often contains interpretative elements. Such a particular interpretation was given to baptism, for example, in the old Roman Catholic rite, when the priest prayed:

> We pray thee, Lord, lead him (the baptisand) to the bath of the new birth, in order that, together with your faithful people, he may be deemed worthy to reach the eternal gifts of your promises.[24]

This prayer defines the rite: it means the beginning of a new human life (it is 'a new birth') and its goal is the eschatological gifts which God has promised.

Although a water rite is commonly understood to denote a cleansing of some kind, its literal and ritual contexts render this meaning more precise. This may be done in the rite, e.g. in proclamations or prayers, but also through other expressions of the religion or tradition concerned, e.g. in the instruction which precedes or follows the rite.[25]

The importance of the context for the meaning of the rite may be illustrated by two simple examples. According to *Vita Adae et Evae* 1–17, Adam and Eve suffered bitter hunger. They took this to be a punishment from God and decided to repent, in order to appease God's anger and, hopefully, to be fed. So they stood neck deep in water, Adam for 40 days in the Jordan and Eve for 37 days in the Tigris (even though Satan deceived her so that she left after half the time). It is explicitly stated (5–6) that here repentance means an almost impossible effort, which may perhaps propitiate God. Certainly this is a water rite, but hardly a cleansing but rather a voluntary asceticism.

Jewish proselyte baptism has a wholly different purpose. Here too the individual is plunged neck deep but, as we have seen, the rite signifies a cleansing from pagan, idolatrous impurity, and is connected with a

---

[22] Éliade 1958, esp. chapter 6.
[23] Cf. Éliade 1949, §64; 1959, 130–141, 184–196; Widengren 1969, 218, 223ff, 385.
[24] Perduc eum, Domine quaesumus, ad novae regenerationis lavacrum, ut cum fidelibus tuis promissionum tuorum praemia consequi mereatur.
[25] Éliade 1958, 110ff; Goldammer 1960, 235–239, 360f, 390ff.

transition from one set of circumstances to a new, radically different way of life. The reading of certain Torah – commandments during the rite makes it clear that, when leaving the baptismal water, the convert has become a member of God's people and is therefore obliged to observe the Torah. In addition, he also receives instruction in the Torah both before his circumcision and before his baptism.[26]

After this preliminary review of the problems which are connected with Christian baptism and of the general religious phenomena among which it is to be reckoned, we turn to a closer study of its prehistory.

[26] See b.Yeb 47a.

1

The baptism of John

1.1. John the Baptist and his baptism

There are good reasons to assume that the first Christians adopted John's baptism, which thereby gradually became a Christian rite. (Gradually, because there is evidence that the first Christians still regarded themselves as Jews.) Such an assumption is by no means original in today's exegetical scholarship; on the contrary.[1] Thus, when we reach the questions concerning the background and origin of Christian baptism, it will prove useful to have discussed John and his baptism.

Our knowledge of John the Baptist is based on the Gospels and on the reports of Josephus.[2] But these sources are difficult to evaluate. Josephus has only a short item, in which he tries to explain to a non-Jewish reader how an external rite of cleansing could be associated with an internal and spiritual reality, viz., conversion, forgiveness, and righteousness. The Gospels, on the other hand, certainly tell us a great deal about John and his work, but their testimonies are thoroughly leavened by Christian interpretation and reinterpretation. In the latter part of this chapter we shall examine these interpretations.

John, his preaching and his baptism were special: the sources verify such an opinion. Nevertheless, John is easily fitted into the spiritual situation of Palestine at the beginning of our era, and albeit unique, he was nevertheless

---

[1] E.g. Dinkler 1962a, 628; Delling 1963, 55; Lohfink 1976, 42f; G. Barth 1981, 37ff.

[2] Josephus, *Antiquities* 18.116–119. The central passage reads: 'John, surnamed the Baptist ... Herod had had him killed; he was a good man and exhorted the Jews to live virtuously: in justice over against each other and in piety towards God, and so to come to baptism. For in this way also the baptism was to be acceptable to God. They must not use it to gain pardon for these or those sins, but to consecrate the body, since the soul was already thoroughly cleansed by righteousness.' The texts of the Mandaeans, for whom John played such an important role, have very little to tell about the history of John himself. But they can illustrate the stage on which he appeared; see Vielhauer 1959, 804ff; Widengren 1982, 10f; Segelberg 1982, 121f.

a child of his time. This situation meant, *inter alia,* that the Jewish religion had for a couple of centuries been under pressure from cultural and political great powers. Moreover, Jewish society felt the impact of so-called Hellenism, i.e. the culture which spread in the fourth century BCE after the conquests of Alexander the Great. But the Jews also defended themselves, or, rather, influential circles among them who came to determine their spiritual history did so. They sought in different ways to protect the Jews' position as God's chosen people. The important features of this dramatic process included several prophetic and eschatological currents (some would label them apocalyptic[3]). The Qumran community has already been mentioned, and should be understood in this light. Its members 'went into the wilderness to prepare the way of the Lord'.[4] This is an echo of Isa 40.3; obviously the community believed that it participated in the fulfilment of Isaiah's prophecy about the approaching time of salvation.

We still have at our disposal several texts from other circles in Judaism in which the author exhorts pious people who feel oppressed: stand fast in fidelity to the covenant which God made with your fathers; the Lord will certainly recompense his faithful one day. Then he will make a new covenant, and, indeed, will do so soon; accordingly the apostates must repent, or destruction will come upon them. We perceive that these texts reveal how their authors struggled with religious questions of their time. They did so under the constant and diligent tutelage of the Scriptures, and the present-day reader who has a keen ear easily recognises the echoes from the Bible. Thus, in an indirect manner, the Scriptures are made to admonish, warn and comfort the listeners/readers.

A couple of examples from such Jewish texts may suggest the spiritual climate in which John appeared. Thus Josephus tells us about prophets – he himself labels them 'deceivers', for he knows the outcome! – 'who convinced the crowds to follow them into the desert; there, they said, they would show them unmistakable wonders and signs which would be

---

[3] The expression is used in several ways. Normally it stands for ideas about 'the last time' describing great catastrophes, cosmic signs, etc., which precede or accompany God's final intervention, his judgment etc. In addition, scholarly tradition as a rule assumes that these 'apocalyptic' ideas are combined with calculations of epochs and of the date of the end, which are, in turn, said to go together with a deterministic view of history. The 'apocalypticists' are also assumed to take a pessimistic stand vis-à-vis the situation of their own time. As, in my opinion, this use of the word 'apocalyptic' all too often leads to simplistic conclusions as to what 'apocalyptic' texts mean, I choose other terms.

[4] 1QS 8.13f.

THE BAPTISM OF JOHN

performed according to God's providence'.[5] The charismatic leader has apparently promised to lead the crowds in a new exodus to see the fulfilment of the divine promises of salvation.

Some texts express the expectation that in the time of salvation the people will be cleansed. Thus we read in the Qumran Community Rule (1QS 4.19–23):

> Truth shall arise for ever in the world, because it has wallowed in the ways of wickedness during the dominion of falsehood until the time of the ordained judgment. Then God will purify all the deeds of man with his truth, and he will cleanse for himself some of the sons of man to obliterate all spirit of falsehood from the inner part of his flesh and to cleanse him of all wicked deeds through holy spirit. And he will sprinkle upon them the spirit of truth as purifying water (to cleanse them) of all abominations of lies and of all wallowing in unclean spirit, in order to instruct the righteous ones in the knowledge of the Most High and of the truth of the sons of heaven and make them wise who are perfect in their way of living. For God has chosen them for an everlasting covenant, and to them belongs all the glory of man (or: of Adam). And there shall be no more falsehood and all the works of wickedness shall be put to shame.

Thus history is approaching an ultimate crisis, in which God will judge the wicked, whereas the elect will be cleansed and sprinkled with the Spirit. This is linked with the remission of their sins: God will 'cleanse him of all wicked deeds'. The reader who knows his Bible catches the echoes from Ezek 36.24–28, a passage which deals with Israel's future restoration:

> I will gather you from all the countries and bring you into your own land. I will sprinkle clean water upon you, and you shall be clean from all your uncleannesses, and from all your idols I will cleanse you. A new heart I will give you, and a new spirit I will put within you ... I will put my spirit within you, and cause you to walk in my statutes and be careful to observe my ordinances. You shall dwell in the land which I gave to your fathers; and you shall be my people, and I will be your God.[6]

The following lines from the *Book of Jubilees* (1.22–25) express similar expectations of a divine intervention:

> The Lord said to Moses: I know their contrariness and their thoughts and their stubbornness (Deut 31.27). And they will not obey until they acknowledge

---

[5] Josephus, *Antiquities* 20.167. Similar reports concerning other such figures: *Antiquities* 20.97 (cf. Acts 5.36), 20.169–172 (Acts 21.38 seems to refer to the same episode). Josephus also mentions some of these events in *Jewish War* 2.259–263, 6.285f, 7.437f.
[6] RSV.

11

their sin and the sins of their fathers. But after this they will return to me in all uprightteousness and with all of (their) heart and soul. And I shall cut off the foreskin of their heart and the foreskin of the heart of their descendants. And I shall create for them a holy spirit and I shall purify them so that they will not turn away from following me from that day and forever. And their souls will cleave to me and to all my commandments. And they will do my commandments. And I shall be a father to them, and they will be sons to me. And they will all be called 'sons of the living God'.[7]

Ideas and expectations like those we encounter in these quotations form, as it were, a sounding board for the appearance of John the Baptist. The circumstance that these passages speak of a purification of the inner man does not mean that they have nothing to tell us about the background of the external rite of cleansing. On the contrary, as so often in the world of religion, an external rite and an interior, 'spiritual', event are closely related to each other. But even though we may locate John's baptism and his preaching within the context of the ideas and expectations of contemporary Judaism, they stand out as typical of him.[8]

In his preaching John insisted on conversion. This is seen both from the brief item in Josephus and from the reports of the New Testament authors (Mark 1.2–6 par; Matt 3.7–10 par). The demand for repentance was nothing new in Judaism. The idea was known from the Bible,[9] and a rabbi from New Testament times, R. Eliezer ben Hyrkanos, stated: 'If the Israelites do not repent, they will never be saved, as it is written: "through repentance and rest you shall be saved" (Isa 30.15).'[10] In this context, repentance, or returning, meant a resolute rejection of those things in life which contravened God's will and did not befit those who belonged to his covenant. During the centuries around the beginning of the Common Era

---

[7] Trans. O. S. Wintermute from Charlesworth, *OTP*.

[8] This is the opinion also of those scholars who believe that John's baptism originated in proselyte baptism; see Lindeskog 1983, 60. Apart from the difficulty of proving that proselyte baptism was practised in the 1st century CE, the following factors speak against the assumption that John's baptism was an adaptation of proselyte baptism (which, of course, also would have implied that John claimed that his fellow-Jews were on the same footing as Gentiles): the latter is not connected with confession of sins and forgiveness, the proselyte performs the rite himself, whereas in John's baptism people are baptis*ed*, and the eschatological perspective of John's baptism clearly distinguishes it from proselyte baptism. The same reasons favour the position that neither was the baptism of the early church an adaptation of proselyte baptism. See G. Barth 1973; 1981, 32f; Legasse 1993, 18, 102–105.

[9] E.g. Deut 30.2, 8ff; Ps 7.13; 51.15; Isa 10.21f; Mal 3.7. See H. W. Wolff 1951 and 1961.

[10] p.Taan 1.1 (63d) (Billerbeck 1922–28 1, 162f).

Jews often directed the demand for repentance to those fellow-Jews who tended to pursue un-Jewish ways of life or paid insufficient attention to God's commandments. (Nevertheless it is wrong to assume that normal Jewish morality in general involved a strict but superficial observance of the Torah, without any serious moral dedication.)[11]

John's preaching of repentance was addressed to the whole people. The individual was to abstain from his former way of life and to offer willing obedience to the God of Israel; and the moral demands which were once proclaimed by the prophets of old concerning human relations were reiterated by this new prophet in the desert. In this way, it seems, John sought to prepare a renewed people of God in the wilderness, the place where once the covenant between God and Israel had been made (Luke 1.17; cf. Mal 3.1; 4.5f).

This proclamation of John also contained the feature that 'the strong one' or 'he who is stronger than I' was to 'come' (Mark 1.7f par.). A lively debate on this designation has provoked several suggestions as to its meaning and to whom it referred in John's preaching. For the present writer the evidence indicates that it stood for God, 'the Strong One of Jacob' (Gen 49.24; Ps 132.2; Isa 49.26).[12] When John proclaimed that he was to 'come', he took into his mouth a phrase which is common in several religions when mention is made of a divine intervention, either in a prayer for a divine liberation to take place or in a warning that a judgement is near. A few biblical examples may suffice: 'The Lord comes to judge the world' (Ps 98.9); repent, 'if not, I will come to you' (Rev 2.5); 'Oh, when will you come to me?' (Ps 101.2).

According to John, God comes to judge and to save. This is expressed through the imagery of threshing: those who refuse to repent are compared to the chaff which is thrown into the fire after the threshing (Matt 3.12 par.), in other words, they will be overtaken by the divine wrath (Matt 3.7 par.), when it will be of no avail to refer to the divine promises given in the covenant with Abraham (Matt 3.9). On the other hand, the crisis which John expected also meant that those who had repented would be separated from the wicked and 'gathered' as the wheat is gathered into the granary (Matt 3.12). This idea of gathering recalls the appearance of this motif in several biblical texts,

[11] See Merklein 1981b, 1025.
[12] The expression stands for God according to Vielhauer 1959, 805; Thyen 1970, 137; Hughes 1972, 218; Lindeskog 1983, 64. It refers to the Son of Man, sent by God, according to Becker 1972, 35ff; Hoffmann 1972, 29; Neugebauer 1974/75, 102f; Pesch 1976–77 1, 84. In the opinion of, among others, Böcher (1988, 176) and Legasse (1993, 38–41) it stands for the Messiah.

according to which God, at the time of his final intervention, will 'gather' his dispersed children (e.g. Deut 30.3; Jer 29.14; Ezek 34.11f, 24).

According to Matt 3.11, John contrasts his own water baptism with a baptism in the Spirit and in fire, which he who will come will perform.[13] In John's preaching baptism in fire was almost certainly just another image for judgment;[14] either the image stands for a painful cleansing (as in Mal 3.2, 'He will be as a refiner's fire') or for an annihilating judgment, also represented by the burning of the chaff.

Although it is often assumed that the combination 'holy spirit and fire' originated with John,[15] the commentators differ when it comes to explaining what a baptism in Spirit may have meant in his preaching. Actually we find a relevant, illuminating example in the passage from the Qumran text already quoted, according to which the eschatological cleansing will take place 'through holy spirit' (1QS 4.21). If this is accepted as a valid analogy, baptism in fire and baptism in spirit both denote the coming divine cleansing. In addition, such an understanding would retain the most common meaning of water-rites, namely, that of cleansing.[16]

The preaching of this message was connected with John's baptism. The somewhat abstract wording of Josephus, quoted above,[17] implies that the evangelists are to be trusted when they report that it was 'a baptism of repentance unto the remission of sins'. Submission to baptism was a sign that the individual repented and bore the fruit of repentance or wanted to bear it (Matt 3.8 par.).

The question may be asked how the remission of sins should be understood in this context. Was it given in baptism, or was baptism only a promise that the baptised person would find remission at the coming of the Strong One?[18] It appears that an external detail is of some importance here. John's baptism was received passively and the penitents did not bathe or

[13] Mark 1.8 only says 'in holy spirit'. Presumably this represents a Christian reinterpretation; thus Pesch 1976–77 1, 84f; Gnilka 1978–79 1, 48; G. Barth 1981, 25.

[14] See e.g. Dan 7.10; Rev 20.10; *4 Ezra* 13.10; *Mekh Exod* 18.1; Lang 1959, 935f, 942–946.

[15] Thus e.g. G. Barth 1981, 25. John spoke only of a baptism in fire, according to Kraeling (1951, 60) and Pesch (1976–77 1, 85). The circumstance that already in the Q-source the combination seems to be so hard to understand, indicates that here the Christians have transmitted the tradition better than they understood it.

[16] Hartman 1976, 98f; Fitzmyer 1981–85, 454, 473f. Cf. Hollenbach 1979, 968. For other interpretations, see Barrett 1947, 126; Kraeling 1951, 61ff; Schweizer 1959, 397 (Spirit and fire = fire-storm); Sint 1964, 69ff (fire = judgment, spirit = gift of the Spirit).

[17] See footnote 2 above.

[18] The former understanding is that of Delling 1963, 43; Thyen 1964, 98; G. Barth 1981, 36; the latter is that of M. Barth 1951, 124.

wash themselves, as was the normal procedure at other ritual baths and cleansings.[19] This fact supports the first of the two ways of regarding the relationship between baptism and the remission of sins. John meant that God had sent him to perform the outer rite of cleansing which was the sign that God forgave those who had repented. In addition, it should be mentioned that the motif of remission fits well into the frame of eschatological expectations which we encountered in the passages quoted above.[20]

The repentance and the baptism unto the remission of sins did not result in John's gathering a closed group like the Qumran community. Nevertheless people baptised by John came to form a group which expected the arrival of the Strong One for judgment and salvation. When New Testament authors mention John's disciples,[21] this indicates that such a group existed, however loosely it was organised. Probably it followed certain rules of conduct, which were marked by the eschatological expectations of the Baptist and by his austere message,[22] just as the life of the prophet himself also seems to have been rather ascetic (Mark 1.6).

Thus the baptism of John also became a *rite de passage*. The group to which it gave entry was not strictly closed, but there are nevertheless reasons to believe that his followers regarded themselves as members, or maybe rather as members-to-be, of a renewed people of God. Not only John's preaching, but also John's appearing in the wilderness fits such a context well. We have seen how other prophets of the time went there to show 'the signs of the salvation' to the crowds they brought with them.[23] The wilderness was the traditional place for the liberation of God's people: thither had they gone from Egypt, there the covenant had been made, through the wilderness they went from Babylon, and there the way of the Lord should be prepared (Isa 40).

1.2. The interpretation of John's baptism in the Gospels

The fact that Jesus joined those who underwent John's baptism also means that, in some sense or another, he belonged to the above-mentioned Johannine group, albeit only for a time.

[19] This is stressed by G. Barth 1973, 140–146; 1981, 34–36, cf. Stommel 1959, 10f.

[20] See also Sjöberg 1938, 62ff; Thyen 1970, 61ff, 73f, §2–4; Hartman 1979, 33ff, 133f.

[21] Matt 9.14; 11.2; 14.12; Mark 2.18; Luke 11.1; Acts 19.3f. Böcher (1988, 172) stresses that John's baptism should be regarded as a rite of initiation.

[22] Thus we hear of fasting (Mark 2.18; although fasting need not be particularly ascetic; cf. Matt 4.2; 6.16f; Acts 13.2f), of cleansing (John 3.25), of how to pray (Luke 11.1). See Thomas 1935, 89–139; Kraeling 1951, 76–80, 161ff, 171ff.

[23] See the passages in Josephus mentioned in note 5, above.

It is possible that Jesus already understood the appearance of John in the light of the expectations expressed in the book of Malachi.[24] The gospel traditions obviously did so.[25] According to the book of Malachi, God would send his messenger to prepare the way of the Lord (3.1), who would come soon (3.1, 5). The coming Lord would purify the sons of Levi (3.3) and be like a refiner's fire (3.2); he was drawing near to judge those who had sinned against their fellow human beings and against God (3.5); the fallen people were exhorted to return to God (3.7) because 'the day' was coming, the one which would be like a burning oven (4.1), in which the evildoers would burn like stubble. But for the God-fearers the sun of righteousness would arise (4.2). Before 'the day' Elijah the prophet would be sent to the people to turn the hearts of the family-members to each other (4.5).

When we use such a text as a clue to the appearance of John, several details of the picture of him fall into place. He appears as one convinced that the world is approaching an immediate, definitive confrontation with the Holy and Righteous One, a confrontation which requires reflection and change, indeed conversion, now, at the critical present instant.

When Christian thinking as reflected in the Gospels dwelt on the Malachi passage, it took one very particular step, in so far as it identified the coming 'Lord' with Jesus. The same step determines the way in which John and his baptism are understood, namely as preparations for the work of Jesus or as a beginning thereof. At the same time early Christian theologians tend to diminish the importance of John and of his baptism.[26]

Thus when *Mark* describes 'the beginning of the gospel of Jesus Christ, the Son of God',[27] he tells his readers about John and his baptism. They are fully integrated into his Christian thinking; so Jesus is said to be the 'stronger' one (1.7), for whom John prepares the way; he 'comes after' John (1.9, 14) and will baptise in spirit, not in water (1.8). According to Mark, John certainly preaches repentance, but this repentance does not precede an impending judgment. The perspective of the definitive crisis or, in other

---

[24] Thus Bultmann 1931, 132, 178; Schürmann 1969, 417; Böcher 1988, 173.
[25] This holds true for the Q-source (Matt 11.7–11/Luke 7.24–28), as well as for the Markan tradition (1.2–6). In Mark there is possibly also an echo of 2 Kings 1.8: Elijah had a leather girdle, and according to Mal 4.5 Elijah was to appear before the end of the time. Luke 1.17, 76 is peculiar to Luke which alludes to Mal 4.5f and 3.1, respectively.
[26] Wink 1968; Bammel 1971/72, 96–113.
[27] I choose to follow the variant reading which contains the words 'Son of God', although they are not found in many important manuscripts.

words, the eschatological perspective of John's work, is instead determined by the contents of 1.14f. There Jesus appears in public, preaching the gospel of God's kingdom, and this message states that 'the time is fulfilled'; the 'time' is the critical time, but the crisis is not caused by an approaching judgment, but by the necessity of turning to the gospel. This picture of the eschaton well fits the fact that the Markan John does not mention a baptism in fire performed by the one who comes after him – assuming that the fire baptism would stand for a judgment.

Mark does not tell us how he understands the clause that Jesus will baptise in the Holy Spirit. But it is a reasonable assumption that he and his readers shared the widespread early Christian belief that Christian baptism was somehow connected with the gift of the Spirit. So they presumably also thought that this was the reference of the Baptist's words on the baptism in the Spirit.[28] At any rate the evangelist knows that the Holy Spirit is active in the Christian community (13.11: it speaks for them in court).

When *Matthew* makes use of the Markan passage on John and his baptism, he changes a few details. Whereas Mark presents John as proclaiming the baptism of repentance for the forgiveness of sins (1.4), Matthew only tells us that he appeared in the wilderness preaching repentance (3.2). Thus Matthew focuses on the preaching of repentance and indirectly denies that John's baptism was for the forgiveness of sins; instead, it is presented only as a baptism 'in water for repentance' (3.11). So Matthew is reluctant to describe the gifts of the Johannine baptism. The forgiveness of sins is instead given by Jesus and through his work; thus Jesus' name is explained by the statement that 'he will save his people from their sins' (1.21), and Matthew also mediates the liturgical tradition whereby Jesus' blood is 'poured out for many for the forgiveness of sins' (26.28).[29]

We noted above that the Matthean John is particularly a preacher of repentance. His preaching and the repentance which it seeks prepare for the future kingdom of heaven (3.2), which will be announced by 'the coming one', that is, by Jesus (4.17, 23). The preaching of repentance and the baptism of repentance form the background for the coming of 'the stronger one' (3.11) and for his baptising in the Holy Spirit and fire (3.11). The Matthean context makes it clear that here baptism in fire stands for judgment, the judgment which will be passed by the coming judge, the

---

[28] Similarly Gnilka 1978–79 1, 48.
[29] Trilling 1959, 286; Thyen 1964, 101–103.

Son of Man, and of which Matthew has much to tell his readers. We may, for example, think of the parable of the tares among the wheat (13.24–30, 37–43) or of the text on the Son of Man who will separate the nations as a shepherd separates the sheep from the goats (25.31–46).[30]

If we ask what baptism in the Spirit may mean in Matthew, the ending of his Gospel may provide us with an answer. There the risen Lord ordains that his missionaries shall baptise 'into the name of the Father and the Son and the Holy Spirit' (28.19). Then the baptism in the Spirit with which the Coming One would baptise was the Christian baptism which the readers/listeners have received. Certain people may commit an unforgivable sin against the same Spirit; it was once in Christ (12.31f) and dwells in Christians so that it can help them when they are persecuted and brought to court (10.10).[31]

In the Gospel of *Luke* the pair John and Jesus are brought together already in the chapters on Jesus' birth and childhood (1–2). They are related to each other as the story goes on, and Jesus is always presented as the superior. The birth of both is announced (1.13–21; 1.26–33); John's father is doubtful (1.20), whereas Jesus' mother is not (1.34–38); the unborn John salutes the unborn Jesus (1.41), etc. Already when John's birth is announced, Luke emphasises his role as a preacher of repentance and, in this function, as the forerunner of Jesus (1.16). In the hymn of Zechariah, which, according to the literary conventions of the time, forms a moment of reflection and interpretation in the narrative, the task of the forerunner is defined: he will 'give knowledge of salvation to his people in the forgiveness of their sins' (1.77). Accordingly, when John comes on the scene in chapter 3, his baptism (as in Mark) is introduced as a baptism of repentance for the forgiveness of sins (3.3). But in accordance with the programmatic lines in the hymn of Zechariah, the baptism of repentance and the forgiveness are also linked with the work of the stronger one. This is also suggested by Luke's treatment of the quotation from Isa 40 which sheds light on John's appearance. The lines which he takes from Mark are applied to John, but he adds a further verse from Isaiah so that the quotation also says: 'All flesh shall see the salvation of God' (Isa 40.5; Luke 3.6).[32] Concerning this salvation aged Simeon in the Temple has already

---

[30] Also otherwise fire stands for judgment in Matt. 3.10ff; 7.19; 13.50; 18.9.
[31] See Luz 1985–90 2, 266f.
[32] In the wider Lukan context the phrase 'all flesh' is important, because both in Luke and in Acts God's salvation is brought about in a world-wide perspective. G. Schneider 1977, 84f.

said: 'My eyes have seen your salvation', namely that 'which you have prepared to be seen by all peoples' (2.30f).

Luke mentions that John baptised, but nevertheless presents him as more of a preacher than a baptist.[33] His preaching largely concerns Christ, even though to some extent indirectly so. Thus Luke introduces the saying that the stronger one will baptise with spirit and fire by inserting a question from the people concerning whether or not John is the Messiah (3.15). John answers that, no, he only baptises with water, but 'he who comes' will baptise with spirit and fire. So both the statement on baptism in spirit and fire and the sentence concerning the clearance of the threshing floor (3.17) become a proclamation of Jesus, the Messiah. In addition, Luke refers to this preaching of John as a preaching of 'the gospel' (3.18), that is the message of Jesus and, later on, of the apostles.

As regarded within the context of the two books of Luke, the expectation of a baptism in spirit (3.16) is fulfilled at Pentecost as described in Acts 2. For in Acts 1.5 Luke reiterates the words of John quoted in Luke 3.16: 'John baptised with water, but before many days you shall be baptised with the Holy Spirit'. But the readers of Luke probably believed that John's words on a baptism in spirit were also fulfilled in their own Christian lives. For in Acts Christian baptism is normally connected with the gift of the Spirit (2.38 etc.), and this differentiates it from John's baptism (19.1–7). Moreover, John's saying that the stronger one would gather the wheat into his granary (Luke 3.17) might be associated with Christian baptism as Luke writes about it in Acts; there baptism is part of the process in which people accept the apostolic testimony, repent and join the Christian community; thus they are 'gathered' into the church.[34]

What then may baptism in fire stand for in Luke? Certainly Acts 2.3 mentions tongues as of fire, which suggests that baptism in fire is a reference to the gift of the Spirit bestowed in Christian baptism.[35] On the other hand, as John's preaching is reported by Luke (and for that matter, by Matthew), the words on baptism in spirit and fire are immediately followed by the prediction that the coming one will not only gather the wheat into his granary but will also burn the chaff in an unquenchable fire. This may indicate that baptism in fire stands for the negative side of John's

---

[33] G. Schneider 1977, 90; Bovon 1989, 179.

[34] Acts 1.5; 2.47. See G. Schneider 1977, 87, 90; Bovon 1989, 177.

[35] Thus Leaney 1966, 40; Grundmann 1971, 105 (doubtful); Hoffmann 1972, 30; Fitzmyer 1981–85, 474 (doubtful); Chevallier 1986, 530; Bovon 1989, 177.

message, viz., that judgment awaits those who do not accept it.[36] In my opinion, the latter alternative is preferable.

In the *Gospel of John*, the evangelist attaches still less significance to the Baptist and his baptism than the Synoptics do. Possibly this relates to the ecclesiastical environment of this Gospel, which may have included people who regarded themselves as the disciples of the Baptist. If this be the case, the evangelist tells them that their master requested that they turn from him to Jesus (1.29–34 etc.).[37] That John baptised with water is mentioned, and we are told that God has sent him to do so (1.33),[38] but there is no information in the Fourth Gospel as to what this baptism meant. It is not called a baptism of repentance, nor is it connected with forgiveness of sins. When John is reported to deny that he is the Messiah or Elijah or the Prophet (cf. Deut 18.18), the audience ask why he baptises (1.19–25), as if any of the persons mentioned was supposed to baptise – which was not the case.[39] But no answer is given as to why he baptised. Nor is anything mentioned in 1.26f which is contrasted with John's baptism with water ('I baptise with water'); rather, the Baptist's person is contrasted with him who is in their midst: they do not know him and John is not worthy to untie the thong of his sandal (1.27). As a matter of fact John has come (to baptise, but these words carry no weight, and) to reveal this unknown man to Israel (1.31) and so to be the forerunner of the Messiah (3.28). Thus John has really 'decreased' (3.30) in the Gospel of John.[40]

It is evident from the preceding paragraph that the Gospel of John reveals some knowledge of the tradition whereby John's water baptism is contrasted with that in spirit (and fire) to be performed by the coming one, whether he takes it from Mark or from another tradition. But in John it is radically transformed.[41] Its first half 'I baptise with water' occurs in 1.26, but is not contrasted with another baptism. In 1.33 follows a counterpart to the second half of the tradition, 'I did not know him, but he who sent me to baptise with water said to me, "He on whom you see the Spirit descend and

---

[36] Schürmann 1969, 175; Schweizer 1982, 49; Nolland 1989 1, 153.

[37] Brown 1966–71, lxvii–lxx.

[38] God has sent John also according to 1.6, but only in order to bear witness to the light (1.7f; see also 3.26).

[39] On the other hand, John's baptism could be regarded as a rite with symbolic eschatological associations. I have touched upon this aspect above, and all three figures can be connected with such ideas.

[40] See Stowasser 1992, 241f.

[41] Haenchen 1980, 171.

remain, this is he who baptises with the Holy Spirit".' So, the meaning of this element seems to have become as follows. According to John the risen Jesus gives (or asks his Father to send) the Spirit to his disciples when his work has been completed.[42] Here the Spirit, sometimes called the Paraclete (or, as in the RSV translation, the Counselor),[43] stands for the gift of divine life which human beings receive because of the work of the Son (also 6.63). The dialogue with Nicodemus (3.1–21) follows a similar line: humans receive eternal life through being born of water and spirit, and this is made possible through the work of the Son.[44] This gift takes several expressions: the work of the Son is continued and related to more people (14.17f, 26; 15.26; 16.13f), and sins are forgiven (20.23). Thus the Baptist tradition has been totally integrated into the Johannine world of ideas.

1.3. The baptism of Jesus

There can be no doubt that Jesus really did join John and was baptised by him, because without the compulsion of historical facts, early Christian narrators would hardly have thought of reporting that their Lord Jesus submitted to the baptism of repentance for the forgiveness of sins. But this being so, it is also probable that his baptism represented far more than a few minutes in his life. Rather it stands for a longer phase of Jesus' life, which must have meant that he accepted John's preaching of repentance at the prospect of the approaching crisis, including the expectation of the coming of the Stronger One.[45]

The tradition that there was a Baptist period in Jesus' life was obviously not transmitted by mere chance in the gospel tradition. There are certainly details in the Gospels which do not seem to be of specific importance to their message. Thus, for example, the remark that Jesus was not the only child in his family (Mark 3.31; 6.3) can hardly be regarded as information to which the evangelist has attached great Christological significance (although, of course a theologian could derive several *theologumena* therefrom). But John, his preaching, and his baptism seem to play an indispensable role in the early Christian material – and so does Jesus' relationship to them. So the so-called Q-source contained material on the Baptist, Mark

---

[42] John 7.39; 16.7; 20.22.

[43] Of course I cannot in this context enter upon a traditio-historical discussion of the different roots of these concepts. Nevertheless it is obvious that in the present form of the Gospel they can be taken as synonyms. See Becker 1979–81, 470–5.

[44] See my further discussion of this pericope in chapter 11.

[45] Braun 1953, 39.

begins his Gospel by telling about him, and Matthew and Luke follow suit. The Gospel of John goes its own way, but nevertheless John the Baptist has a place in its presentation. The circumstance that John enjoys such a position supports the opinion that both Jesus and the Jesus movement were decisively influenced by him. We have already examined some examples of how the early church tried to cope with this heritage. We shall encounter more examples of this kind as we turn to the evangelists' narratives of the baptism of Jesus.

The descriptions of Jesus' baptism in the Synoptic Gospels all have a primarily Christological function. In their position at the beginning of each Gospel the narratives of Jesus' baptism bring out essential features of the main character, and in particular Matthew interprets in this connection what it meant that Jesus was baptised.[46] If, for a moment, we direct our interest to the time before the gospels, it is a precarious enterprise to reconstruct the prehistory of the *narrative*.[47] But as to the prehistory of the *motifs* we can state with some certainty that they are rooted in that Jewish soil of ideas and expectations which we considered when investigating the religio-historical background of John's baptism. In wide Jewish circles it was hoped that when God intervened in the last days, he would purify his people and give them a new or holy spirit; this was also a sign that he had chosen them and was often combined with the idea that they would be God's sons. We recognise all of these motifs in the narratives of Jesus' baptism. The fact that this constellation of eschatological motifs is so important in the baptism story indicates a conviction on the part of those who composed and transmitted these traditions that with the advent of Jesus the expected time of salvation had come or was at hand. Such a conviction must have been connected with this tradition at the beginning of its history. But apart from this everything is uncertain.[48] At the very root

---

[46] Sabbe 1967, 193f; Haenchen 1968, 61; Pesch 1970, 123f, 129; Lentzen-Deis 1970, 177f.

[47] For an attempt see Lentzen-Deis 1970. I made another attempt in Hartman 1976.

[48] Thus for example the dove-like form of the Spirit is puzzling; for a survey see Lentzen-Deis 1970, 170–183. Was Jesus' baptism described in this way, e.g. because he was regarded as the representative of the whole people to be saved? Or was it because the Christians who gave the tradition its first form thought that they themselves, as baptised, possessed the Spirit, were God's sons and his chosen? Their baptism had been performed 'into the name of the Lord Jesus', i.e. Jesus was understood as being the fundamental referent of the rite (more about this below, in chapter 3). If this was so, we might assume that the account of how Jesus was baptised was so told as to stand out as the beginning of the work which made available the eschatological gifts that they had received: Spirit, sonship and election.

of the tradition lies, not only the event of Jesus' baptism, but possibly also some visionary experience of Jesus himself. But concerning the contents of this experience we can only speculate.[49]

But, as stated, when we encounter the story of Jesus' baptism in the Synoptic Gospels, it has a clear Christological function. In *the Gospel of Mark* the evangelist first says simply that Jesus came and was baptised by John (1.9). This is the first time that Jesus is mentioned after the introductory headline in 1.1. As compared with the headline he is very briefly introduced, only by his name, with no Christological titles, and by the geographical notice 'from Nazareth in Galilee'. But details of the narrative of the baptism (v. 10f) give Jesus attributes which convey to the understanding reader the same message as some Christological titles. So Mark tells his readers that Jesus has a vision when coming out of the water, seeing the heavens opened and the Spirit descending upon him like a dove. In the vision a heavenly voice also proclaims him to be God's son. The words allude to Ps 2.7 ('You are my son . . .') and to Isa 42.1 ('my chosen, in whom my soul delights'). Thus the omniscient author gives his reader insight into something which, according to the narrative, was Jesus' personal experience. The message of the vision is that now a communication is established between heaven and earth, between God and man (the opened heavens, the voice). It is made through Jesus, the Galilean from Nazareth, who is the anointed one whom God has promised to send (Ps 2.7; Isa 42.1). His work was performed in God's power and on God's commission (the Spirit, the sonship).[50]

On the whole, Jesus' divine sonship, which is so central to the baptism story of Mark, plays an important role in this Gospel, and the weighty proclamations of this sonship reach their climax in the comment by the centurion after Jesus' death (15.39). The Christological implications of the baptismal narrative also provide the reader with an early answer to the questions concerning Jesus' authority which recur in the Gospel of Mark (1.22, 27; 2.7, 10 etc.).[51]

[49] Marcus (1995) suggests that Luke 10.18 represents the content of Jesus' baptismal vision.

[50] E.g. Haenchen 1968, 61; Pesch 1976–77 1, 89–94.

[51] It has been suggested that Jesus is depicted as an example to Mark's readers in so far as he (like the Christians) underwent a water baptism. Here everything depends on how we think of these readers. The Gospel itself contains little on which to build an answer. But it is hard to assume that this Gospel, which was so quickly and unproblematically accepted, should be located in a church which, in the 60s or 70s, did not baptise converts. On the contrary, I think it did. Then the horizon can be widened further than Schenk (1990, 11) is willing to allow, when he stresses that Mark makes no other mention of a Christian baptism in water.

In the *Gospel of Matthew* the readers receive several pieces of information about the main character of the narrative before he is baptised by John. Thus Matthew tells them that Jesus' birth meant the fulfilment of the Messianic prophecies (1.23; 2.6, 15, 18). So also the appearance of John, his forerunner, is predicted by the Scripture (3.3). Jesus is of the Holy Spirit (1.18, 20), he will save his people from their sins (1.21), indeed, he is 'God with us' (1.23). The evangelist also quotes a passage from Hosea on God's son and applies it to Jesus (Hos 11.1; Matt 2.15).

In the Matthean narrative on the baptism of Jesus (3.13–17) the voice from heaven is not directed to Jesus as in Mark ('You are...'), but rather contains a proclamation about him: 'This is...'. It seems primarily to be addressed to John. Indirectly, however, it becomes a message to a wider audience, i.e., the readers/listeners of the Gospel.

Before Matthew reports the actual baptism he inserts a dialogue between Jesus and John, according to which John refuses to baptise Jesus, who should instead baptise him. Here the evangelist hints at the uneasiness which could arise in the minds of those who maintained that Jesus was the Stronger One and their saviour: it was a stumbling-block that he submitted to the repentance-baptism demanded by the weaker one.[52] The Matthean solution of the problem is indicated in Jesus' answer: 'Thus we (i.e., both Jesus and John) have to fulfil all righteousness' (3.15). Evidently the answer at least says that both of them perform God's will. It is, however, difficult to be more precise.[53]

But there are reasons which support the following suggestion:[54] God's all-encompassing will must be obeyed, by Jesus and by John, as well as by Christians (5.20; 12.50; 25.37; 28.20). In Jesus' case this is realised throughout; in the full sense of the word, he 'fulfils' the will of God (5.17; 23.32). In addition, when Matthew presents Jesus as God's Son, a dominant feature of this Matthean Son-Christology is that the Son performs his Father's will (4.1–11; 26.39; 27.43, 54). When the baptismal narrative delivers the first example of his 'fulfilment' of God's demand for

---

[52] *The Gospel of the Nazarenes* expresses the problem more precisely: 'Look, the mother of the Lord and his brothers said to him: "John the Baptist baptises for the remission of sins. Let us go and be baptised by him." But he said to them: "What have I sinned that I should go and be baptised by him?"' (Jerome, *Dialogus contra Pelagianos* 3.2).

[53] As Luz (1985, 154) says: 'In dem kurzen Aussprach Jesu ist jedes Wort strittig'.

[54] Strecker 1966, 179f; Sabbe 1967, 185ff; Luz 1985, 154f; Gnilka 1986–88 1, 76f. Several of these authors have reservations about O. Cullmann's interpretation (and rightly so; Cullmann 1958, 13–17), according to which Jesus' baptism means his becoming the Servant of God who will suffer for others. Thus also Legasse 1993, 61.

righteousness, this nicely fits the circumstance that there he is proclaimed as God's Son.[55] Jesus complies with the will of the Father and submits to baptism in solidarity with other human beings; however, he also becomes an example of obedience and humility to the Matthean Christians. They too were God's sons (5.9, 45). Indeed, they might very well have regarded Jesus as an example also in as much as he had been baptised with water, as had they and other new disciples (28.19).[56]

When the readers of the *Gospel of Luke* come to the story of Jesus' baptism (3.21f), they recognise some attributes of Jesus which they have encountered earlier in the Gospel. He has already been called the Son of the Most High (1.32), in whom are fulfilled the promises concerning the Anointed One, the Messiah (1.32; 2.11, 26). In the beginning of the Gospel the accounts of John and Jesus run parallel, but after the baptismal narrative Jesus alone is the protagonist. Indeed, this is the case already in the account of the baptism, because Luke reports beforehand that John was taken captive (3.19f). Accordingly, John is not even mentioned in connection with Jesus' baptism. But also the baptism itself loses some of its weight,[57] for the grammatical construction of the account is such that it focuses on the descent of the Spirit and the heavenly voice; even a translation may convey how the sentence hurries on, quickly leaving the baptism behind: 'It happened, when Jesus had been baptised and was praying, that the heaven was opened and that the Spirit came down . . . and that there was a voice from heaven: "You are. . ."'. The point that Jesus prayed becomes more prominent than the mention of the baptism, so that the descent of the Spirit is linked with Jesus' prayer rather than with his being baptised (3.21c).

The vision of the dove is more concrete in Luke than in Mark and Matthew, so that Jesus' possession of the Spirit becomes apparent to a larger public.[58] A particular light is shed on Jesus' filial status when the

[55] Luz 1985, 156; Gnilka 1986–88 1, 79f. Gerhardsson (1973) sees a close connection between the proclamation of Jesus' sonship in the baptismal story and the motif of his sonship in the temptation narrative.

[56] Strecker 1966, 181; Chevalier 1986, 534; Legasse 1993, 66f.

[57] Bovon 1989, 183; Nolland 1989, 160f. Nevertheless Luke is of the opinion that John's baptism belonged to those events concerning which the witnesses of Jesus, the apostles, should be able to testify (Acts 1.22).

[58] The focusing on Jesus' divine sonship may possibly be sharper through another Lukan particularity, namely that the heavenly voice quotes Ps 2.7 more extensively: 'You are my son, today I have begotten you'. This variant reading is controversial but, albeit with some hesitation, I prefer to follow it, applying the principle that a more difficult reading is to be preferred to an easier one. In this case it would have been easier for the copyists to follow the Markan version, as in the majority of the manuscripts, including those which are generally regarded as the best. Grundmann (1971, 107) makes the same choice.

words of the heavenly voice are directly followed by his genealogy, the last links of which are '(son) of Enos, (son) of Seth, (son) of Adam, (son) of God' (3.38).

Thus the baptismal narrative of Luke's Gospel occurs immediately before his report on Jesus' public appearance, which begins in 4.14 ('Jesus returned in the power of the Spirit to Galilee'). The audience is informed that a divine act is imminent, to be performed by the promised Messiah, who works in the power of the Spirit and under its guidance (see also 4.1, 18). Thus Peter also is made to proclaim later on in Luke's second work: 'God has anointed him (Jesus) with the Holy Spirit and with power' (Acts 10.38). This agrees with a general feature in Luke's presentation in the Gospel and in Acts, namely that the Spirit directs and guides the course of events.[59] Thus, as we have seen, the baptism itself is not connected with either the endowment of the Spirit or the proclamation of Jesus' sonship. These are rather bound to Jesus' prayer after his baptism. (Cf. 11.13: the Father gives the Holy Spirit to his children who ask him.)[60]

In his baptismal narrative Luke says nothing of what Jesus' baptism meant. But in the light of the whole Gospel, it is evident that when Jesus was baptised like 'all the people' (3.21), he did something that God wanted, indeed, something which derived from the divine purpose behind his mission. This is indicated by 7.29f: 'All the people including the tax collectors listened (to John), and they justified (ἐδικαίωσαν) God and were baptised with the baptism of John. But the Pharisees and the lawyers rejected the purpose (τὴν βουλήν) of God and did not undergo the baptism.' This statement implies that Jesus, when being baptised, did something required by 'righteousness' (cf. Acts 3.14). In Luke's church too God was 'justified' when people accepted the proclamation and were baptised, albeit in their case with Christian baptism. Thus Jesus' baptism could also be an example to be imitated by converts to Christianity.

In the *Gospel of John*, finally, it is never explicitly mentioned that Jesus was baptised by John, even though 1.32–34 seems to presuppose a knowledge that the baptism occurred (see also 3.26). In these verses the Baptist 'bears witness' that he has seen the Spirit descend and remain on Jesus, who is the one who will baptise with the Spirit. For this reason John can testify that Jesus is God's chosen. We recognise the elements from the

[59] Luke 12.12; Acts 4.8; 5.32; 10.19; 13.2; 15.28 etc.
[60] Grundmann 1971, 107f; G. Schneider 1977, 92; Nolland 1989, 160. Also in Acts baptism and gift of the Spirit are combined in the indirect manner we encounter in the baptismal narrative. See Acts 2.38; 8.15–17; 10.44–48; 19.5f.

Synoptic Gospels, and the similarity becomes even greater if we read 'the Son of God' instead of 'the chosen one'. The latter is, however, preferable.[61] Here the Christological interest predominates, as well as a determination to make the appearance of the Baptist subservient to this interest. Accordingly, John is fully subordinate to Jesus.

Of the deliberations in this chapter particularly the presentation of John and his baptism are crucial. The interpretations of his baptism and of the tradition of Jesus' baptism teach us, on the one hand, how important John and his baptism were in these early Christian circles, and on the other, that the account of Jesus' baptism could also have a bearing on the baptism which the Christian readers had undergone.

---

[61] The manuscripts which generally are regarded as best (and in this case, also the majority) read 'the Son of God'. But precisely the similarity to the Synoptics suggests that this reading is secondary in comparison with 'the chosen one'. Possibly John here represents a tradition which is parallel to that which first appears in Mark. It could even be the older of the two. See Hartman 1976.

2

The origin of Christian baptism[1]

There are good reasons to believe that from the beginning entrance into the early church normally meant that the neophyte was baptised.[2] This is self-evident to Luke in Acts, and other independent traditions point in the same direction: the Johannine (John 3.5), the Matthean (28.19), and, before these, Paul and those Christians before him and contemporary with him, of whom he bears indirect witness in his letters (e.g. Rom 6.3). When asking how early the first Christians baptised, it is useful to remember that Paul takes it as a matter of course that he himself was baptised (1 Cor 12.13). This means that about five years after the death of Jesus there were Christians to whom it was natural that newly converted persons should be baptised, for this is the time of Paul's conversion.[3]

Two particular reasons have been adduced to support the assumption that the very first Christians did not baptise, or at least that there were early Christian circles which did not. On the one hand, these scholars refer to the pericope about Jesus' commissioning of the disciples (Mark 6.8–11/Matt 10.5–16/Luke 10.1–12), in which no mention is made of baptism, although otherwise these speeches in their present form contain details which seem to reflect the missionary work of the church. On the other hand, they refer to the episodes in Acts 18.24–19.7, in which Luke mentions Apollos and some 'disciples' who knew only of John's baptism. As to the commissioning speeches, both Matthew and Luke are evidently of the opinion that the death and resurrection of Jesus were the necessary presuppositions of a wider mission and of baptism. In their view, Jesus' death and resurrection were so fundamental to the missionary preaching

---

[1] For a survey of the discussion see Lohfink 1976 and G. Barth 1981, 11–43.
[2] Thus Dinkler 1962a, 629; Conzelmann 1967, 64; G. Barth 1981, 11ff; Chevallier 1986, 529. Differently Barnikol 1956/57 and Haufe 1976, 566.
[3] For a concentrated discussion of Pauline chronology see Koester 1982 2, 99–106.

after Easter that it was impossible to have Jesus say anything in these speeches like, e.g., the command of the risen Lord to his disciples in Luke 24.47: 'Repentance and forgiveness of sins will be preached in his name (i.e., that of the risen Messiah) to all nations'.[4]

If, then, it is not too difficult to explain why a commission to baptise is not found in the speeches of the earthly Jesus as represented in the Gospels, the two passages in Acts raise slightly harder questions. To a great extent this depends on the circumstance that their value as sources is by no means clear. Does 19.1–7 really testify to the existence of Christians in the 50s who did not know of Christian baptism? Or only to after-effects of the Baptist's circles which Luke wanted to neutralise? Or to something else? Does the passage on Apollos (Acts 18.24–28) tell us not only of a missionary work that we can also surmise behind 1 Cor 1–4, but also of a missionary who performed baptism in another manner than Paul, i.e. baptised with John's baptism? In the latter case, does Luke, so to speak, correct Apollos and assign him a place in the Pauline group?[5] It is hardly possible to find strong grounds for an opinion as to how far these passages reflect an extraordinary but existing attitude on baptism. Therefore the questions are too numerous and the attempts to answer them too various. But evidently Luke could at least imagine a Jewish Christian missionary who did not know of Christian baptism, and furthermore think that there were 'disciples' (i.e. in his usage, Christians) who were only baptised with John's baptism. Indeed, he could imagine such things, but as something unacceptable.

Thus, if at least it was normal that baptism was required of those joining the church, and if this was the case from the beginning, then the question becomes even more urgent: why? To some Bible readers the question may seem unnecessary: when the risen Lord sent his apostles to make the nations his disciples, did he not explicitly command them to baptise new converts (Matt 28.19)? But there is a far-reaching unanimity among New Testament scholars that the evangelist has laid this commission in the mouth of the risen Jesus.[6] It is often suggested that it reflects the view held by the church in Syria (where Matthew's Gospel is assumed to

---

[4] Grundmann 1971, 453; Goppelt 1976, 547, 607ff.

[5] See the discussion in Haenchen 1977, 531–534; Pesch 1986 2, 159–166; Weiser 1981–85, 505–509, 512ff.

[6] In the commission the injunction to baptise is actually secondary to the overall command to go and make disciples of all nations.

have its origin) that it baptised in accordance with the Lord's will when baptising in the name of the T·riune God.[7] One of the strongest reasons in support of this opinion is the trinitarian formula; other material in the New Testament, particularly Pauline material, indicates that the formula is comparatively late. Furthermore, the passage contains more traces of the evangelist's personal idiom than is usually the case when he takes over older traditions.[8]

As an explanation of why the followers of Jesus baptised the people who joined the church it has been suggested that they learnt the practice from Judaism, which compelled Gentile converts to undergo a rite of purification, proselyte baptism.[9] This baptism was treated in the introductory chapter above. The practice may possibly have begun sometime during the first century CE.[10] But several reasons contradict such an opinion on the origin of Christian baptism. Certainly proselyte baptism was a kind of transition rite (a 'rite de passage') which was performed only once in a person's life. In this respect it was more similar to Christian baptism than the purification baths which were prescribed by the Old Testament or otherwise observed by the Jews, and which have also been adduced to explain why the Christians began to baptise.[11] Moreover, proselyte baptism could certainly be called a purification rite – such was the meaning of many water rites, as we saw in the introduction above – and this holds true also of Christian baptism. But proselyte baptism was not associated with forgiveness of sins, nor was it connected with conversion and repentance in a critical, eschatological perspective. Finally, and more important than we may perceive at first: proselyte baptism was performed by the proselyte himself, whereas in Christian baptism the one baptised was passively being baptised by another person.[12]

When the present writer holds the view that the first Christians adopted and christianised John's baptism, this is not very original; it is a common

---

[7] G. Barth 1960, 123; Strecker 1966, 208ff; Grundmann 1972, 576; Schweizer 1973, 348; Goppelt 1976, 332; Lohfink 1976, 38. Differently J. Schneider 1960, 533f; Beasley-Murray, 1962, 77–92. This assessment is not contradicted by the fact that a redaction-critical analysis suggests that there are older patterns behind the passage; see Bornkamm 1964, 173f; G. Barth 1981, 15f.

[8] See Schweizer 1973, 348; Kingsbury 1974, 577.

[9] Cullmann 1958, 6f; Jeremias 1958, 28ff.

[10] See Schürer 1973–87 3.1, 174. Nevertheless, as mentioned in the introductory chapter, it is uncertain whether proselyte baptism was being practised when John and, soon after him, the early church began to baptise.

[11] G. Barth 1981, 32f. Cf. Thiering 1979/80 and 1980/81.

[12] G. Barth 1973. See also above, on John's baptism, chapter 1 footnote 8.

opinion among contemporary exegetes.[13] In the preceding paragraph a number of features of Christian baptism were mentioned which bring the two baptisms close to each other and which point to some thoughts and ideas common to them both. On the other hand, the differences between Christian baptism and proselyte baptism which were adduced in the same paragraph are all details in which Christian baptism resembles that of John.

But the enumeration of a series of similarities does not answer the question of why the Christians began to baptise with the Johannine baptism. Presumably it was of some importance that Jesus, as well as some of the disciples, had undergone John's baptism.[14] John 1.35 mentions two disciples of John whom John directed to Jesus, one of whom is Andrew.[15] But the belief that the ultimate crisis was at hand must have been more important. Such a view was crucial to John and a fundamental reason for his appearance, and this was also true of Jesus, both of the Jesus who was caught up by the Baptist's preaching and of him who himself preached God's kingdom and lived and died for it. The disciples of Jesus must also have shared this view and perceived the world in an eschatological perspective.[16]

In so far as Jesus' disciples had once adhered to the preaching of the Baptist, their encounter with Jesus did not involve radically new expectations. His preaching, too, had as a centre the message that God's kingdom was critically near, even though his picture of God had features of warmth not found with John. Nevertheless, this was the crux: soon the radical change would come, and new conditions would be created by God, either through a cosmic catastrophe or through an intervention of some other

[13] See Dinkler 1962a, 628; Delling 1963, 55; Lohfink 1976, 42f; G. Barth 1981, 37ff.

[14] But we cannot prove that early Christians reported from the beginning that Jesus underwent John's baptism, and furthermore, interpreted this event as meaning that the epoch of the new covenant was imminent and maintained that people who were brought into this new covenant should be baptised with the same rite of purification. We observed, however, that Matthew is probably of the opinion that the baptismal narrative contains this among other messages (see the passage in the previous chapter on Matthew's usage of the baptismal narrative).

[15] It is probable that Jesus baptised for some time before beginning his proper work (John 3.22, 26). In John 4.2 the evangelist changes this earlier remark and asserts that Jesus' disciples baptised, not he himself. In any case he came to a point where he left off baptising and respectfully distanced himself from the Baptist in the conviction that he had a different mission of his own. See Becker 1979–81, 152 (+ literature); Legasse 1993, 71–87.

[16] Lohfink 1976, 47ff; G. Barth 1981, 43; Pokorný 1980/81, 374f; cf. Dinkler 1962a, 629.

kind. The new age was dawning, or, with other images: a new covenant between God and his people was in the making. This approaching new situation determined Jesus' preaching and his perception of his own person and mission. He even said that God's reign was already manifest in what he did and said. His ethical message too is to be understood in such a context. His command that people repent and believe in the good news was of course also born out of the same expectation that the time was imminent when God would take all power into his hand. The fact that Jesus and his followers were convinced that God's Spirit was at work through him (Matt 12.28/Luke 11.20) must also have given rise to eschatological expectations. This may be inferred from the fact that many of the Jews then were of the opinion that the Spirit had been taken from Israel with the last of the prophets, Malachi, and that it would not return before the time of salvation.[17]

When individuals who saw the world in this perspective were convinced that their executed master had risen from the dead, this must have given further substance to their eschatological expectations.[18] For although there was no fixed Jewish doctrine that the dead would rise at the end of time, such a view was well represented among Palestinian Jews of those days.[19] Thus the conviction that Jesus had risen must have implied that the new age had drawn even closer. The disciples were themselves to share in its blessings together with their living Lord.[20] This could per se have had as a result that the group coalesced firmly and like the Qumran community withdrew from the rest of the world. Instead they entered upon a mission, first among their fellow Jews and eventually also among Gentiles. Leaving aside the questions of the origin and early history of Christian mission,[21] we may content ourselves with stating that it began early. This has a counterpart in the circumstance that the stories of the encounters with the Risen Lord often contain a command to engage in mission.[22] Thus the followers of Jesus thought of the new situation in such a manner that they

[17] See Greenspahn 1989.
[18] Thyen 1970, 147; Conzelmann 1971, 27f.
[19] Cavallin 1974 and 1979, esp. 260ff, 266ff, 310–319.
[20] It is difficult to know in precisely what categories they first thought of this communion. One mode of thinking seems to have been inspired by the image of the Son of Man brought to the Ancient of Days in Daniel 7. 1 Thess 4.13 bears witness to an old tradition (thus Dupont 1962, 103; Hoffmann 1966, 212ff) according to which the risen Christ is understood as this Son of Man and the believers are 'brought with' him. See Hartman 1966, 186f.
[21] E.g. Kasting 1969.
[22] Matt 28.16–20; Luke 24.36–49; John 20.19–23.

became convinced that it was of importance to all people, although first to their fellow Jews.

It fits well into this eschatological pattern that the disciples moved to Jerusalem. According to traditional expectations Jerusalem and/or its temple were to be the centre of the people of the new covenant or of the age of salvation. The following quotation from a vision reported in *The First Book of Enoch* (*1 En.* 90.29–33)[23] is a good illustration:

> I went on seeing until the Lord of the sheep brought about a new house, greater and loftier than the first one, and set it up in the place of the first which had been covered up ... All the sheep were within it. (30) Then I saw all the sheep that had survived as well as all the animals upon the earth and the birds of heaven, falling down and worshipping those sheep, making petition to them and obeying them in every respect. (32) Those sheep were all snow-white, and their wool abundant and clean. (33) All those which had been destroyed and dispersed, and all the beasts of the field and the birds of the sky were gathered together in that house; and the Lord of the sheep rejoiced with great joy because they had all become gentle and returned to his house.[24]

The imagery is easily interpreted. The sheep of course stand for God's people, Israel, and the beasts for the Gentiles. 'The house' is a new temple in Jerusalem. The dispersed people of God are gathered, and are all righteous (32, 33). Gentiles join them (30, 33), and there are also, as it seems, people risen from the dead (33a).[25]

This text reflects an overall perspective which seems to have suggested itself to Jesus' disciples after Easter; it also provided a reason to pick up John's baptism of repentance unto the remission of sins (note that the purity mentioned in the *Enoch* passage [32] might very well stand for forgiveness). What John had expected was now beginning to be realised. Was the threshing floor now to be cleansed and the wheat to be gathered into the granary?

In our discussion of the religio-historical background to the baptism of John we encountered a bundle of expectations associated with the hope of the new covenant. It is now time to recall them. They were alive in the Jewish environment of the early church.[26] But now the followers of Jesus had had experiences of their own which fitted into these patterns of

---

[23] Other texts which give Jerusalem a position in the eschatological expectations are Isa 2.2ff; Jer 3.14–17; Ezek 47; *1 En.* 25–27; *Ps.Sol.* 11.1–3; 17.28f; *2 Bar.* 39.7–40.4. See Billerbeck 1922–28, 4, 883, 919f.

[24] Trans. by E. Isaac in Charlesworth, *OTP*.

[25] Cavallin 1974, 40.

[26] See Baltzer 1960; Hartman 1979; 1980.

expectations, and they came to believe that a renewed people of God were being gathered, who repented and turned to the Lord, were purified in water, received a new Spirit, and were called the sons of God as he was their Father.

Christian baptism was characterised above as a christianised Johannine baptism. We have also encountered some features which are common to both of these baptisms, particularly the eschatological perspective in which both of them should be understood. Between the two baptisms lay the life and work of Jesus and the events which led to the conviction that he had risen from the dead. This was also understood in the same eschatological perspective, but had the result that Christian baptism became something more than a renewed Johannine baptism. So it may be justified to label the adopted Johannine baptism 'christianised', even if the first Christians did not regard themselves as belonging to a religion other than Judaism. This can be seen from the formula which has been associated with Christian baptism as far back in time as we can follow it: it was performed 'into the name of the Lord Jesus'.

3

'Into the name of the Lord Jesus'

3.1. The formula

For some reason the first Christians spoke of their baptism as one 'in the name of Jesus Christ' or 'into the name of the Lord Jesus'.[1] There are several forms of such a baptismal formula in the New Testament:

> into the name of the Lord Jesus (Acts 8.16; 19.5; εἰς τὸ ὄνομα τοῦ κυρίου Ἰησοῦ)
>
> in the name of Jesus Christ (Acts 10.48: ἐν τῷ ὀνόματι Ἰησοῦ Χριστοῦ)
>
> because of the name of Jesus Christ (Acts 2.38: ἐπὶ τῷ ὀνόματι Ἰησοῦ Χριστοῦ)[2]
>
> into the name of the Father and the Son and the Holy Spirit (Matt 28.19: εἰς τὸ ὄνομα τοῦ πατρὸς καὶ τοῦ υἱοῦ καὶ τοῦ ἁγίου πνεύματος)

Compare the following with the first two phrases:

> into the name of Paul (1 Cor 1.13: εἰς τὸ ὄνομα Παύλου)
>
> into my name (1 Cor 1.15: εἰς τὸ ἐμὸν ὄνομα
>
> (you were justified) in the name of Jesus Christ, the Lord (1 Cor 6.11. ἐν τῷ ὀνόματι τοῦ κυρίου Ἰησοῦ Χριστοῦ)[3]

Luke, when writing Acts, hardly thought that there was any difference in the meaning of the different formulae.[4] But how then to explain the variety? Possibly Luke knew of several forms actually in use, in which case the differences could depend on tradition. The phrase which Paul uses in 1 Cor 6.11 may indicate the existence of such a tradition, different from that which he echoes in 1 Cor 1.13–15. But although this is a possibility, we

---

[1] Campenhausen (1971) was of another opinion; but see G. Barth 1981, 45ff.

[2] Some manuscripts read 'in', but this must be regarded as an easier reading and therefore inferior.

[3] 'Into the name of the Lord' (εἰς τὸ ὄνομα [τοῦ] κυρίου) stands in *Didache* 9.5 and *Hermas*, Vis. 3.7.3. In *Did.* 7.1 also 'into' (εἰς) is used, but with the 'name' of the Trinity as in Matthew. 'Into Christ' in Rom 6.3 and Gal 3.27 may be regarded as an abbreviated form (cf. 1 Cor 10.2, 'into Moses').

[4] But cf. Delling 1961, 84ff, 90ff.

should also consider another explanation of Luke's formulae (which need not, however, contradict the existence of different traditions).

This explanation involves considering Luke's modes of expression. Luke encountered the phrase 'in the name (of somebody)' in Mark (see e.g. Mark 9.37ff/Luke 9.48f); the same holds true of 'because of the name (of somebody)' (Mark 13.6/Luke 21.8). But, more importantly, he knows of them from the Septuagint. There they are also used of acts of worship: e.g. somebody prays 'in (God's) name' (Deut 10.8) or brings a sacrifice 'because of (God's) name' (Mal 1.11).[5] Now, it is well known that Luke wants to keep a biblical style. This is particularly visible in the first part of Acts, in which he describes the Jerusalem community. For this purpose he employs a number of somewhat peculiar turns of phrase which are found in the Septuagint. There they have their roots in the underlying Hebrew original. Thus when, in Acts 2 and 10, Peter uses 'in' and 'because of' 'the name (of somebody)', Luke lets the prince of the apostles speak with biblical turns of phrase.

The expression '*into* the name (of somebody)' is, however, un-biblical in so far as it does not occur in the Septuagint.[6] In addition, it is at odds with Greek style, and actually in normal Greek used only in banking language. There the 'name' stood for the owner of a bank account, and when somebody paid money into this account, it was done 'into the name' of the owner.

Now, a simple inquiry reveals that Luke uses the 'into' form when he himself is the narrator. This means that the form corresponds to his natural style, presumably the mode of expression he has learnt from his own Christian surroundings. This observation can be combined with another insight, namely that Luke, when writing Acts, followed the rules and conventions of contemporary historiography. The rules were, so to speak, in the air, but somebody could also formulate them, as Lucian did.[7] One such convention was that the principal characters' utterances, and especially their speeches, should meet the expectations of the reader concerning the speakers and their behaviour in the depicted situations.[8] A good general should, for example, speak to his troops in a particular manner before a battle.

[5] See Hartman 1985.
[6] That somebody can utter blasphemies 'against (εἰς) his (i.e. God's) name' (2 Macc 8.4) is of course no exception. Here the 'name' is the object of the action contained in the noun, not its circumstance.
[7] His book is entitled *How To Write History*.
[8] See Plümacher 1972, 39; van Unnik 1979, 59; Gempf 1993.

Returning to the baptismal formulae, we find that the different forms 'in the name (of somebody)' and 'because of the name (of somebody)' are well suited to Luke's authorial techniques. Apparently he found it fitting that Peter's language should sound biblical. As suggested, this does not exclude the possibility that these turns of phrase, or at least that with 'in', were actually in use in some circles. 1 Cor 6.11, quoted above, supports such an assumption.

A similar approach is natural when it comes to the Christological terminology of the different baptismal formulae.[9] Thus Luke makes Peter say 'in the name of *Jesus Christ* (or: of *Jesus, the Messiah*)'. The combination 'Jesus Christ' was established and known before Luke, particularly by Paul.[10] It is entirely possible that, say, in Jewish–Christian circles, baptism was performed 'in the name of Jesus the Messiah'. Be that as it may, Luke is almost totally consistent, and in his book particularly the Jewish–Christians use this Christological title when talking to other Jews.[11] Thus Luke obviously thought that this was how Jewish–Christians should speak.

We can regard 'the Lord Jesus' in the 'into the name' formula in a similar way, as corresponding to Luke's authorial technique.[12] The phrase not only represents Luke's own idiom,[13] but also belongs to the language which the Christians speak among themselves in his account.[14]

Thus we can, on the one hand, conclude that Luke seems to choose his expressions with regard to the principal characters of his account and their expected behaviour. On the other hand, the expressions are rooted in the tradition in different ways, although such roots are more probable in the case of the 'into' formula than of the others.

The formula 'into the name of the Lord Jesus' may thus be well established, but the fact remains that it is peculiar: it is both un-biblical and un-Greek. This calls for an explanation, and one such was advanced by Wilhelm Heitmüller at the beginning of this century.[15] It was then that scholars in the fields of antiquity gained access to the vast finds of papyrus

---

[9] Hartman 1985, 735ff. Delling (1961, 85ff) hints at the problem as also does Hemer (1989, 382).

[10] E.g. Wilckens 1974, 157.

[11] 2.38; 3.6; 4.10; 8.12; 9.34; 10.36, 48; 16.18. In other combinations: 11.17; 15.26; 28.31. An exception is 16.18; does it depend on the circumstance that there we encounter a conjuration formula (cf. 3.6 and 4.10, where the subject is similar)?

[12] Hartman 1985, 737f.

[13] 4.33; 8.16; 11.20; 19.5, 13, 17.

[14] 1.21; 7.59; 15.11; 16.31; 20.21, 24, 35; 21.13.

[15] Heitmüller 1903.

manuscripts from Egypt, largely documents from everyday life. In business documents they found the formula 'into the name of somebody', used in banking terminology in the manner already mentioned. Heitmüller advanced the idea that the Greek-speaking Christians had adopted this technical term in order to claim that the baptised persons became the property of the glorified Lord like a sum of money which was transferred to a new owner. They were, so to speak, paid into his account.

Heitmüller's explanation and the understanding of baptism he deduced from it have been widely accepted.[16] Nevertheless they have been criticised by some scholars who think it is too far-fetched to assume that these early Christians described their relationship to Christ by borrowing an image from the technical language of banking.[17] To the present writer this criticism appears to be justified. Heitmüller's construction seems to be founded on a questionable assumption as to the function of so vague an expression as 'into the name of somebody'. Every time it is used, its specific meaning depends wholly on its literary context. Accordingly, it can hardly bring its meaning in banking into a baptismal context so as to function as an image there.[18] The distance between the two fields of association is too great and the term is too vague. The following simple example may illustrate the point. In Job 35.3 the RSV makes Job ask: 'What advantage have I?' When somebody attends a tennis match and the umpire shouts, 'Advantage Peterson', nobody would imagine that the umpire answers Job's question, any more than anyone would think of Job as a tennis player. Certainly the expression is the same, but it is vague, and the two contexts are too far apart to allow any interplay between the two texts.

There is, however, another suggestion as to the origin of the formula 'into the name of somebody', that it is a translation of a Hebrew phrase *l^eshem*, or of its Aramaic equivalent *l^eshum*, which literally means 'into (somebody's) name'. The meaning of the phrase is 'with regard to', 'bearing ... in mind'. This explanation is as old as Heitmüller's and seems to the present writer to be the correct one.[19] Nevertheless it has been applied in a questionable manner, to which we will return in a moment. Its

---

[16] Oepke 1933, 537; Bornkamm 1938, 47; J. Schneider 1952, 32; Bultmann 1968a, 42; Dunn 1970, 117f; Thyen 1970, 147; Dinkler 1974, 116f; Haenchen 1977, 186; Fitzmyer 1993, 430.

[17] Bietenhard 1954, 275; Delling 1961, 32ff; G. Barth 1981, 50f.

[18] Hartman 1973/74, 433.

[19] Heitmüller too takes into account that in some cases the Semitic phrase lies behind the 'into the name'; thus in Matt 10.4 ('bearing in mind that he is a prophet'; Heitmüller 1903, 113f).

defenders have regularly adduced the following sacrificial regulation from the Mishnah:

> An offering must be slaughtered into the name of (with regard to) six things: into the name of the offering (what kind of offering is it?), into the name of the offerer (on whose behalf is the offering made?), into the name of the Name (with regard to God), into the name of the altar-fire (bearing in mind that it must be a valid burnt offering), into the name of the fragrance, into the name of the pleasure (bearing in mind that it is to please God) (m.Zeb 4.6).

After some deliberations[20] the scholars who propose this solution conclude that as the offering is presented to God, so in baptism the baptised person is presented to Jesus as his property.[21] Accordingly, the upshot is remarkably similar to that of Heitmüller.[22]

But to the mind of the present writer, the scholars who have advanced this explanation have dealt with the comparative material somewhat improperly.[23] Indeed, the question may be raised whether in this case too it has been assumed that the 'into the name'-formula has a more fixed meaning than it actually has.[24] Already the phrase in the quoted Mishnah passage 'into the name of the Name' does not mean (offered) 'unto God', but (offered) 'with regard to God', that is, in his service, not in that of other gods.[25]

---

[20] They try to differentiate between a causal and a final meaning of the formula and find that it has a purpose-defining application. There is a risk that here scholars expect the language to have more grammatical precision than it actually has; they might even be unconsciously influenced by their way of thinking in their own mother tongue. See Hartman 1973/74, 434f.

[21] Billerbeck 1922–28 1, 1005; Bietenhard 1954, 275.

[22] This was also observed by some authors, who consequently felt less disturbed by the historical problem. See Leenhardt 1944, 36; Beasley-Murray 1962, 90ff, 100; Kuss 1963a, 98.

[23] Billerbeck 1922–28 I, 591, 1054ff; Bietenhard 1954, 275. Before them Brandt 1891 and Dalman 1898. They have been followed by, among others, Jeremias (1958, 35), Beasley-Murray (1962, 90f), Kretschmar (1970, 18, 32f), Goppelt (1976, 331).

[24] Hartman 1973/74, 434ff.

[25] In *Die Zueignung des Heils in der Taufe. Eine Untersuchung zum neutestamentlichen 'Taufen auf den Namen'* (1961) G. Delling presented his own solution to the 'name'-phrases. In a way, his study is text-immanent, at least in so far as he does not adduce extra-Christian material to shed light on the problem. He discusses all New Testament passages where 'name' appears and concludes that in the New Testament the name expressions ('into the name' etc.) in most cases have to do with Jesus. So he maintains that 'the person through whom God acts eschatologically cannot be separated from the work that God performs through him' (43). This may be an acceptable theological statement, but I am not sure that it can be deduced from the way the vocable 'name' is used in connection with the name 'Jesus' in the NT. Nor can the use of precisely the vocable 'name' carry the conclusion at the end of the book: 'Baptism "into (in) the name" introduces one into the salvific event which is associated with the name (Jesus)' (97).

There is, however, a Jewish-rabbinic usage of the phrase 'into the name' which seems to solve the problem of the original wording and meaning of the baptismal formula. As mentioned above, the expression is basically a general one, 'with regard to', 'having in mind'. But it is also used in a particular kind of context which is of interest in our case, contexts concerning religious rites. The rites are performed 'into the name' of the god, to whose cult the rite belongs or who is otherwise associated with the rite in question. This god is the fundamental referent of the rite; he/she is the one whom the worshipper 'has in mind' or 'with regard to' whom the rite is performed and who thus makes it meaningful.[26]

One element in the sacrificial rule just quoted may serve as an example. It says that the offering was to be offered 'into the name of the Name', i.e. it should be in worship of the God of Israel, not, say, a Zeus-cult like, for example that which Antiochus Epiphanes demanded according to 1 Macc 1.41–47. Other examples: the Rabbis discussed the validity of religious vows which are made by youngsters who say: 'We know into whose name (*lᵉshem mi*) we have given our vows' (m.Nid 5.6). Moreover, it is said that a Samaritan circumcises 'into the name of Gerizim' (t.Ab Z 3.13); the holy mountain of the Samaritans here stands for the Samaritan form of Judaism, which is the framework which gives the rite its meaning. Of course the scribes deny the validity of the sacrifices which are offered 'into the name of the mountains, of the hills, of the seas or of the desert' (m.Ḥul 2.8; cf. Deut 12.2); the rites do not belong to the worship of the one, true God. The last-mentioned Mishnah ruling is included in the Babylonian Talmud (b.Ḥul 40a), where stars, planets and Michael are added to the list. But neither in the Mishnaic nor in the Talmudic rule do the 'names' primarily represent deities who *receive* the offerings. Instead they stand for the worship of the gods of nature, including fertility gods, and, particularly in the Talmudic version, for the astral religion of antiquity. There was much speculation concerning cosmic beings and their power, and astrology was an important feature thereof. The speculation was widespread and played a role in most religions, even in Judaism. Moreover, the astral religion had a place for such heavenly powers as angels and archangels.[27] Thus the 'into the name' formula of the Talmudic rule in b.Ḥul 40a refers to the basic religious framework of the sacrifices. We also encounter the 'into the name' formula in the following two quotations, which deal with worship more generally: 'Every gathering into the name of heaven (i.e. God), will be

---

[26] Hartman 1973/74.

[27] See Philo, *De somniis* 1.140; Plutarch, *De fato* 572 F-574 C; Rom 8.38.

established' (Ab IV.11),[28] and 'there are two ways of drawing near (i.e. to one's god in worship),[29] one into the name of heaven, one not into the name of heaven' (S.Num § 136).

Finally it should be mentioned that the phrase 'into the name (of somebody)' could appear in another form, namely 'in (*bᵉ*) the name (of somebody)'. The expression is relatively common in the Old Testament, also in the Greek translation, and is used of acts of worship as well.[30] The meaning of this formula hardly differs from that of the phrase 'into the name'. One could also abbreviate the 'into the name' form into the simple 'into', with no change in meaning in this case either.[31] These possibilities are interesting to the student of the New Testament, as they represent analogies to the different formulas (to be baptised) 'into the name', 'in the name' and the short Pauline 'into' (Rom 6.3).

This comparative material suggests the following conclusions concerning the Christian baptismal formula. The formula, linguistically peculiar though it may be, is a literal translation of a Hebrew–Aramaic idiom, which the Aramaic-speaking early church used when speaking of Christian baptism. Accordingly we are brought down to a very early period of the church. In its Greek version the formula became a Christian technical term. It is difficult to be positive as to the time of the translation, but already the so-called Hellenists (Acts 6–7) could have been the circle within which the Greek form originated. According to Luke (Acts 11.19f), they were dispersed to Antioch in Syria and to other places and may have brought the term with them. Both Paul and Matthew (and even Luke) may have become acquainted with it in Antioch.[32] The 'in'-form may also be old, but here the material is less conclusive.

When early Christians spoke of the christianised Johannine baptism as one 'into the name of the Lord Jesus', the phrase probably implied that 'the

---

[28] Matt 18.20 ('gathered into my name') uses the same language.

[29] Cf. Heb 4.16; 10.1, 22.

[30] Thus it can be said both that young people give promises 'into the name (of God)' and that an idolator does so 'in its (i.e. the idol's) name' (m.Sanh 7.6). As to the OT, see above the discussion of Luke's Septuagintal idiom.

[31] Thus it is said in m.Ab Z 3.7 that a certain person trims a tree 'into the name of idolatry', but when this line is quoted in the Gemara (b.Ab Z 48a) it only says 'into idolatry'. Luke can behave in a similar manner. In Luke 21.12 he makes use of Mark 13.9, which mentions being brought before kings 'for my sake'. But Luke writes 'for the sake of my name'. Similarly, in Acts 10.43 he writes that forgiveness of sins is given 'through his name', whereas in Acts 13.38 it is given 'through him'. In these cases too the different expressions obviously mean the same thing.

[32] Hartman 1985, 733f.

Lord Jesus' meant the same to baptism as 'the Name' or 'Heaven' meant to the worship, the gathering, the sacrifice or the vows which were mentioned in the Jewish examples above. These rites were performed within the framework of the worship of God and in the light of what he meant to his people. Here a similar statement is made concerning the Lord Jesus. In all these cases the name refers to a deity which is the presupposition of the rite; its deeds and power, its promises or obligations to its adherents, its precepts or its blessings belong to the referential frame which dictates the meaning of the rite.

If this is the principal meaning of the name-phrases, they also acquire a defining, delimiting function: sacrifice 'into the name of the Name' was not offered within the framework of idolatry, circumcision 'into the name of Gerizim' was to be distinguished from that of orthodox Judaism. Then, in the case of Christian baptism, the name-phrase should, at least indirectly, have differentiated it from other baptismal rites. Among such rites, Johannine baptism comes first to mind,[33] but once Jewish proselyte baptism was in use, it would also be a ceremony from which the formula distinguished Christian baptism. But this, so to speak negative, delimiting manner of speech is presumably less important than the positive definition.

3.2. The meaning of the formula

So the question arises what it really means when a baptism is designated as 'into the name of the Lord Jesus'.[34] Generally speaking, it is more reasonable to assume that a formula of such a cultic technical usage had significance than to presuppose that it was meaningless, empty wording.[35] Although any answer is bound to be uncertain, the uncertainty is no worse than that inherent in the suggestion that the baptised person thereby became the property of the glorified Lord like a sum of money paid into his bank account or like a sacrifice brought to him.

When we attempt to answer the question of the original meaning of the formula, we should begin by recalling the eschatological perspective of the disciples' conviction that Jesus had risen from the dead. The kingdom of God and its imminence had played an important role in the preaching of Jesus. Now, when such a miraculous event seemed to have occurred, this

---

[33] Note the demarcation in Acts 19.1–7.
[34] The following account represents much of what is said in Hartman 1974.
[35] 'Nur eine Formel' writes Marxsen, assuming that it was not given any meaning until later (1964, 174).

nearness must have seemed to be even more relevant. But the belief that Jesus was risen did not only sharpen eschatological awareness, nor did it merely involve the hope that after Jesus, the first risen one, others would share the blessings of the kingdom (cf. 1 Thess 4.16f; 1 Cor 15.20; Col 1.18; Acts 26.23). As a technical, ritual formula, the baptismal formula presupposed more: its 'name' referred to an authority behind the rite, who conferred significance on the rite and made the formula meaningful.

The authority mentioned was probably an important subject of the disciples' preaching. For the baptism must have been coupled with the preaching in the same way as was the case with John the Baptist. His baptism was closely linked with his preaching of the approaching crisis and of repentance and remission of sins. This preaching and its reception had a ritual application in baptism. There the remission of sins was given, not by the Baptist, but by God who had sent him. There was a similar linkage on the part of the audience: they heard John proclaim the necessity of penitence and of baptism, they took this message to heart and repented. But this interior event had an external counterpart, in that the penitents made their way to the Baptist and to the water and were baptised, so receiving the forgiveness of their sins. When John's baptism was adopted by Jesus' followers, it was still probably combined with a preaching which demanded repentance and conversion to the same God, but which also dealt with Jesus and his teaching. For the baptism was one into his name, i.e. he stood for facts and circumstances that were basic to the rite and its meaning. His followers regarded his resurrection as the vindication of a man who had been despised and executed.[36] But now he had a lasting authoritative status as one who had been 'exalted' or 'glorified'.

At the same time, the conviction that Jesus had been vindicated must have prompted the first Christians to regard the historical Jesus, his preaching and work, in a new light.[37] Since many of the preachers of the earliest church must have known Jesus during his life on earth, it would have been strange if they had preached a baptism into his name and had not related it to this Jesus, even if they proclaimed that he had risen. Such a connection with the work of Jesus would have been natural with respect to the motif of the remission of sins, for a preaching which led to baptism must also have touched on the remission of sins given there. As with John's baptism, God was the one who forgave; but now the divine forgiveness was bestowed at a baptism into the name of Jesus the Lord. Under the sign of

---

[36] Thüsing 1967–68, 214ff; Kümmel 1969, 91ff.
[37] Thüsing 1967–68, 208ff, speaks of a 'transformation'.

God's kingdom this Jesus had brought sinners into communion with him and eaten with them; he had forgiven their sins – as God alone could do (Mark 2.5ff) – and, *inter alia*, his preaching had contained such features as are illustrated by the parable of the prodigal son.[38] This Jesus of the past was now understood in the light of the new eschatological situation. In the present, critical time, he was a living authority who gave validity and meaning to the rite which was the exterior sign that sins were forgiven.

Furthermore, there are good reasons to assume that the preachers proclaimed, as John (and Jesus) had done, that people must repent and turn to God in view of the eschatological crisis. It is difficult even to guess, but it seems fair to say that the proclamation that conversion was necessary also implied moral demands. This was, of course, the case in John's preaching, but also in that of Jesus, although with Jesus the message of salvation preceded the moral demands.[39] 'Faith' was a positive expression of what conversion meant.[40] Moreover this call to faith constituted a connection with the historical Jesus, in whose preaching the demand for faith, or an invitation to it, seems to have played an important role.[41] When individuals believed, they took the 'gospel' to themselves, placed themselves at the disposal of the kingdom, and let themselves be brought into a new relationship to God. The 'name' in the baptismal formula, 'the Lord Jesus', became a new prism through which all these motifs were refracted.

The preaching and/or the reflections on baptism probably also touched upon the Holy Spirit. John the Baptist had in some sense spoken of a future baptism in the Holy Spirit, and we remember that Jewish expectations concerning the age of salvation could also contain a hope for the gift of the Spirit. It seems that the first Christians prided themselves on their possession of this gift, which the followers of John lacked. In this respect too they may have linked up with Jesus, who was convinced that his work was borne by this Spirit (Matt 12.28/Luke 11.20). Now, his followers claimed, it was given in his name.

Finally, we can discern a further aspect of the christianised Johannine baptism. It was not only a 'rite de passage' for those who entered a new

---

[38] On the remission of sins in the work of the historical Jesus see e.g. Fuchs 1956, 220; Becker 1964, 199–217; Perrin 1967, 102ff, 139ff; T. Holtz 1979, 60f.

[39] See Leroy 1978, 78–87; T. Holtz 1979, 70–83; Stanton 1989, 192–203.

[40] Behm 1942, 999. It is, of course, venturesome to speak of early Christian preaching in statements as sweeping as these, as though we knew more about it than a few reflections, visible especially in the writings of Paul and of the considerably later Luke.

[41] Behm 1942, 998; Bornkamm 1956, 119–12; G. Barth 1983, 223f.

phase in God's history with his people. It was also the door into a new human community. We found something similar in connection with John's baptism. Several motifs in the eschatological expectations are related to such a community. Here the people of the new covenant were gathered, cleansed, forgiven, sanctified and equipped with a new spirit. Indeed, the gathering itself can also be regarded as occurring 'into the name of the Lord Jesus'. In a new key the early church could link up with the gathering work of her Lord, who gathered people to himself, not in order to form a closed group or a sect, but to assemble a people of God under God's present and imminent sovereignty.[42]

These deliberations represent a few features of what a baptism 'into the name of the Lord Jesus' may have meant already when it was understood as a christianised Johannine baptism performed by individuals who were convinced that Jesus had risen from the dead. When we now enter upon a discussion of the Christological designations of the formula, we embark on a task which is at least equally complicated, namely determining the contours of the earliest Christology. For our present purpose we must limit ourselves to aspects which are of direct significance to our subject.[43]

There are good reasons to believe that the Semitic prepositional construction of the formula 'into the name of the Lord Jesus' is very old. It is slightly less certain that it was connected from the beginning with the Christological designation 'the Lord Jesus'. (We saw that Luke assumed that Peter spoke of a baptism 'in the name of Jesus Christ' [or: in the name of Jesus the Messiah; Acts 2.38]). But when we encounter the designation 'the Lord Jesus', it must be somehow connected with the early confessional formula 'Jesus (is) the Lord' (κύριος Ἰησοῦς).[44] This in its turn is rooted in ideas which are to be surmised behind the Aramaic prayer *maranatha*, 'Come, our Lord!'[45] They are similar to those at which Paul hints in 1 Thess 1.9f when he reminds the Thessalonians of their conversion: 'You turned to God from idols to serve the living and true God and to wait for his Son from heaven, whom he raised from the dead, Jesus, who delivers us from the coming wrath'. When Jesus was called 'Lord' in the baptismal formula, it meant that he was confessed as a heavenly authority, not as the God to whom the Thessalonians had turned, but yet as a Lord with divine

---

[42] See Goppelt 1976, 254–260.
[43] A fine discussion is found in Pokorný 1984.
[44] See Rom 10.9; 1 Cor 12.3; Phil 2.1. See Fitzmyer 1981 (+ literature).
[45] Like so many others I prefer to read the phrase in this way, although it is also possible to interpret it as 'our Lord comes'. For the discussion, see G. Schneider 1981.

power who was active among human beings. This was expressed in different ways: he was called the Son of God, as, for example, in the aforementioned passage from 1 Thessalonians, and Psalm 110 was read as referring to him: 'The Lord said to my Lord: Sit at my right hand';[46] he was described as God's wisdom[47] or God's word[48] who carried out God's plan. We need not discuss these problems here, but can be content with stating that a baptism 'into the name of the Lord Jesus' presupposed a belief in a glorified Jesus who had power which he now exerted on earth. It is probable that the conviction expressed in 1 Thess 1.10 was shared by many, that this power would deliver people in the ultimate crisis, which John the Baptist had likened to a threshing, and which Paul some twenty years later called 'the coming wrath'. To belong to Jesus' flock meant to belong to those who were or who would be saved.

We have already seen that this heavenly power of Jesus was also exerted in as much as sins were forgiven. This was presumably regarded as another aspect of his saving capacity.

The passage from 1 Thessalonians also supports an assumption that the eschatological climate involved the expectation that he would come relatively soon 'from heaven'. Since the imagery of this so-called return is not wholly clear,[49] we may express ourselves in somewhat vaguer terms and say that the near future would bring a confrontation with the divine authority which was also the fundamental referent of baptism.

It is conceivable, but hardly more than this, that this Christology which was 'localised' in heaven was preceded by one using Messianic categories, according to which the risen Jesus would reign in an established kingdom of God. It is also conceivable that a 'heavenly' Christology existed parallel with a 'Messianic' one. Be that as it may, we have already touched on the possibility that at an early stage baptism could also be performed 'in the name of Jesus Christ' or 'in the name of Jesus the Messiah'. Thus Jesus' being the Messiah becomes a framework of decisive importance for baptism. But for the early history of the early church, into the mists of which we now peer, it is difficult to determine what Messiahship may have meant in connection with baptism.[50] But the manner in which Luke uses

[46] Mark 12.36 par.; Acts 2.34f; 1 Cor 15.25; Heb 1.3, 13. See Hay 1973.
[47] Suggested in Matt 11.19 par.
[48] John 1.1–14, etc.
[49] The 'direction' of the 'parousia' of the Son of Man may first, as in Dan 7.13f, have been towards heaven. See Lagrange 1929, 402f (ad Mark 14.62); Glasson 1945; Robinson 1957; Taylor 1966 (ad Mark 14.62); Hartman 1966, 186f.
[50] See Pokorný 1984, 36–40, 65–67.

the Christ-title in a later time may indicate something. As we have seen, he makes Jewish Christians use it when they speak to other Jews. Jewish Christians would then claim that the risen Jesus was the fulfilment of God's promises to his people of a coming ruler in his kingdom. At the same time they must, however, have reinterpreted the Jewish expectations in order to include the fact that this Messiah must suffer, die and be raised.[51] A baptism referring to such a Messiah would also have been associated with the other motifs to which I have just referred, and which were taken over from the Baptist (forgiveness, conversion, faith, and the gift of the Spirit).

In previous research the question was often raised whether 'the name' was mentioned at baptism. W. Heitmüller took this for granted, as he built his reconstruction in large measure on a particular position of baptism in the history of religions in antiquity; thus, he was of the opinion that it should be understood in the light of how different holy names were used for exorcisms and magic, or, sometimes, to mark ownership by the person named.[52] If my attempt to explain the background of the formula 'into the name of the Lord Jesus' is correct, Heitmüller's answer to the question is unacceptable. Instead we are referred to such ritual analogies as I quoted earlier in this chapter, that is, even if we do not assume the existence of a fixed ritual of baptism, the rite must have contained such prayers, allocutions and acclamations as made clear that the Lord Jesus was its fundamental referent. The circumstance that the formula, despite its linguistic oddity, was so widespread, may signify that the phrase was used in the rite in such a way that it stuck in the mind of the participants.[53]

We now turn to the New Testament passages which deal with baptism; the discussion of each book or group of texts will conclude with a few

---

[51] Pokorný 1984, 66 (there also further references).

[52] Heitmüller 1903, part 2. See also Dibelius 1964, 175ff and cf. Mussner 1964, 122f. In later texts it is expressly mentioned that a name was pronounced over the person who was baptised (*Hermas, Sim.* 8.6.4, and Justin, *Apology* 1. 61.10–13). This ritual detail may be of early origin. But when Jas 2.7 is adduced for support, this makes a weak argument. The passage says that some people 'blaspheme the good name that has been mentioned (ἐπικληθέν) over you'. (The verse from James resounds, by the way, in the *Hermas* passage.) The expression is, however, biblical, and, in the OT it is used of God's chosen people (2 Chron 7.14; Jer 14.9; Bar 2.15; Dan 9.19), as well as of the temple sanctified to God (1 Kings 8.43; Jer 7.30). Thus in Jas 2.7 the expression hardly refers directly to baptism, but rather says that the Christians addressed are sanctified and dedicated to God and so belong to him, like the old Israel. Cf. Galling 1956.

[53] One analogy could be the usage which is indicated in b.Pes 60a whereby, at an offering in the temple, the offerer stated which sort of sacrifice he was performing, saying e.g. 'I slaughter the Passah into its name' (i.e., this is a Passah-offering).

paragraphs in which the results of the preceding deliberations are compared with the above reconstruction of the motifs which were linked to
baptism into the name of the Lord Jesus in the earliest phase of the early
church. We encountered most of them already in the preliminary glance at
Galatians 3 in the Introduction, and then in a particular form in our study
of John the Baptist. Briefly, the motifs which I shall examine to determine
how far they play a role in each text or group of texts discussed, are the
following: first, the overall *eschatological perspective*: on the one hand, a
conviction that the end was near, on the other, a belief that salvation was
already being realised. This perspective was determined by the Lord Jesus:
converts were baptised into his name, into the name of him who once lived
on earth and whose present lordship was confessed by the Christians, *kurios
Iesous*, Jesus is the Lord. This means that I shall ask how the author
perceives the *relationship of Jesus to baptism*. Since the belief in Jesus'
resurrection and his present authority played a major role in the picture I
tried to paint of the early thinking on baptism, I shall also enquire what
part these features play in our material. Furthermore, we noted how the
new situation prompted the followers of Jesus to *preach* a gospel determined by their belief in Jesus, a gospel aiming at *conversion* and *faith*. Both
were connected with baptism in a manner reminiscent of how conversion
and baptism belonged together in the mission of John, but also somehow
in the preaching of Jesus. Moreover, we encountered the motif of the
remission of sins with John, and it was also crucial for Jesus' preaching and
approach to sinners. When discussing the background of John's baptism
we also observed that remission of sins was one of the motifs which
appeared among the expectations for the age of salvation. Finally, we found
both with John and with Jesus, as well as in connection with the baptism of
the early church, the idea that a new *people of God* was being gathered; in
addition, this people possessed the *Holy Spirit*, a gift which was also
expected in the age of salvation by John among others.

4

Paul

4.1. Introduction

A discussion of the individual baptismal texts of the New Testament could follow a chronological line. It would start with the inception of the rite, tentatively reconstructed above, then continue with the material from the oldest phase and with the first Pauline texts from the beginning of the fifties. Such an approach would mean that before discussing Paul we would investigate the pre-Pauline material which can be extracted from the Pauline letters, in which Paul's turns of phrase are often such as to imply that he refers to opinions and traditions older than the text in question and which obviously derive from others. However, I prefer not to deal with this pre-Pauline material until after the treatment of the passages in Paul's letters which refer to baptism. The main reason for such an arrangement is that an attempt to treat the material in a strictly chronological sequence could easily convey the impression that we followed a discernible historical development. This would, however, be a false impression. Certainly we can surmise chains of thought and particular accents in different texts and groups of texts, but the material is too scanty to allow us, e.g., to distinguish between different phases in the development of the primitive motifs which I presented in the previous chapter, reconstructing, say, how baptism's eschatological aspects changed from the very first period and onwards until the Pastoral Letters or the Gospel of John. We should not assume that reflection on baptism and the development of such reflection occurred in a steady progression, which proceeded at the same pace everywhere in the early church, following the same tracks. Instead it is reasonable to reckon with the serious possibility that different motifs were differently developed in different contexts, and that thus there was no gradually advancing historical growth which had the same appearance everywhere. (Nevertheless we shall find that the diversity did not exclude a number of similarities.) Thus it is preferable to direct our attention to one text and text-group in turn and only in certain cases to discuss how a development has taken place. One such particular case is the step from Paul to his disciples.

Paul mentions or alludes to baptism relatively often. But it is worthy of notice that in the texts he left behind we never encounter a passage over which could be put the title 'On Baptism', and in which Paul explicitly presents a few fundamental features of his theology of baptism. Instead, in the cases where he comments on baptism, he is actually discussing something else, and he adduces baptism to use elements of his and/or others' thinking thereon as arguments in the treatment of the problem which is being discussed in the occasional epistolary context.

In such contexts Paul often indicates that his statements are accepted by the other party or acknowledged by the addressees as part of their own belief. Such indications are expressions such as 'do you not know that we ...' (Rom 6.3), 'you were not baptised, were you ...?' (1 Cor 1.13), 'for all of us were baptised ...' (1 Cor 12.13), 'what will they (among you) do who are being baptised on behalf of the dead?' (1 Cor 15.29). In the first examples here Paul certainly shares the opinion of the addressees. (If the argument is to carry weight, they must actually be of the opinion which he ascribes to them.) But in the latter case Paul probably refers to an opinion held by some of the addressees in order to make use of it when refuting the ideas of his opponents.

When scholars, using Paul's letters, want to reconstruct a Pauline theology of baptism, they must be aware of the historical difficulties. The ideas we encounter are only fragments which are not cited in their contexts as main features of Paul's baptismal thinking but adduced as effective arguments in discussions of other matters. In other words, the Pauline theology of baptism which we may reconstruct with the help of this material is based on the statements of the Paul of the letters. But the Paul of the letters may be more or less dissimilar to the historical Paul. The latter Paul may have had much more to say on baptism, perhaps points which were very important to him. But, for different reasons, he did not see fit to include these in his letters.

The historical problem, outlined in the preceding paragraph, has another side. Already the passages which deal explicitly with baptism may be challenging to the interpreter. But as a matter of fact there are other texts which may allude to baptism or even such as were originally parts of a baptismal liturgy or of a relatively fixed baptismal catechism. If, for example, Phil 2.5–11 was a text connected with baptism, known as such by both Paul and his early Christian readers,[1] this passage would increase our knowledge not only of Paul's baptismal thinking but also of that of other theologians. But we do not know enough to be certain. It is also possible that Paul alludes here and there to his own teaching on baptism, but that we simply do not catch the allusion or are not sure whether such an allusion is there. Is, e.g., 2 Cor 1.22, '(God) who put his seal on us', such an allusion?[2] Given this situation I preferred to risk dealing with too small rather than too large a number of texts. Then we can at least be certain that our material reflects Pauline thinking on baptism, even though we cannot be sure how representative it is either of the historical or of the epistolary Paul. Such a procedure seems preferable to one in which we reconstruct a Pauline baptismal theology, the correspondence of which to reality is even more fragile, namely the reality both of the textual world and the world of history, than is the case when we adhere to a more ascetic approach.[3]

Thus we shall deal with those Pauline passages which explicitly mention baptism or most probably allude to it. They will be treated in both their literary and their actual contexts. The latter normally pertains to a Christian community founded by Paul, but it should be mentioned that the reconstruction of such situations is not always easy.

Another context which must be considered is that of Paul's theology. Nor is this unproblematic, because his theology is not an unequivocal, clear, consistent ideology, but rather a pulsating organism full of tensions.[4] Nevertheless I allow myself to treat these passages without asking whether the apostle changed his views on baptism over the years. I do so, not to conceal possible tensions, but because it seems to me that the material does not provide us with a basis steady enough for such an attempt. The texts were written within a relatively short interval, and, above all, Paul's remarks on baptism in the specific cases are to such an extent adapted to particular problems and rhetorical situations that it seems wiser to regard

---

[1] Thus Käsemann (1960b). He is of the same opinion concerning Col 1.15–20 (1960a).

[2] Thus e.g. Dinkler 1962b; Furnish 1984, 148.

[3] J. Schneider (1952, 43–57), Delling (1963, 108–131), and G. Barth (1981, 92–106) make use of the following texts from the undisputed letters when discussing Pauline theology of baptism: Rom 6.1–14; 1 Cor 1.13–17; 6.11; 10.1–4; 12.13; Gal 3.27. But Schnelle (1983) also deals with Rom 3.25; 4.25; 12.5; 1 Cor 1.30; 2 Cor 5.21; Gal 2.19f, as well as with the formula 'in Christ'.

[4] Several exegetes have recently discussed the tensions of Pauline theology; see, among others, the works by J. C. Beker, H. Hübner, H. Räisänen, E. P. Sanders.

the statements on baptism as variants of a view which, fundamentally, is relatively coherent.[5]

4.2. Gal 3.26f

In the first pages of this book Gal 3.26f was cited to demonstrate the combination of motifs which we have since encountered in different forms, both when considering the background and prehistory of baptism and when attempting to reconstruct beliefs concerning baptism 'into the name of the Lord Jesus' in the earliest phase of the church.

In Gal 3.26f Paul is involved in an argument which is not wholly transparent in all its details.[6] He seeks to prove that the Gentile-Christian Galatians need not be circumcised in order to belong to God's people. Certain individuals possessed of considerable authority appeared in the Galatian church arguing that such a circumcision was necessary. Thus it is a main object of the letter to persuade the addressees not to yield to these teachers but rather to stand by Paul's gospel. Paul is obviously not of the opinion that the demand for circumcision only concerns an external ritual detail without any serious theological significance. Instead he sees it as a matter of principle which is of prime importance.

One part of the argument is 3.6–29, where Paul uses the figure of Abraham for his purpose. He has three aims: first, *(a)* he would attach decisive importance to 'faith', i.e. to the facts that the Galatians have accepted the missionary preaching, converted to Christianity, and now adhere to Christ. Furthermore, *(b)* he would show that God's promises of blessing and heritage to Abraham are valid for the Galatians. Finally, *(c)* he must find a meaningful place for the law in his thought-system without being forced to the conclusion that the Galatians are bound by it. All three items will serve the general purpose of the context, namely to show that the demands for circumcision are unjustified.

First, then, faith *(a)*. Abraham 'believed God', Paul writes, quoting Scripture (3.6), and received a promise from God: 'In you will all the nations be blessed' (3.8). Thus, Paul maintains, they are blessed through 'believing', and not through doing what the law demands (e.g. in Gen

---

[5] Betz (1995, 85) is of the opinion that there are considerable theological differences between the passages on baptism in the Pauline letters and is optimistic as to the possibility of reconstructing a development in Paul's attitude concerning baptism.

[6] For an attempt at analysing it, see Hartman 1993.

17.10, where the commandment of circumcision is found). This thesis is argued in 3.6–14.

But, furthermore, *(b)* Paul also wants to demonstrate that the inheritance which was promised to Abraham belongs to the believers. Thus, resorting to a scribal device, Paul makes use of the detail that according to the Abraham narrative the heritage was promised also to Abraham's 'seed'. So, as a Christian interpreter, wholly convinced that Scripture must be on his side, he writes: 'To his seed, that is, to Christ' (3.16). But he must still link this promise to the Galatians, not only to Christ (and, possibly, to the Jews). Before doing so, Paul finds a place for the law *(c)*: before the promise – the covenant – came into force, the law functioned as a 'custodian' such as the slave-attendant who supervised free-born boys during their schooling until they had come to age. But now, Paul maintains in 3.25, the time of the 'custodian', the law, is over, because with Christ the age of faith has come. So the law no longer has jurisdiction over 'us'.

So Paul has arrived at the stage of his argument concerning the inheritance where it is applied to the Galatians. This is closely related to the need to explain why 'we' are no longer under a custodian when the age of faith has come (3.25). As a reason he claims: 'because through faith all of you are God's sons in Christ Jesus' (3.26). In order to function as an argument – note the 'because' (γάρ)! – this must be further explained. One part of the explanation is not explicitly stated, but is presupposed; we also encounter it in the context. When namely the Galatians became Christians, 'believers', they also received the Spirit (3.2–5, 14; 4.6). This had apparently taken such forms that Paul can refer to it as an undisputed, experienced fact; probably charismatic phenomena had occurred (3.4; 6.1). This should be combined with the fact that according to Paul one who possessed God's spirit could rightly be called a son of God (Gal 4.6f; also in Rom 8.15f). Whereas this explanation of the Galatians' sonship on the basis of their spiritual endowment is only implicit, in 3.27 Paul presents an explicit reason for his saying 'all of you are God's sons through faith, in Christ Jesus', that is: 'For as many of you who were baptised into Christ, have put on Christ'. Thus Paul explains what he says about faith with a statement on baptism,[7] which is feasible only if Paul presupposes a close connection between the two concepts. The pivot of his argument is apparently the Galatians' communion with Christ. Baptism and faith seem to be two sides of entrance into this Christ-communion. This is also why

---

[7] Dunn (1993, 203) is virtually alone in regarding 'baptise' as a metaphor here.

Paul can refer to baptism in order to arrive at the conclusion that through faith the inheritance which belongs to Abraham's seed Christ, also falls to the Galatians.

Above, the phrase 'Christ-communion' was used. This phrase can have more than one meaning, as can the wording of the text to which it refers. It can stand for 'communion with Christ', or for 'the communion of people who belong to Christ'. Probably we should let both nuances determine our understanding of the Galatians passage. It refers to this Christ-communion in several ways, one of which appears in the sentence which mentions baptism, namely that it means to 'put on Christ'. The image of clothing stands for life conditions;[8] to have Christ as a garment means to have entered life conditions created by him, conditions which also confer a life 'with' him. In other words, 'Christ' stands for a particular identity of the baptised person; his or her 'I' is fundamentally determined by Christ, by what he did, was, and is, and this should be the point of departure for a self-consciousness of considerable gravity. The context incorporates another expression for the same Christ-communion when Paul says that 'in Christ Jesus' the Galatians are the sons of God through faith ('in Christ' recurs in 3.28). Here Christ and his work are a fundamental reason why faith can have this effect, and the preposition 'in' has the additional nuance of 'through'. But Christ is also active in the present, and the believers live under his dominion. Thus Christ now enables the Galatians to be God's children and determines the conditions of life in this filial relationship. Baptism, the ritual side of faith, brought the Galatians 'into' all this, because it was a baptism 'into Christ'. 'Into Christ' led to 'in Christ'. 'Into Christ' is certainly derived from the baptismal formula 'into the name ...', but here the phrase succinctly describes how faith and baptism lead to this close relationship with Christ.[9]

These conditions of life, determined as they are by Christ, have consequences for the human community, which owes its existence to them. Indeed, it lives by them. This is seen from the immediate continuation of Paul's text: 'There is neither Jew nor Greek, neither slave nor free, neither male nor female, for you are all one in Christ Jesus' (3.28). Possibly the verse was originally a proclamation within a baptismal liturgy.[10] Be that as

---

[8] On the image, see the material and the discussion in Mussner 1974, 263, and Betz 1979, 187ff.

[9] Consideration of these nuances of the phrase 'in Christ', taken from the context, indicates that the idea is similar to that in 1 Cor 12.13. There Paul speaks of being baptised into one body, i.e. the body of Christ.

[10] Betz 1979, 181ff.

it may, it brings out the radical consequences of the new Christ-conditions. They eliminate structures and differences imposed by religion, society and cultural conventions.[11] In the argument of Galatians it is particularly relevant that the distinction between Jew and Greek is declared invalid, since such a statement questions the position of the chosen people, Israel, vis-à-vis other nations.

On the other hand, the new Christ-conditions effect a unity of those who live under them and by them: they are 'one'. In the Greek 'one' is masculine, which also indicates how intensely Paul links it all with Christ. The people who are encompassed by the Christ-conditions share a trans-individual life, the name of which is Jesus Christ.[12] (Here Paul does not mention a further factor of this life, though we encounter it in 4.6, namely, that those who belong to this communion have the same Spirit, the Spirit of the Son. This subject is not developed here, but in 1 Corinthians 12, which will be treated below.)

In Gal 3.29 Paul draws the conclusions of his argument so far and (at last!) applies to the Galatians the promise to Abraham: 'If you are Christ's, then you are Abraham's seed, heirs according to the promise.' His presupposition is evidently that the Galatians can, so to speak, be identified with the heir, the seed, Christ. For this purpose Paul uses a further phrase to characterise the Galatians' Christian life-conditions, namely, they are Christ's.[13] The other passages in which Paul expresses himself in this manner,[14] and particularly the context in Galatians, suggest that again we should think of the close relationship, indeed somehow the identity, between Christ and the Christians. The genitive is of a kind which is common in Greek, and which indicates possession, but also membership of a group, kinship, or close fellowship.[15] The usage can also be illustrated by a phenomenon encountered in many religions,[16] in which a god is represented as the lord of his adherents (e.g. Isa 44.5), in

---

[11] Betz 1979, 190ff.

[12] We may compare this with the simile of the body of Christ (1 Cor 12); although Paul does not use it here. See Betz 1979, 200f.

[13] This being Christ's should hardly be understood in the light of Heitmüller's way of interpreting the baptismal formula; cf. my criticism in the preceding chapter.

[14] 1 Cor 1.12; 3.23; 2 Cor 10.7. Cf. 1 Cor 7.22 ('he who was called as a slave is a freedman of the Lord').

[15] It can denote 'son of', 'daughter of' (Mark 1.19), 'wife of' (John 19.25), 'mother of' (Mark 15.47). And see 1 Cor 1.13, where it means 'follower of'.

[16] van der Leeuw 1956, § 69, 99.

as much as he reigns over them and takes them under his protection.[17] This is how in Gal 3.29 the Galatians belong to Christ: he determines their identity and their life-conditions.

Thus, when Paul mentioned baptism in Galatians 3, he used the following elements of his baptismal thinking for the discussion. First, baptism is a pendant to faith. To become a believer and to be baptised are two expressions of the movement 'into Christ'. On the other hand, the consequences of this step are not attributes which the individual, so to speak, acquires, but gifts, i.e. the heritage, the blessing, the Spirit, the life-conditions. They can be summarised in the formula 'in Christ'. Paul mentions these gifts in order to identify the Galatians with Christ, the heir par excellence. This close Christ-relationship has as a result that the Christians are one. Thus this collective, determined by Christ, is also one of the features which Paul associates with baptism. Its unity depends on the fact that all those who belong to it share the same source of life. When this unity is expressed by the formulaic sentence 'Here is neither Jew nor Greek, neither male nor female' etc., the phrase 'neither Jew nor Greek' becomes important in the situation envisaged in the letter. Finally we can also note that baptism is regarded in an eschatological perspective, for the age of faith which followed upon the age of the 'custodian', the law (3.23, 25), is 'the fulfilment of time' (4.4), the age when the promises of the new covenant are fulfilled. Paul applies this perspective when, with some scribal artifices, he proclaims that the Gentile-Christian Galatians are exempt from obedience to the law of Moses. The idea of the fulfilment of the promises is given a deeper dimension when we also remember that the Jews expected the age of the new covenant to coincide with the bestowal of a new Spirit upon God's people, who would be called his sons and daughters and would really be his property. Paul attaches all of these expectations to the Galatians.[18]

---

[17] Cf. the Old Testament and Jewish concepts of the covenant between God and his people. A typical feature occurs in Exod 19.5: 'You shall be my possession among all peoples' (cf. Deut 29.12; see Perlitt 1969, esp. 102ff). The same holds true for the new covenant: 'At that time I will be the God of all the families of Israel and they shall be my people' (Jer 31.1). See also Jer 32.38; Deut 27.9; and *1 En.* 1.8 ('they will belong to God'). In addition, from Qumran: 1Q22 13.9 ('you [God bou]ght us to be an eternal people to you') 1Q22 2.1 'today [you will be a peo]ple to God your [God]'); 1Q34bis 3 2.5 ('you have elected for you a people at the time of your pleasure') and cf. 1QS 4.18–23 and *Jub.* 1.22–25, which are quoted in chapter 1, above.

[18] See the beginning of chapter 1, on John the Baptist; furthermore, Hartman 1980, 109–112.

4.3. 1 Cor 1.12–17

In 1 Cor 1.12–17 too Paul must resolve an acute problem of his addressees, namely that the community is divided, ascribing authority to different individuals. In a seemingly half-parodic mood, he quotes the slogans of the Corinthian Christians: 'I am Paul's, I am Apollos', I am Cephas', I am Christ's' (1.12). Faced with this situation Paul asks the rhetorical questions: 'Is Christ divided?, or was Paul crucified for you?, or were you baptised into the name of Paul?' (1.13). For some reason he then adds that he is thankful that he has baptised only a few people in Corinth (1.14–16), 'for Christ sent me, not to baptise but to preach the gospel, not with eloquent wisdom, lest the cross of Christ be nullified' (1.17). The latter words introduce another topic, which presumably is one of the reasons why the Corinthians are divided: they have been charmed by learning and rhetorical elegance.

We should certainly wish to know more about the situation for which this was written. Were there real parties in Corinth? If so, was there actually a Christ party? What is the relation, if any, between the divisions, on the one hand, and, on the other, baptism and the fact that Paul has only baptised a few? We need not answer all these questions in order to glimpse Paul's thoughts on baptism in this passage. But it would have been an advantage to know at least why he raises the topic of his own baptising activity. Did the person who performed the baptism become an authority to those whom he baptised, similar to the situation in some mystery cults, where the individual who initiated the converts would be revered? Is Paul criticising such reverence?[19] But Peter is also mentioned, and he has hardly baptised any Corinthians. It seems reasonable to assume, as inferred by several commentaries on 1 Corinthians,[20] that the argument, and not least its conclusion (2.4–16; 3.22f), indicate that it is particularly the respect for wisdom that is at issue and that has given Apollos a circle of admirers. Apollos is described by Luke as follows: 'From Alexandria, an eloquent man, well versed in the Scriptures' (Acts 18.24–28). Whereas some Corinthians, then, are charmed by him and gather around him, others still cling to their first missionary, Paul. In the background we may surmise still others who remain loyal to Peter, the leader of the apostles. It seems that the latter play no part in the conflict. If the Christ group existed at all and

---

[19] Mentioned as a possibility by Conzelmann (1981, 49f). Cf. the brief discussion in Schrage 1991, 148f; Horn 1992, 162–165.

[20] Barrett 1971, 43ff; Fee 1987, 56ff; Lang 1986, 24f; Schrage 1991, 142–152.

its place on the list does not result from a rhetorical exaggeration by Paul, it may have been composed of people who had withdrawn from the debates of the others, and maybe even detested them. The theories are numerous, and we need not linger on them.

Behind these verses of 1 Corinthians we can surmise a missionary practice. Paul was the herald, the pioneering missionary. He did not disregard baptism, but normally seems to have left others to perform it. Such a practice was natural when baptism was not a brief rite which immediately followed on acceptance of the message, i.e. on 'belief'. The narrative in Acts of how, for example, the Philippian jailer and his family were converted and baptised in a few hours (Acts 16.30–33) hardly reflects the practice which was followed in Corinth. There those who were to be baptised were probably first instructed over a long period, doubtless by the missionary who performed the baptism. Presumably Apollos was one of these teachers, and when Paul left Corinth, he continued to instruct the catechumens and also worked as an inspiring teacher. Paul describes such activity in a couple of images: 'I planted, Apollos watered' (3.6), 'I laid the foundation, someone else is building on it' (3.10). If the background in Corinth was like this, it is easier to understand why Paul can write that he is happy that he has baptised only a few.

Before examining the contents of these verses in greater detail, we can state that Paul evidently assumes that the Corinthians accept his way of thinking when he juxtaposes the ideas that Christ was crucified for them and that they were baptised 'into' Christ (1.13).[21] This implies that the underlying idea is not particularly Pauline, for the adherents of the other 'parties' would also accept it; otherwise they would refuse to follow him in his argument. In consequence, the motif will be discussed also in chapter 5, under the rubric 'Before Paul and not only Paul'.

Moreover, it should be noted that our passage from 1 Corinthians contains a trace of the old baptismal formula, that is, in Paul's travesty thereof, 'Were you baptised into Paul's name?' The fact that Paul can allude to the formula in this manner indicates that, in all its linguistic ruggedness, it was established ritual technical terminology when Paul arrived as a missionary in Corinth in the first years of the fifties and his first converts were baptised.

Indeed, the allusion to the baptismal formula may explain the short step between the idea of Christ's crucifixion 'for you' and the idea of a baptism

---

[21] Of course both ideas are only implicit, hidden as they are behind the rhetorical questions whether Paul was crucified for them or whether they were baptised into Paul's name.

into his name.[22] This association of the two is possible if also in this case the formula indicates the fundamental referent of the rite, that the 'name' marks basic features of its contents and significance. Here Paul summarises the meaning of Christ and his work in the phrase 'crucified for you'. In the same 1 Corinthians (11.24) he quotes the eucharistic tradition which contains the line 'my body (which is) for you', and in 15.3 he refers to a tradition concerning the resurrection which says: 'Christ died for our sins according to the Scriptures'. 1 Cor 15.17 ('you are still in your sins') shows that he thereby not only cites traditional material, but also himself is of the opinion that Christ died vicariously for the sins of others.[23] (This is only one aspect, although an important one, of Paul's thinking on the impact of the death of Jesus, but this is another matter.) The same 1 Cor 15.17 warns us against isolating the concept of this atoning death of Jesus from the meaning of his resurrection (see also e.g. Rom 4.25), but here in 1 Corinthians 1 the focusing on the cross is well suited to the issue, since the motif, including its associations with shame, fittingly illustrates that God, when saving the world, does not use that which is elevated, noble or wise.

Thus the allusion to the baptismal formula enables us to understand how, in 1 Cor 1.13, Paul can connect the idea of baptism and the interpretation of the death of Jesus: it was 'for you'. Elsewhere Paul combines baptism and forgiveness of sins (1 Cor 6.11; Rom 6.11), but here the idea of forgiveness is only in the background of the text, in that it is one of the effects of Jesus' saving work and is implicit in the formula 'for you'. Baptism is based on this work of Christ and brings it home to the person baptised.

In 1 Cor 1.13 we encounter two pairs of motifs, one pair dealing with the Christ-event, the other with baptism. Thus, on the one hand, it is said that 'Christ was crucified' and 'it was for you', on the other, 'you were baptised' and 'it was into his name'. From what Paul says about the apostolic message in 1.17b–25 we can extract some statements reminiscent of the pairs of 1.13: 'Christ was crucified' (1.17b, 23) and 'this is proclaimed as a gospel' (1.17f, 23), and on the other hand, 'people accept the message, i.e. believe' (1.21, 24) and 'thus God saves them' (1.18, 21). To some extent the pairs of 1.13 and 1.17b–25 are parallel, and it may be instructive to compare them. Both mention that *Jesus was crucified*. This is an objective event in the past. But when *it is proclaimed*, it is made relevant in the present. Something similar also happens in baptism, because it is

[22] For the connection, see Schrage 1991, 153f. Cf. Fee 1987, 61.
[23] See also Rom 3.24f; 2 Cor 5.14f.

performed *into the name of Jesus,* i.e. with regard to the one who was crucified and who is the fundamental referent of baptism. To define the crucifixion as an action which was performed *'for you'* signifies that it brings salvation to those addressed. In a corresponding way the other chain of thought contains the claim that *God saves* (through the preaching, 1.21). Two concepts of the list have not yet been discussed, *baptism* (in the first line of thought) and (in the second) *faith.* As in Gal 3.26f, they are closely related to each other. Together they belong to the same divine, saving act. Faith becomes the subjective element which involves acceptance of the salvation which is preached in the message of the cross, whereas baptism becomes the objective means whereby the same salvation is conferred on a person.[24]

The Christ-proclamation, the folly of which Paul defends in 1 Corinthians 1ff, has an obvious eschatological ring.[25] Thus, that some are saved through faith and that others perish (by dismissing the proclamation, 1.18) should be understood in the light of Paul's belief that the final confrontation between God and the world is imminent (Rom 5.9; 1 Thess 1.10; Phil 3.19). Indirectly baptism is included in the same short temporal perspective, because when God called and gathered people into the *ecclesia* in Corinth (1.2) and they received baptism as a crucial element thereof, this occurred with the ultimate crisis hanging over the horizon like a thundercloud. Later on, 1 Corinthians 10 and 15 will show us Corinthians who seem to have understood their baptism in such a way that already in the present it had given them the complete eschatological salvation. Paul rejects such an idea, but the probable presence of such thinking in Corinth makes it the more likely that in 1 Corinthians 1 too, baptism is loaded with eschatological associations.[26]

One more aspect should be mentioned. Paul's first rhetorical question to the 'parties' is: 'Is Christ divided?' Irrespective of how this relates to the preceding context (a moot point), the question presupposes that the Christians belong together in a unity, because they are one with Christ. In the same 1 Corinthians (12.13) Paul reiterates that the addressees have been 'baptised into one body', and in order to illustrate what he means he elaborates on the image of the body as an organic whole. Through their divisions, the Corinthians deny this unity by declaring their loyalty to

---

[24] G. Barth 1981, 105.
[25] Barrett 1971, 51f; Schrage 1991, 172f.
[26] See also 1 Cor 1.8: Christ 'will sustain you to the end, so that you are not accused on the day of our Lord Jesus Christ'.

different human authorities. When Paul arrives at the conclusion of his debate on the divisions (3.21–23), he states something wholly contrary: 'Thus no one shall boast of men. For all things are yours, whether Paul or Apollos or Cephas ... But you are Christ's and Christ is God's.'

Thus, in his discussion of the divisions in Corinth, Paul uses the feature of his thinking on baptism that Jesus' death 'for' those baptised is thereby realised or made relevant. So they are closely connected to Christ. Against this background the divisions appear to be an actual denial of the unity with Christ and in Christ.

4.4. 1 Cor 6.11

In Gal 3.26–29 Paul dealt with the close affinity, indeed, the unity, between Christ and the person baptised. The image of putting on Christ refers to the radically new conditions under which the Christians live with Christ and 'in' Christ. Paul uses wholly different language when, in 1 Cor 6.11, he treats both these new conditions and their acceptance: 'You were washed,[27] you were sanctified, you were justified in (or: through) the name of the Lord Jesus Christ and in (or: through) the Spirit of our God'. The sentence may contain established turns of phrase,[28] but it nevertheless fits perfectly in its context. If it was a phrase which the Corinthians recognised, its possibilities of being an effective argument were increased. For the context deals with moral problems, more precisely with the circumstance that some Christians took each other to court in civil actions. To Paul such behaviour constitutes a relapse into the ways of life which belonged to the Corinthians' pagan past and were incompatible with their Christian status.

Not all the commentators on 1 Corinthians maintain that this passage refers to baptism,[29] but it seems to me that there are good reasons in favour of such an contention. This is so although the baptismal rite *per se* is not in focus, but rather the whole process of leaving the old pagan life behind and entering the Christian community.[30]

---

[27] I read the form as passive voice instead of middle voice ('you washed yourselves'). See Halter 1977, 581; Conzelmann 1981, 136; cf. Beasley-Murray 1962, 163; Schenk 1990, 14ff; Schrage 1991, 427. But if the middle reading is preferred, the form can also be translated 'you had yourselves washed' (thus e.g. Schrage, ibid.).

[28] For good reason it is regarded as a tradition, which is independent of Paul, by, among others, Hahn (1976, 105f) and Schnelle (1983, 39–42). But cf. Schenk 1990, 14ff.

[29] Fee (1987, 246f) is one of those who are doubtful.

[30] Cf. Schenk 1990, 17, who maintains that if baptism is mentioned at all, it should be regarded as part of the whole process of becoming a Christian.

First, the Corinthians were washed. The imagery of washing was naturally inspired by the fact that baptism is a water rite. The image stands for cleansing, from the sins of the past. The introductory 'but' in 'but (ἀλλά) you were washed ...' contrasts the clause to the list of vices in the preceding vv. 9f. Before becoming Christians the Corinthians are said to have indulged in idolatry, adultery, etc. But the context also suggests that the vices represent not only various sinful actions in the past which are now forgiven, but also earlier, basic conditions of life which were dictated by evil powers and paganism. From those conditions the addressees are now liberated.

Secondly, entrance into the church meant that the Corinthians were 'sanctified'. Already at the beginning of the letter Paul addressed them as 'the church of God', 'those sanctified in Christ Jesus, the holy, called ones' (1 Cor 1.2). To be holy means that a person or an object belongs to God and to the realm which is reserved for and dedicated to him. There he is also present in a particular manner. Therefore the holy person or the holy object is separated from the secular world (see e.g. Rom 12.2; 1 Cor 5.9f; Gal 1.4). It behooves those who belong to this divine sphere to be holy,[31] i.e. to live in a manner which is worthy of the divine. According to 1 Corinthians 6 the opposite has occurred when the Corinthians' conduct is incompatible with their holy state.

Thirdly, the transition from old to new is characterised by the phrase 'you were justified' (ἐδικαιώθητε). In the context it is contrasted to verse 9, which claims that 'unrighteous (or: unjust, ἄδικοι) people will not inherit the kingdom of God'. To have been 'justified' here means that the transgressions of the past have been forgiven. But we should also allow the whole of Paul's thinking on justification to colour our understanding of the passage. The entrance into the church of God meant that the Christian was delivered from the power of sin and entered a realm where God's creative Spirit held sway.[32] The fact that all the verbs in the passage are in the passive voice implies that the underlying agent is God. It is he who cleanses, sanctifies, and justifies. Paul expresses the same opinion in other places when dealing with people's entering the church. The entrance is actually performed by God: people are 'called' (see 1 Cor 1.26; 7.18ff, etc.), and God is the one who calls (cf. the active use in Rom 8.30; 1 Cor 7.17; Gal 1.6; 1 Thess 2.12).

[31] Barrett 1971, 142; Halter 1977, 149; Schnelle 1983, 39f; Schrage 1991, 433.
[32] Schweizer 1970, 196; Lohse 1973, 242; Hahn 1976, 107; Halter 1977, 150; Lang 1986, 80.

Finally, the washing, the sanctification, and the justification are said to have taken place 'in (or: through)[33] the name of the Lord Jesus Christ and in (or: through) the Spirit of our God'. Probably the first half of the phrase echoes a baptismal formula.[34] Above, we saw that the meaning was probably the same whether one said 'baptise into the name...' or 'baptise in the name ...'. Thus it also fits well into this context to assume that 'the Lord Jesus Christ', that which he has done, and that which he means in the present, are the foundation of the baptism and of the other phases of the entrance into the church.[35] They make it meaningful to speak of a cleansing, of being sanctified and dedicated to God, and of being justified in the profound, Pauline sense of the word.

But it is also claimed that the entrance into the new conditions occurred 'in (or: through) the Spirit of our God'. Paul seems to take for granted that there is some connection between the gift of the Spirit and entrance into the church/baptism (1 Cor 12.13 appears to testify to that); this aspect however is disregarded here. The context (6.17, 19) rather suggests that the Spirit represents God's activity among people and is a manifestation of God's power experienced in the present. It mediates and effects the purification, the sanctification, and the renewal and justification which belong to the entrance into the new conditions of life. In this process baptism has a given, central position, being its objective, ritual factor.[36]

The transition from the old to the new life conditions has an eschatological perspective also in the case of 1 Cor 6.11. The new life which the Corinthians have received and which must now be lived, is contrasted with Paul's warning in 6.9, 'The unrighteous will not inherit the kingdom of God'. Thus he says in effect, 'You who are washed, sanctified and justified will inherit the kingdom – provided that you hold on to being what you are'.

In this passage Paul uses that feature of his baptismal belief that baptism mediates the remission of sins and 'sanctifies' those who are baptised. In

---

[33] Instrumental and local nuances of meaning cannot be clearly differentiated (Lang 1986, 80).

[34] Cf. chapter 3.1, above (towards the end). That the text says 'in' instead of 'into' can be explained in two ways, which need not be mutually exclusive. For it can be assumed that it comes naturally to use the rough 'into' together with the established formula 'baptise into the name ...', whereas the expression with 'in' goes better with other verbs. On the other hand, an 'in'-phrase may have appeared even more natural if there was also a baptismal formula 'in the name of ...'.

[35] Cf. Schrage 1991, 434: '*onoma* [repräsentiert] auch hier die Wirklichkeit und Gegenwart Jesu Christi selbst'.

[36] G. Barth 1981, 72; Horn 1992, 146.

consequence the baptised person must lead a life which corresponds to this status. This is Paul's main interest in this context. But since he uses established turns of phrase, other aspects of his baptismal thinking also come to the fore, namely, the central importance of Christ and of the Spirit.

4.5. 1 Cor 12.13

Paul mentions baptism in one further passage in 1 Corinthians, in 12.13. In chapters 12–14 he treats the problem of spiritually gifted persons or spiritual gifts; both translations are possible.[37] These Christians – or the gifts on which they pride themselves, particularly ecstatic glossolalia – have caused problems in the community; they seem, moreover, to have regarded themselves as superior to their fellow-Christians. They may even have thought of themselves as instruments played by God's Spirit.[38] In consequence, the gatherings of the church were threatened by disorder.

Before our passage, Paul maintained that all the different spiritual gifts, faith, wisdom, glossolalia, and the rest, are the effects of the one and only Spirit. In 12.12 he introduces the image of the body, which is one but has many co-operating members. In a similar way the Corinthian church consists of many members with different gifts and tasks, all given by the Spirit. All of them are necessary and they must co-operate for the good of the whole:

> For as the body is one and has many members, but all the members of the body, though many, are one body, so it is also with Christ. For in one Spirit we were all baptised into one body, whether we are Jews or Greeks, slaves or free, and all were made to drink of one Spirit.

Thus, once more in 1 Corinthians, Paul focuses on unity in Christ. This is also why he mentions baptism here.[39] From Gal 3.28 we recognise

---

[37] The genitive plural of the Greek can be either masculine ('the spiritual persons') or neutral ('the spiritual things').

[38] With this image I allude to what may have been an opinion among these Corinthians, which was represented in the Greek culture, according to which a soothsayer in a trance functioned as the instrument of a god playing it. See Schweizer 1959, 345ff.

[39] Fee (1987, 603ff) and Dunn (1970, 127–131) doubt that Paul thinks of baptism in water here, and assume instead that 'baptise' is figurative and that the passage concerns conversion, referring particularly to the gift of the Spirit at conversion. But we have already seen how Paul in 1 Cor 1.13 naturally resorts to ideas on baptism when he has to argue for the unity of the church (cf. Eph 4.4–6). It seems that baptism represented an objective sign of the unity in Christ. Also in the third place where the phrase 'nor Jew, nor Greek' recurs (Col 3.11), it is used in a baptismal context.

the formulaic sentence which illustrates how the new conditions into which the Christians are baptised question social and religious circumstances which were self-evident under the old conditions. But this time Paul uses the sentence to stress the unity behind the diversity in the church.[40] Again we note how closely he connects Christ and the group of persons who live by and under the new conditions. He does not say: 'As the body is one and has many members, so it is with the church', but 'so it is with Christ'. The conditions which have been established by Christ provide a Christ-life, which is damaged when the unity of the church is impaired.

But because problematic spiritual gifts are particularly at issue, Paul pays special attention to the Spirit. Thus he stresses that the Corinthians were baptised into the new Christ-sphere 'in (or: through) the Spirit'. As in 6.11, speaking of the Spirit means speaking of the work and active power of God who is present and at work in and among humans. This power is one. To Paul it is obvious that not the water itself but the Spirit of the near and active God brings the baptised persons into the Christ-communion and makes them share its new conditions of life. When Paul underlines that this Spirit is one, he reiterates what he has written before in vv. 4, 9, 11, but also emphasises to the Corinthians that, in their baptism, they, for all their differences, are subject to the work of the one Spirit. The less extraordinary Christians are no exceptions to this rule.

The last clause of the verse, 'We were all made to drink of one Spirit', could as well be translated 'We all had the one Spirit poured over us'.[41] The Spirit not only brought the baptised persons into the body of Christ, but also remains with them as a divine active presence. Paul does not explicitly combine this gift of the Spirit with the rite of baptism, stating that baptism mediated the spiritual gift, and we should not be too quick to read First Corinthians in the light of Acts (e.g. 2.38; 19.1–7). But nevertheless there is a connection between the two. The image of pouring may indicate how baptism was practised, that is, by pouring water over the baptismal candidate;[42] then the connection between the rite of baptism and the gift of the Spirit becomes closer. At any rate, Paul seems to be of the opinion that baptism is the focal point of the whole procedure of conversion, calling (1.2, 9; 7.17 etc.), and entrance into the Christ community. One important element of this procedure, with baptism as its focus, is that the

---

[40] Halter 1977, 170f; Conzelmann 1981, 258.
[41] Cuming 1980/81; also C. Wolff 1982, 189. Cf. Rogers 1983; Horn 1992, 174.
[42] Cuming 1980/81, 284f.

new Christians not only are the subject of the work of God's Spirit but also share in this divine power, the Spirit.

Such a way of regarding baptism is apparent in 2 Cor 1.22. This verse does not explicitly deal with baptism, but there are good reasons to assume that baptism is envisaged.[43] Here Paul compares baptism with sealing. When a person seals something, it becomes his property. So God 'put his seal upon us and gave us the Spirit in our hearts as a warrant', as a warrant of his promised salvation. As in other baptismal contexts, Paul does not explicitly say that the rite of baptism conferred the gift of the Spirit, but he presupposes a close, self-evident connection between them.

Thus in 1 Cor 12.13 Paul uses the element of his baptismal theology whereby baptism brings people into the Christ-community which has been created by Christ, is carried by him, and receives its life from him. This is made possible through the Spirit which is at work in this community. In his argument against the Corinthians, Paul employs an aspect which, apparently, he does not feel needs to be proven, that the Spirit of God is one.

4.6. Rom 6.1–14

It remains to treat the Pauline text on baptism which, more than any other, has been the basis of attempts to reconstruct his baptismal theology, Rom 6.1–14.

Before tackling this passage, we should, however, locate one of its features in the wider field of the phenomenology of religion, more precisely the way in which Paul relates Jesus' death and resurrection to baptism. Actually this recalls a phenomenon which is often encountered in the world of religion. Human beings tend to ask what the acts of their god or gods in the past, including a mythical primeval time, have to do with their present life. Or, in more existential terms, they seek to understand their present life and so to relate it to a mythical past. Examples of such past divine acts are the creation of the world, the death and rediscovery of Osiris, the Exodus of Israel, and the death and resurrection of Jesus. The question is rarely asked consciously or explicitly, but ways are nevertheless found to bridge the gap between past and present. The past is made present and real in rites or in proclamation, and the present is understood in the light of the past or of the myth which describes the age-old divine acts.[44] Indeed we have already encountered something similar in 1 Corinthians 1, where Paul combined

---

[43] Dinkler 1962b; Haufe 1976, 562; G. Barth 1981, 69f.
[44] See Éliade 1954, esp. chapter 2; 1958, chapter 10f; van der Leeuw 1956, part 3 A.

the death of Jesus with baptism and with the proclamation of the cross. In both cases the death of Jesus was made relevant or even re-enacted in the present, not simply as a remembered event, but also as a salvific act in the present time. In the same 1 Corinthians, Paul discusses the Lord's Supper, which apparently he also regards as a rite which re-enacts a past divine act or makes it relevant (1 Cor 11.17–34).

Romans 6.1–14 is obviously based on the belief that baptism makes the saving act of the past topical and effective in the present. Here too Paul turns to baptism in order to find arguments for a debate on another subject. I need not determine the aim of Romans as a whole – is it, for example, Paul's theological will?,[45] or does it seek to provide basic guidelines for the coexistence of Jewish and Gentile Christians, justified by faith as they all are?[46] For the purpose of the present study it suffices to say that in this part of Romans Paul is defending the principle of justification through faith apart from works of the law.

In chapter 5 Paul depicts the new situation of the Christians. In 5.1–11 he describes the peace of God which prevails because of the new righteousness – the new possibility of being righteous – which was brought about by Christ, and in 5.12–21 he delineates the new situation by using the concept of the primordial man who incorporates and represents all the later generations who are descended from him. Now Paul presents Christ as the new primordial man, the second Adam, who mediates life and righteousness to the human generations who have their origin in him, rather than the death which Adam brought to his offspring. So Paul can conclude in 5.20f: 'Where sin increased (through the law), grace abounded all the more. For, as sin reigned and brought death, so grace shall also reign through righteousness and lead to eternal life through Jesus Christ, our Lord.'

When Paul reaches this point, he must deal with a real or imagined objection from those who retort that such a view favours immorality. He formulates their question himself: 'Are we to remain in sin in order that grace may abound?'.[47] The whole of the sixth chapter is devoted to

---

[45] Bornkamm 1971.

[46] Stendahl 1976, 29; see also Donfried 1977 and Karris 1977a and b.

[47] As Paul in Rom 3.8 defends himself against the accusation of weak morality, it is probable that this is also the kind of resistance he imagines here, whether or not it is realistic. See Michel 1963, 204; Tannehill 1967, 8; Käsemann 1973, 157; Schlier 1977, 190f; Wilckens 1978–82 2, 8f. Cf. Frankemölle 1970, 19. Paul's situation when writing Romans points in the same direction: he is on his way from Corinth to Jerusalem (15.30–32); Jervell 1971, 67ff. Such an assessment seems to me preferable to one whereby Paul attacks libertinists who say: 'Let us sin, so that grace may flow the more abundantly'.

countering this objection. The text is unusually awkward and many are the suggestions to solve its problems.[48] We shall now try to follow the steps of Paul's argument in order then to consider what he there says about baptism.[49]

In 6.1 Paul introduces the objection which he is about to refute: 'let us remain in sin'. Already the fact that he does not have the opponents say 'let us sin' is noteworthy, for actually he has them say, 'Let us remain under the realm of sin'. So he implies that becoming a Christian really means the abandonment of a realm where the power of sin holds sway, for according to Paul sin is precisely a power, a potentate. Then, in verse 2, he presents his own counter-thesis in the form of a rhetorical question: 'How could we, who died to sin, still live therein?' Rewritten as a thesis it becomes: 'No, we who died to sin cannot live in it any more'. When he writes 'not . . . any more'(ἔτι), he links up with the 'remain' in the thesis of the opponents.

Paul now has to prove his counter-thesis, and, in addition, as some of its elements are apparently not evident to his addressees, he must explain them. There is no need to demonstrate that a dead person is not alive, but Paul must prove that the Christians have died to sin. To establish this claim, he must first show that a death has occurred, in order then to argue that it was a death to sin (whatever this may mean). This second step is not taken until verses 6f and 10–14.

Thus it must be proven that a death has taken place. Paul begins by making a statement on which he assumes that he and the Romans agree – or should agree: 'Or do you not know that all of us who were baptised into Christ Jesus, were baptised into his death?' (6.3). From Gal 3.27 we recognise the phrase 'baptised into Christ (Jesus)', which apparently has its origin in the baptismal formula 'into the name of'.[50] But determining its origin tells us little or nothing of what the phrase means in this passage.

---

[48] Analyses of the chain of argument are of course to be found in the commentaries, also in Lamarche 1980; Frid 1986. I learnt much from Hellholm 1995, or rather from earlier forms thereof which I have had the opportunity to study.

[49] This manner of dealing with Rom 6 primarily as a piece of argument differentiates my discussion from that of Betz (1995), who maintains that here Paul's aim is to present his (modified) doctrine of baptism (110f). Hellholm (1995) even labels it a 'misunderstanding' when somebody assumes that 'Paul here is introducing the doctrine of baptism or a new understanding of baptism instead of realizing that he is arguing his case. . .' (142). To Fitzmyer (1993, 429) the chapter is a theological presentation rather than an argument in defence; its purpose is, however, to demonstrate that the gift of life described in chapter 5 demands fulfilling of duties (i.e. neither to Fitzmyer is it primarily a teaching on baptism).

[50] Barrett 1962, 122; Schnackenburg 1971, 374; Cranfield 1975–79, 1, 301; Wilckens 1978–82 2, 11.

Here, as in Galatians 3, it stands for 'baptised into the Christ-communion'.[51] In this case the nuance 'communion with Christ' prevails over that which could be paraphrased 'the human communion which is determined by Christ'. As compared with Galatians 3 and 1 Corinthians 1 Paul here places the emphasis differently; he refers to the Christian's common life with Christ and focuses upon the death of Jesus. In 1 Cor 1.13 it was natural to translate the established turn of phrase ὑπὲρ ὑμῶν as '(Christ was crucified) for your sake'. Had Paul used this phrase in the present case, it should have been paraphrased 'on your behalf, so that, when he died, it counts as if you had died'. Actually Paul expressed himself in these terms in 2 Cor 5.14: 'One died for (ὑπέρ) all; therefore all died'. The thought of a new identity of the Christians which we encountered in Galatians 3 is here used by Paul in another, more dramatic way. For here the Christian is, so to speak, condemned to death with Christ.[52] The introductory words, 'do you not know that' indicate that Paul presupposes that this connection between baptism and communion with Christ is known to the addressees or at least acceptable to them.[53] Otherwise his argument becomes untenable.

In the first half of verse 4 Paul repeats what he has just said of baptismal death, but varies it by exchanging death for burial: 'That is, we were buried with him in baptism into death'.[54] Here Paul follows a pattern of thought which he has learnt from other early Christian theologians and which he quotes in 1 Cor 15.3f, namely, Christ died, was buried, and was raised.[55] Then he goes one step further: the fate which Christ and the Christian shared is not only one of death (and burial), but also means something more – it had a purpose: 'In order that, as Christ was raised from the dead by the glory of the Father, thus we also were to walk in newness of life' (4b). Since Christ was raised, the communion with him which is established in baptism also has as a consequence that the one baptised is

---

[51] Or possibly 'into the body of Christ'; thus Schnackenburg 1950, 151f; Tannehill 1967, 23ff. See further Halter 1977, 536f, and his own discussion 46ff. The field of associations around this turn of phrase may also contain the idea of Christ as the second Adam.

[52] See further Merklein 1990, 90f.

[53] There is far-reaching agreement among exegetes that verse 3 contains tradition, but opinions differ as to how and how much.

[54] I prefer such a translation for the following reasons: the statement is presented as a conclusion of the preceding one, and therefore it is natural to understand βάπτισμα εἰς τὸν θάνατον as a repetition of εἰς τὸν θάνατον (αὐτοῦ) ἐβαπτίσθημεν. Similarly Frankemölle 1970, 54. Others take εἰς τὸν θάνατον as adverbial to συνετάφημεν; thus Bornkamm 1952, 38; Kuss 1957–78, 298; Frid 1986, 191.

[55] Kramer 1963, 24; Fitzmyer 1993, 434.

made to participate in a life. No doubt Paul is of the opinion that this life is something already real and not only something promised for the future. This is indicated by his reference to the Christ-communion, which we encountered when discussing other passages, although Paul did not there speak in terms of life and death. But he does not write 'as Christ was raised, so were we' (cf. Col 2.12), but uses vaguer terms.[56] The new life becomes an aim or a moral duty rather than an automatic consequence of baptism. For 'to walk' here means 'to lead a life'. This obviously pertains to the purpose of the argument, directed as it is against people who accuse Paul of preaching immorality.

Once again, however, Paul has taken such a long step in his argument that he must adduce new evidence for it. In other words, he must answer the question why the baptismal death had the purpose that the baptised persons were to lead a new life. So he continues in verse 5 by giving an explanation which first goes on through verse 7 and then, in vv. 8–11, is almost repeated,[57] albeit then with regard to sin (a subject he left in v. 2). Why, then, this duty to lead a new life? The beginning of v. 5 hardly gives a clear answer, although it is introduced as an explanation, 'because' (γάρ); it turns the readers' attention to a future event which was implicit in the baptismal death, namely, the resurrection: 'For, if we have been united with the counterpart of his death, we shall also be so with that of his resurrection'. The sentence is problematic, as to both language and contents, and although I believe that it looks forward beyond this life, i.e. to the resurrection (or glorification) of the Christian, this interpretation is

---

[56] One gets the impression that Paul, so to speak, turns aside at the last moment; it has been suggested that he actually modifies a mode of thinking which allows of a closer parallelism between Christ and the one baptised, so that the latter is also regarded as being raised with Christ in baptism. This is how the author of Col 2.12 understands Paul. Several scholars assume that Paul picks up an opinion which was held by some Corinthian Christians who thought that in baptism the Christian died and was raised with Christ, and this resurrection was held to be definitive. In other words, these Corinthians held too optimistic a view of the realism of the new life and failed to realise that they did not yet fully possess it. Nor did they look forward to an eschatological fulfilment. This topic will be discussed in the chapter on views beside and before Paul.

But this is not the only explanation of why it seems that Paul in 6.4 avoids saying that the Christian has been raised with Christ in baptism. His views on what a resurrection might be like may have been closely bound to the idea that a resurrection cannot take place without a body. Then it would have been difficult for him to think only of a symbolical resurrection in baptism (thus Wedderburn 1983, 347ff; 1987, 184f). These questions concerning origin and background should however not hide the fact that Paul's awkward wording actually functions well in the argumentative context.

[57] Bornkamm 1952, 38ff. But Bornkamm stresses the parallelism much more than I do.

by no means certain.[58] How, then, is the thought of the Christians' resurrection related to their duty to live the new life? Possibly the answer is that Paul consistently thinks in terms of the Christ communion (v. 4) and only now extends its framework to embrace an eschatological outlook on the present time in which the Christians live with Christ; it gives an eschatological reason for the duty.[59]

If v. 5 did not make it clear why those baptised are to lead a new life, there is an explanation in v. 6: 'Because we know that our old man was crucified with (him), in order that the body of sin should be destroyed, so that we might no longer serve sin'. Here Paul develops negative reasons for the moral duty. 'Our old man' is contrasted to 'newness of life', which is mentioned in v. 4. Paul links up with his remarks in chapter 5 on the first Adam, and refers to the old conditions of life under which the powers of sin and death held sway. These old structures have now been stripped of their power. That the 'body of sin has been destroyed' means liberation from sin's dominion over the body.[60] This does not mean that Paul thinks that the Christians do not or cannot sin; this is evident already from the paraenetic sections of his letters. But here the argument concerns a principle: power structures and life conditions now prevail which did not exist before.

Now Paul must demonstrate that baptismal death brought precisely such a liberation. Thus he presents a further explanation (γάρ), maintaining: 'Because the one who has died is no longer guilty of sin' (or, more

[58] The word I translated as 'united' actually means 'grown together' (σύμφυτοι). Is this too 'free' a translation (notwithstanding that RSV has it!)? And shall 'grown together' be taken together with 'counterpart' (ὁμοιώματι) or with an implied 'him', so that the result is 'grown together (united) with him through the counterpart ...'? Furthermore, what does the word behind 'counterpart' (ὁμοίωμα) mean: 'image', 'similarity', 'form'? and for what does it stand: for the death of Christ, for baptism, for baptismal death, for the person of Christ, for the church (thus Schrage 1980)? How ought the second half of the verse to be understood: 'So we shall belong to the resurrection'; or 'so we shall be united (grown together) with the counterpart of his resurrection'? Finally, is 'we shall' a logical future tense? Then it aims at life after baptism, in which the Christian should lead a life inspired by the resurrection of Christ. Or is it clearly temporal and eschatological? See Bornkamm 1952; Tannehill 1967, 10–12; Frankemölle 1970, 71; Halter 1977, 51–55, 537f; Schnelle 1983, 81f, 211; P. Müller 1988, 89. Paul's short eschatological perspective may have contributed to his cryptic expressions when writing '(counterpart)' of his resurrection'. When in Romans he used eschatological concepts, he was convinced that the end was near. Thus he could be of the opinion that not all of his addressees would die before the parousia and would therefore not be raised from the dead. (Cf. 1 Cor 15.51: 'We shall not all sleep, but we shall all be changed').
[59] Similarly e.g. Wilckens 1978–82 2, 15f; Dunn 1988, 331; Fitzmyer 1993, 435f.
[60] Wilckens 1978–82 2, 17; Fitzmyer 1993, 436.

73

literally: 'is justified from sin'). Here Paul presupposes a juridical rule, which also has its counterpart in the Talmud.[61] This liberation is, however, not simply a theoretical matter or a principle deduced from a legal ruling which has been adapted for the present argument. As a matter of fact it builds on the fundamental conviction that the step into the Christ communion, with its ritual focus in baptism 'into his death', made this death a death 'for us' and 'for our sins' (Rom 5.8; 1 Cor 1.13; 15.3). Baptism made this death relevant in the present, applying it to the person baptised, and was the external (we might even say, the sacramental) sign of the forgiveness of the sins.[62] In this context the statement means that sin has lost its former power, under which Paul's slandering opponents said that one might as well remain, so that grace would abound (6.2).

With 6.8–11 Paul begins the positive argument to prove that the Christians have received a new life which they must also lead. As in vv. 5–7, he uses the 'with'-motif: 'If we die with Christ, we also believe that we will live with him, since we know that Christ, risen from the dead, dies no more; death has no dominion over him' (vv. 8f).[63] The latter half of the sentence tells the reader the reason for the contents of its former part: the Christ-event became a model for that which holds true for 'us' through baptism. But as yet the argument has not advanced beyond what is claimed in vv. 5–7 (which, as we noted, are parallel to 8–11); the final salvation and the future (resurrected) life with Christ are still the centre of interest. Verse 10 keeps to the Christological pattern and develops it: 'For the death which he died, he died to sin, once for all, but the life which he lives, he lives for God'. Thus Christ's death deprives sin of the possibility of affecting him. Although Paul still, so to speak, has his mind in heaven, this Christological statement is crucial to his conclusion concerning the present of the Christians. For baptised persons are closely connected 'with' this Christ, who lives 'for God'. They will share his life one day, but indeed already do so. So Paul can press on to his goal and apply the Christological statement to the addressees: 'Thus it is also with you (this is a slight paraphrase of 'thus you also', οὕτως καὶ ὑμεῖς): consider yourselves dead to sin and alive to God in Christ Jesus' (6.11). It is easy to undervalue the last words, 'in Christ Jesus', but they mark out the foundation of Paul's argument, in other words that the Christian is connected with Christ in a

---

[61] Cf. b.Shab 151b: 'When a man is dead, he is freed from fulfilling the law'. See further Kuhn 1931.

[62] Hahn 1976, 111; Wilckens 1978–82 2, 16.

[63] Verse 8 also contains expressions from tradition; see Hahn 1976, 109f.

real, decisive way. At the entrance into that Christ-communion baptism played an important role as a symbolic action and an effective sign.

On reaching this conclusion Paul has proven all the elements of his argument in 6.2: those who have died to sin cannot rightly live in it any longer. Now he draws the moral consequences of the proof, and we can also hear an echo of the last lines of chapter 5 which formed the starting point for the objection in 6.1. So he concludes (6.12–14):

Thus (οὖν) sin must not reign in your mortal bodies so that you obey their passions. Do not yield your members to sin as instruments of wickedness, but yield yourselves to God as people who have been brought to life from death, and your members to God as instruments of righteousness. For sin shall not have dominion over you, since you are not under law but under grace.

Having thus completed his refutation of the opponents' thesis and proved his own counter-thesis, in 6.15–23 Paul presents another series of arguments for the same thesis, now using the imagery of the slave-market.

Having followed Paul's winding argument in Rom 6.1–14, let us focus more closely on those elements of his baptismal theology which have emerged. Obviously Paul raises the issue of baptism because he can use it for the debate concerning justification by faith which he argues is valid for Jews and Gentiles alike. The ideas on baptism on which Paul and the addressees agree provide the foundation for his proof that the principle of justification by faith will not lead to moral bankruptcy. Probably this topic also determines Paul's mode of expression in this passage. Thus we may note that the life–death theme occurs already in chapter 5. It may be that Paul then found it all the easier to resort to the theology of baptism, since life–death associations were already to be found there too; in addition he could assume that such a view was shared by the Romans. Another possibility is that he stretched his thinking on baptism, so that it could be formulated in terms of life and death.[64] Romans 6.3 and 6 can be adduced in favour of the former alternative: Paul writes as if their contents are known to the addressees: 'Do you not know that . . .', and 'since we know that . . .', respectively. Another assessment of these two statements assumes that Paul, so to speak, takes his chance and hopes that the Romans will not only approve of his opinion that baptism means entrance into Christ-communion, but also that they will follow him when he claims that it means to die and to obtain life with Christ.

One may ask whether Paul's thinking on baptism developed and

[64] Wedderburn is of this opinion (1987, 50).

75

Romans 6 represents a change from what we encountered before. In such a case, Paul would here apply to baptism the ideas which he otherwise has concerning the conditions of Christian life in general; examples include passages such as 2 Cor 5.14 ('one died for all, therefore all died') and Gal 2.19f ('through the law I died to the law, that I might live to God; I am crucified with Christ; it is no longer I who live, but Christ who lives in me').[65] Or did Paul hold the same beliefs on baptism throughout, and were his words to the Romans not new to them (or do his statements go farther than the addressees were used to, but were statements that they might nevertheless accept)? As long as we are only concerned with Paul himself, as in this chapter, these questions are of little relevance, provided we do not attempt to reconstruct a development in Pauline baptismal theology.

Nevertheless it is evident that in Romans 6 we find a baptismal thinking which is very similar to what we have already seen in other Pauline passages. But there is more. Here Paul's view on baptism is also fitted into his theology concerning sin, law, grace, righteousness, and sanctification. Being brought 'into Christ' – and this process has its ritual focus in baptism – means to be freed from the realm where sin and death hold sway and to be exempt from the claims of the law. The concept 'our old self' (v. 6) indicates that the former existence of those who are now Christians is outdated; formerly they led lives of which Paul has but negative things to say. In those earlier days his Gentile-Christian addressees lived in darkness and under the wrath of God (1.18–32). Even though the Jews possessed the privileges of God's covenant and his promises (3.1–3), the right relationship to God, the true righteousness, was given only under the new conditions of life. It had been established by God through Jesus and his work, and people entered it by faith. In baptism it was emphasised that these old conditions belonged to the past, for they were cast out of the life of the Christian as a criminal was cast out from human society by being crucified. But the crucifixion whereby this occurred was that of Christ, which was made topical or re-enacted in this rite. These old life-conditions were contrasted with the new life (6.4) and the new conditions. Entry upon this life meant entry into a sphere of divine favour and energy. There God reigns, and he could make justified claims that this new life should be

---

[65] Fitzmyer 1993, 430. See also Gal 5.24; 6.14. Betz (1979, 187) emphatically denies that Gal 2.19 refers to baptism. The thesis in Betz 1995 is that Paul did not fully develop his baptismal theology until writing Romans. The new aspect in the baptismal theology of Romans would then, according to Betz, be that baptism is characterized as a rite of initiation.

a reality in the life of the Christians who lived there. The contrasting motifs of life and death deepen the perspective around this new life and around the Christians' close relation to Christ. Their new identity, determined as it is by Christ, is radically new, for the life-and-death contrast underlines that, when the work of Christ is applied to a person at the entrance into the new conditions, this means a thoroughgoing change. The Christians must realise that the application has such far-reaching consequences and live according to this insight.

The wording 'with Christ' plays an important role in Romans 6. It also has a place in Paul's eschatological expectations, as we encounter them already in his oldest letter, 1 Thessalonians: 'If we believe that Jesus died and rose, God will also, through Jesus, bring (to himself) those who have fallen asleep with him' (1 Thess 4.14). In 1 Thessalonians faith in Jesus Christ, the dead and risen one, is the point of departure for salvation 'with Christ'. In Romans 6 Paul looks to baptism, which means a participation in a life 'with Christ' (which is to be lived out). But it also anticipates an eschatological 'with him' (6.5, 8). In other words, as was the case in the Pauline passages we discussed earlier, in Romans too baptism has eschatological associations.

We have also seen how Paul in Romans 6 uses the vague formula 'into the name ...', but in an abbreviated form, 'into Christ'. On the one hand we could observe how Paul in this context binds the meaning of baptism to Christ and to his work, which is made relevant and effective in the rite. He is, to use the terms of the preceding chapter on the formula, the fundamental referent of baptism, which gives it its significance. On the other hand, the expression also acquires a local meaning: 'baptised into Christ' also equals 'baptised into Christ-communion'.[66]

If, finally, we ask ourselves why in this context Paul takes his arguments precisely from the theology of baptism, an answer could be as follows. He wants to demonstrate that the power of sin shall not rule over Christians, even if the law no longer holds the Christians in check. The associations with baptism should then be obvious, as it was apparently a common belief in the early church that baptism was performed unto the remission of sins (because of Christ and his work). Paul can enlarge this idea so as to mean that the one baptised not only received remission of the sins of his pre-Christian past, but was also liberated from the power of sin.[67] On such a

---

[66] The scholarly debate has seen many pros and cons concerning such a 'local' or 'mystical' interpretation, see Halter 1977, 46ff; G. Barth 1981, 99.

[67] Käsemann 1973, 154.

basis Paul can formulate the thesis that it would be wrong to surrender again to that power instead of living in righteousness for God with Christ. In a way which is not found in other Pauline baptismal texts, he sharpens this thesis by stressing the significance of baptism as a participation both in Christ's death and in his resurrection. As regards the latter element he combines it with a reservation that the glorious completion is not yet realised but is expected. But this does not diminish the duty to live with Christ the life which the Christian has received.

4.7. The primitive motifs

After this walk through Pauline baptismal texts, it is time to return to those main motifs I suggested were inherent in the baptismal practice of the first Christian generation when it adopted and christianised John's baptism. We have encountered all of them: the eschatological perspective, the thought that Jesus Christ and his work are the fundamental referent of baptism and render the rite meaningful, furthermore, the context of a proclamation aiming at conversion/repentance and faith, the forgiveness of sins, and the gift of the Spirit; moreover all these aspects are connected with the belief that the one baptised enters a collective which expects salvation (in some sense of the word) to ensue soon.

Before continuing, however, we should recall that, at the time when Paul wrote or dictated the letters we have now assessed, the church had taken the step into the wider world. This is true in several respects. On the one hand, the church now lived in the Jewish, Greek-speaking diaspora, which must have meant new conditions for the Christians' relationship to the Judaism. Among these diaspora Jews, both those who had become Christians and those who had not taken this step, the Jewish religion provided a sounding board under Christian modes of thought and speech. Nevertheless these Christians thought and spoke with other cultural and religious presuppositions than did the 'saints' of Judaea, because here Judaism was a minority religion. On the other hand, Christians had preached the gospel to Gentiles of different religious and cultural backgrounds, a procedure in which Paul as much as anyone had been involved. Among these Gentiles were also those whom Luke called God-fearers, that is Gentiles who, without becoming proselytes, sympathised with Judaism and observed some of the Jewish rules.[68]

---

[68] A lively debate has taken place concerning this group. For a balanced discussion see Cohen 1989 and Hemer 1989, 444–447.

The step into the wider world also involved a challenge in terms of linguistic usage, concepts, thought forms and vocabulary. Already such terms as conversion/repentance and forgiveness of sins have other meanings when they no longer function within such frames of reference as the ideas of God's covenant with his people. This holds true, whether or not the speaker is convinced that the age of the new covenant has dawned. For Gentile Christians conversion/repentance and forgiveness meant that they had turned to another religion and so had changed their basic religious value system. (In this perspective, it did not mean a change of religion when Jews became Christians.)

The step into the wider world also meant that the perspective concerning eschatology, church and Christology was enlarged. At the time when the texts we have studied were written, the church had already passed through two decades or so of intense theological work. Presumably this involved confrontations between different outlooks, inside and outside the church, not to mention that it was by no means clear where the borderline between inside and outside was to be drawn. Probably several interpretative patterns were tested when, for example, it came to answering the questions of who Jesus was, what his importance once was, what it was now in the present, how to understand the multifarious eschatological concepts, or what the Christian community was as a local phenomenon and in a wider perspective.

As regards the primitive motifs connected with baptism, *the eschato-logical perspective* remains with Paul. It is not a relic or a matter of routine or tradition but essential and self-evident.[69] It dictates how Paul regards the situation after Christ. With Christ the time has come when God's promises of future salvation are fulfilled (Gal 3.24f; 4.4–7). Thus, when Paul proclaims his gospel, he does so having the approaching, ultimate, and decisive crisis in prospect. The people who accept his preaching are 'saved'[70] in or from this ultimate crisis, whereas those who reject the gospel are lost.[71] (This is one reason why the problem of the Jews' fate, dealt with in Rom 9–11, is so burning to Paul.) Becoming a Christian and being baptised not only means having hope in this ultimate crisis, but also having a share in the gifts of life which are bestowed by the communion with the saviour who has inaugurated the final phase. However, everything hastens

[69] E. P. Sanders (1977, 434f) rightly stresses that no theological interest should be allowed to hide the importance of eschatology in Paul's theology not least in his Christology.
[70] Rom 1.16; 1 Cor 1.18; 1 Thess 2.16 etc.
[71] 1 Cor 1.18; 2 Cor 2.16; 4.3 etc.

towards the definitive renewal, and to the baptised Paul holds out the prospect of life with the risen Lord, whether such a hope is to be fulfilled via their own death and resurrection or through a glorification without an intervening death.

Christ, 'into' whose 'name' the Pauline Christians have been baptised, is the fundamental referent of their baptism. Not only is his resurrection the point of departure for the Christian proclamation of the Gospel, but his death and resurrection are also a work 'for us' which is made present in baptism (1 Cor 1.13). Indeed, the new, already inaugurated eschatological conditions of life which belong to the baptised are so closely linked up with Christ and his work that baptism is called a baptism 'into Christ' (Rom 6.3; Gal 3.27) or 'into his body' (1 Cor 12.13). Thus the Christ who is the referent of baptism does not simply, so to speak, stand outside when his work in the past is made present and effective. Instead 'Christ' also denotes a divine sphere, or a divine realm of power, which God has established through him and his work. The connection between the work of Christ once and their baptism two decades or so later impinges on the Christians when Paul maintains that in baptism they both died with Christ from the reign of sin and followed him in his resurrection in so far as already in the present they have received a new life 'with Christ'. This is so, even though this life looks forward to an eventual 'with Christ'. In addition, the present state of Christ (he 'lives to God') lays the baptised person under the obligation also to live to God (1 Cor 6.11; Rom 6.3–14).

The close relationship between Christ and the baptised is also linked up with *the church*. Those who share the new conditions of life compose a unity which can almost be called organic. For Christ is not divided (1 Cor 1.13). But the same Christ is also the origin of a new humanity, in which religious, social and other barriers are eliminated: 'There is neither Jew nor Greek ' (1 Cor 12.13; Gal 3.28).

The entrance into these new living conditions took place in a situation in which the church was still growing, above all through mission. Thus *the proclamation* of the Gospel plays a major role as a background of baptism (1 Cor 1.17ff). That the Christians had accepted this proclamation, i.e. had *believed*, and so had abandoned their earlier life were self-evident pre-suppositions of baptism (1 Cor 1.13; 6.11).[72] In this rite justification by faith is represented objectively (or, if you prefer, sacramentally; Gal 3.26f).

[72] In his baptismal passages, Paul never explicitly mentions conversion, and, as a matter of fact, it is only in 1 Thess 1.9f that he unambiguously uses such terms when speaking of what happens when people become Christians. But cf. Gal 4.9; of Jews, see 2 Cor 3.16.

The gift of *forgiveness* already belonged to John's baptism. Paul makes it dependent on the death of Jesus 'for you' (1 Cor 1.13; 11.24) or 'for our sins' (Rom 4.25; 1 Cor 15.3). In baptism the effect of this death is applied to the baptised (Rom 6.11f; 1 Cor 6.11). 'Sacramentally' it mediates the remission which Paul also can claim to be a gift of faith (Rom 4.5–8; this passage is, however, almost alone in portraying such a relation between faith and remission).

Finally, we have seen that Paul was one of the Jews who expected that in the age of the new covenant God's *Spirit* would be active in a new way among his people (Ezek 36.26; Jer 31.33). Thus in 1 Cor 12.13 he presupposes that entrance into the flock of Christ, with its focus in baptism, also confers a share in this divine gift. On the one hand, this view of the Spirit should be associated with Paul's conviction that the communion in Christ and with Christ means life; there exist real, new conditions of life and freedom from the power of sin (1 Cor 6.11). On the other hand, the eschatological perspective impels Paul to regard the Spirit under the tension of 'already but not yet': it is a first-fruit of the eschatological gifts and so also a guarantee of the salvation to come (Rom 8.23; 2 Cor 1.22; 5.5).[73]

Thus, in the Pauline baptismal passages we have encountered all the motifs which were tentatively assigned to the background of the first baptismal practice of the church. But they are integrated into Paul's theological thinking.[74] This integration may be taken as a sign that the ideas and motifs which we have perceived were central in Paul's baptismal theology, although it is evident that he mentions them because he has to find arguments when discussing other matters, particularly moral and pastoral matters. We should also note that as a rule he presents his ideas concerning baptism in such terms as overtly to remind his readers that they are of the same opinion as he is, or that they are already acquainted with the motifs which he uses. Nevertheless, strange as it may sound, the above-mentioned integration of Paul's statements on baptism into the rest of his theology is a fact.

---

[73] Horn 1992, 399–404.

[74] G. Barth 1981, 92–106. The heading of his chapter is very apt: 'Die Integration der Taufe in Rechtfertigungsbotschaft und theologia crucis bei Paulus'.

5

Before Paul, and not only Paul: Material in the Pauline Letters representing the views of other theologians

On several occasions we have encountered opinions on baptism which seem to have been held by the addressees of the Pauline letters or by groups among them. When, as in the case of Romans, Paul had no close connections with the addressees, we can assume that very probably they were of this opinion irrespective of any Pauline influence. Of course the idea in question can nevertheless belong to the apostle's own theology, but others accept it without having learnt it from Paul. In Galatians and 1 and 2 Corinthians he is writing to communities founded by himself, yet turns to people of convictions other than his own; in these cases he also seems to assume that they regard baptism in the same way as he does, at least as he represents them. They may have learnt their view from Paul and then combined it with other thoughts with which he does not agree. But it is also possible that their baptismal thinking does not derive its origin particularly from Paul.

When trying to choose between these possibilities we are not dependent on sheer arbitrariness. On the contrary a meticulous study of details of the texts has led biblical scholars to the conclusion that certain formulas and statements are 'traditional', i.e. they represent or reflect expressions or established turns of phrase which were used in Christian communities and not derived from the author of the individual text.[1] In our cases the traditional clauses or phrases are of course older than the Pauline letter in question, but when they are labelled 'pre-Pauline' this sometimes means that they may even belong to a time earlier than Paul's missionary work. The criteria of such datings are, however, insecure. But the baptismal formula 'into the name of' is an example of a tradition which is certainly pre-Pauline.

Whereas in most cases Paul seems to agree with the contents of the

---

[1] 'Pre-Pauline' thought on baptism is treated in Bultmann 1968a, 136–146 (pioneering); Braumann 1962; Kuss 1963a and 1963b; Hahn 1976; G. Barth 1981, 80–89; Schnelle 1983. As to criteria, see Vielhauer 1975, 11f.

formula to which he refers, there are instances in which are cited or implied opinions on baptism which are held by some people but almost certainly not by Paul. In such cases we learn of theological thinking other than Paul's and which, in addition, differs from his. But it is important that we note its existence and also that it appeared as an element of Christian thought.

Thus there are good reasons to assume that *1 Cor 6.11* goes back to a not-only-Pauline approach to baptism and its consequences: 'You were washed, you were sanctified, you were justified (ἐδικαιώθητε) in (or: through, ἐν) the name of the Lord Jesus Christ and in (or: through) the Spirit of our God'.[2] In the preceding chapter I discussed this passage as we read it in its Pauline context. But when we now regard it as representing a theologian other than Paul, we have no literary context which determines its meaning and which can help us to understand it. Nevertheless, it gives us some idea of how Christians other than Paul could think of the transition from paganism to Christianity.

The image of washing presupposes a picture in which the pre-Christian way of life is characterised as filthy and unclean. Presumably the tradition not only refers to defiling, immoral acts, but also picks up ways of thought whereby that which falls outside the correct or true religion is unclean. Such thoughts are found, e.g., in Ezra 9.11, which refers to 'a land unclean because of the pollutions of the peoples of the countries, with their abominations ...', and in 1 Macc 1.48, which describes the attempts of Antiochus Epiphanes to introduce other religious customs among the Jews: 'They were to defile their souls with all kinds of impurity and abomination'. When Apuleius lets his hero gradually approach his initiation into the Isis mysteries, at critical stages of the procedure he is cleansed from his former lowly and defiled life.[3] The tradition in 1 Cor 6.11 uses the same imagery for the life which the newly converted have left behind.

Purity and holiness are closely related: the person or the object 'sanctified' is consecrated and reserved for a deity, and in order that this relationship continue, the deity in question must not be degraded through any impurity. However, to be sanctified or consecrated, in 1 Cor 6.11 'to our God', also has a positive meaning, viz. to belong to the reign of God, to be in his service and to share in his gifts. To Christians all these blessings are brought about by baptism.

[2] The passage is discussed in Schnelle 1983, 37–45. The same tradition seems to be reflected in 1 Cor 1.30 ('Christ became our righteousness, sanctification and redemption') – Hahn 1976, 107; Schnelle 1983, 44f.

[3] Apuleius, *Metamorphoses* 11.1.4; 11.23.2.

Finally, 'you were justified' or, 'made righteous'. Here righteousness is probably a positive description of an aspect of the washing, the washing away of the defiling sins of the past in baptism. This is to say that the concept does not have the same wide connotations as in Pauline theology.

The transition which is described by these three verbs took place 'in the name of the Lord Jesus Christ'. As shown above, the prepositional phrase can be regarded as a variety of the formula 'into the name of'. There is nothing to contradict the assumption that 'the Lord Jesus Christ' is the fundamental referent of the baptismal rite and of the whole transition of which it was a focal point.[4] But it is more difficult to narrow down this importance of the Lord Jesus Christ. Does the 'Lord' designation mean anything? And does the Christ/Messiah-title? Is the work of the earthly 'Jesus', including his death, understood as the work of the ruler and saviour whom God promised to send, i.e. of 'Christ', the Messiah? And is such a conviction complemented by the view that he is now 'the Lord', the living and exalted One, to whose reign the baptised persons have submitted and whom they confess to be their Master and Ruler? Should we not also adduce the early confessional formula, 'Jesus is Lord' (Rom 10.9; 1 Cor 12.3; Phil 2.11)? But as purification and remission (1 Cor 6.11a!) are essential aspects when the work of Jesus Christ is made present, then it may not be too far-fetched to assume that this tradition also includes an understanding of Jesus' death as being 'for us/you' (1 Cor 1.13; 11.24) or 'for our sins' (1 Cor 15.3), that is, interpretations which are also traditional. Nevertheless it must remain uncertain whether the tradition in 1 Cor 6.11 implies that Jesus was the referent of baptism in precisely this way.

It is doubtful whether 'in/through the Spirit of our God' belongs to that which Paul has taken over in 1 Cor 6.11.[5] It is uncertain what the phrase meant outside the context of 1 Corinthians. We are probably wise to

---

[4] Kramer (1963, 73) follows instead Heitmüller's thesis that the phrase refers to the pronouncing of the *kurios* title over the baptisand.

[5] Schnelle (1983, 37–44) seems to be positive. The expression 'the Spirit of our God' is not found elsewhere in Paul, whereas 'the Spirit of God' is (Rom 8.9; 1 Cor 2.11ff, 14; 3.16). This circumstance can support the opinion that the phrase belongs to the tradition. But it is also feasible that Paul added the adverb to the tradition with regard to the Corinthians' deep appreciation of spiritual gifts. This would go well with the literary context, in that the presence and the work of the Spirit among the Corinthians would stand out in contrast to their unspiritual behaviour which is blamed in 6.1–10. On the other hand, it seems to have been a common view in early Christianity that the Spirit was given at the entrance into the church (with a ritual kernel in baptism) or that it was at work in this procedure and/or in this rite. The latter would strengthen the assumption that the words on the Spirit were part of the tradition.

content ourselves by stating that, if it is traditional, the tradition is related to the other passages in which the Spirit plays a role when people enter the Christian community. But does the adverb mean that the Spirit is perceived in baptism, mediating purification and sanctification? Or should we think of spiritual gifts? Several Christians in Corinth seem to have been of the latter opinion, because their handling of the spiritual gifts was so problematic that Paul must devote three chapters of 1 Corinthians to their amendment. But the tradition hardly derives from them. The underlying ideas are perhaps rooted in Jewish traditional expectations like those expressed in Ezek 36.25ff: 'I shall pour clean water upon you, and you will be cleansed . . . I shall put my spirit in you and make you keep my laws'. In such a case, does the tradition reflect a conviction that the expectations concerning the age of salvation are being fulfilled? And if so, should we surmise a Jewish-Christian source? The wisest thing is presumably to retain the question-marks.

The baptised person as the Lord's property. 1 Cor 6.11 uses the *kurios* (Lord)-title, and in the chapter on the baptismal formula I mentioned the common scholarly assumption that the persons baptised were dedicated to the Lord, whose name was contained in the formula: thus they became his property. Reasons were advanced for another understanding. Nevertheless, we have encountered phrases which describe the relationship between the Lord and the Christian in terms of possession. This is the case in Gal 3.29 ('You are Christ's') and in 1 Cor 1.12 ('I am Apollos' . . . I am Christ's'). We could also think of Rom 6.15–23, where Paul uses the imagery of the slave market to demonstrate that the Christian has been set free from the power of sin in order instead to be slave to righteousness; a slave was of course the property of his master. When discussing Gal 3.29 I referred to the wider field of the history of religion, where we often find the idea that the adherents of a deity are called his/her slaves or servants. Biblical and Jewish texts reflect the same view: 'You shall be my possession' (Exod 19.5), or, about the servant of the Lord in Isaiah: 'You are my servant (or: slave, *ebed*)' (Isa 41.9), and about Israel in the same book: 'I have called you by name, you are mine' (43.1; *li attah;* LXX ἐμὸς εἶ σύ). Thus, when we come across such phraseology in baptismal passages, this is only another, widespread and traditional manner of speaking of the relationship to God. Here it describes the far-reaching consequences of becoming a Christian.

2 Cor 1.22 ('God . . . has put his seal upon us') uses imagery which belongs to the same circle of associations. Setting a seal upon an object

means claiming it as a possession. This passage is another of those which are held to represent a tradition independent of Paul,[6] and there are good grounds to assume that it refers to baptism.[7] Thus there are indications that other theologians than Paul also spoke of baptism and of becoming a Christian in terms of acquiring a status which could also be described as being God's or Christ's possession.

Above, I briefly mentioned the traditional baptismal formula, *'into N.'s name'*. As a whole chapter was devoted to this formula above, including its pre-Pauline connotations, I refrain from discussing it further here. When Paul alludes to it in 1 Cor 1.13, he closely connects it with another traditional formula, *'for you'*. This indicates that Paul attributes also to his opponents the view that the work of Christ, including his death 'for us', was made present and effective in baptism. (When, however, in the same 1 Cor 1.13, Paul stresses that this death was a crucifixion, this accent might very well be due to his unique theological profile.)

In Gal 3.28 and 1 Cor 12.13 Paul cites with some variation the list 'there *is neither Jew nor Greek'* etc., and here he may also be using tradition.[8] Reasons in favour of such an assessment include the proclamation style and the fact that in both contexts the list contains more than is necessary for the argument. Both in Galatians and in 1 Corinthians the context mentions baptism and deals with the Christ-community and its unity (Gal 3.28 'You are all one in Christ Jesus'; 1 Cor 12.13 'We were all baptised into one body'). The Pauline disciple behind Colossians also quotes the proclamation and makes the same association with unity in Christ: 'You have put on the new man' (Col 3.10). It is scarcely possible to do more than guess the meaning of this proclamation in its usage before Paul. Indeed, we cannot even be totally certain that it was connected with baptism, and even less, if so, how it was connected. If we assume that it was not a particularly Pauline fancy to combine it with the thought of unity in Christ, we may surmise a conviction that the new conditions of life, which were dependent on Christ and his work, gave the converts a new identity, which was more important and more substantial than the social and religious conditions under which they lived before.[9] Attempts at a realistic assessment of the sociological structure of the first Christian communities

---

[6] Dinkler 1962b.

[7] Dinkler 1962b. At the end of the first century CE 'the seal' can be used to denote baptism (*Hermas, Sim.* 9.16, 3–5; *2 Clement* 7,6; 8,6). See Lampe 1951, 103–106.

[8] Becker 1976b, 45f; Betz 1979, 181; Schnelle 1983, 58–61 (+ literature).

[9] Betz 1979, 189–200.

indicate that they represented the average of the society.[10] But even so, it seems a realistic assumption that the proclamation shows how radically the Christ community questioned traditional structures, even such as were sanctioned by religion. It is also probable that the proclamation represented something more than an idealistic or hopeful vision concerning the approaching age of salvation; somehow it should also be realised in the present.[11]

After Gal 3.26 ('You are all the *sons of God* through faith in Christ Jesus') immediately follows 3.27, which refers to baptism into Christ under the image of putting on Christ. Both verses are held to represent a tradition on which Paul draws.[12] In our discussion of the Galatians passage above, the claim concerning God's sons was understood as expressing the new identity which resulted from the communion in Christ. In that context, as well as in the chapter on John's baptism, we were reminded of the Jewish expectation concerning the coming age of salvation that God's Spirit would be given to his people and that they would be his children or his sons. In Rom 9.26 Paul quotes Hos 2.1 ('They shall be called the sons of the living God') concerning those whom God has called from among Jews and Gentiles, i.e. he believes that the prophecy deals with the new age and that it is now fulfilled. Gal 3.26 testifies to the fact that other theologians, probably Jewish Christians,[13] regarded the situation in the same way and, in so doing, also connected this idea with baptism. To be the son of God means to have one's life from him, to depend on him, to live at his service in his work among human beings. Paul maintains that this close relationship with God depends on the Spirit; it is relevant here to observe that his statement on this issue in Gal 4.6 and Rom 8.4 is also not-only-Pauline: 'Those who are led by the Spirit of God are the sons of God'.[14] The idea is biblical: this close relationship to God is created through the invisible, powerful action of God, when he bestows his power on those humans who belong to him or are commissioned by him.

At the beginning of the discussion of Rom 6.1–14 we remarked on the phenomenon found in several religions that a cultic ceremony makes present an action which the deity or deities once performed and which is crucial for the cultic community. This *cultic re-enactment* could also be

---

[10] Meeks 1983, chapter 2.
[11] Schnelle 1983, 60 (on Gal 3.26–28).
[12] Becker 1976b, 45f; Betz 1979, 181.
[13] The reason is of course the connection with Jewish eschatological expectations.
[14] Käsemann 1973, 216; Becker 1976b, 49.

perceived in terms of the community sharing the experience or fate of the deity. On different grounds it has been assumed that Rom 6.3–8 is not-only-Pauline and is evidence that other Christians regarded baptism in a similar manner, i.e. that it represents a ritual sharing with Jesus in his death and resurrection.[15] Above, in the chapter on Paul, I did not pass judgment on whether this motif is not-only-Pauline. Does Paul refer to a view which he attributes to the addressees, or does he silently hope that they will consent to his suggestion that they 'know' that in baptism they died and were buried with Christ? I am inclined to believe that the former option is preferable, because so much is at stake in the argument that taking a chance or attempting to persuade already at the point of departure would be too risky. Accordingly Paul seems to be earnest and, for one reason or another, certain that the people at Rome hold these beliefs.

Particularly in the so-called History of Religions school it was thought that Romans 6 was influenced by contemporary mystery religions, in which the initiate shared the fate of the deity in one way or another. Such a view still has its defenders.[16] But there is no lack of opposition, and the authors of several investigations try to explain Rom 6.3–8 by referring to Pauline or other early Christian ideas.[17] When dealing with Rom 6.1–14, above, I also mentioned such material. But, as demonstrated in the first chapters of this book, already the practice of baptising 'into the name of the Lord Jesus' (or similar words to this effect) means that the rite is regarded in a manner which comes close to what we so often encounter in the world of the religions, viz. that a rite re-enacts a divine action.[18] Then the tradition behind Romans 6 represents only a particular variety of this general phenomenon. But here we go beyond what is found in other passages according to which the work of Jesus is re-enacted or made present in baptism; Jesus not only died and rose 'for us/you', but we died and were raised 'with him'. Nevertheless we should not be surprised to find phenomenological similarities between Christian and non-Christian views on this point. After all, there is no reason not to regard early Christianity as one religion among others in the Mediterranean Roman Empire. But it

[15] A survey of the debate with abundant references to the literature is given in Schnelle 1983, 204–214.

[16] E.g. Tannehill 1967, 10; Gäumann 1967, 64f; Käsemann 1973, 153; Dinkler 1974, 87; Becker 1976a, chapter 7. Betz 1995, with modifications (esp. 108f).

[17] Particularly marked was the opposition in Wagner 1962. See further Larsson 1962, 52–80; Siber 1971, 213; Wilckens 1978–82 2, 59ff; Schnelle 1983, 76–88; Wedderburn 1983, 198; 1987, esp. 37–69, 363–392; Fitzmyer 1993, 431.

[18] In Wedderburn 1987 I miss precisely this outlook on the phenomenology of religion.

becomes more difficult to answer the historical question whether it should be assumed that Christian theologians were subject to an influence from 'outside' in this respect. This is true, not least because we cannot reconstruct the origin of the tradition – it is of little help to speak generally of the Hellenistic church ('die hellenistische Gemeinde') or of the Hellenistic-syncretistic society.[19] But that there are similarities in thought patterns should not be denied.[20]

In a footnote to the discussion of Rom 6.4 above, I mentioned the suggestion that there was in Corinth a way of thinking which could be labelled *'over-realised eschatology'*.[21] A crucial point in this thinking is that already in baptism the definitive life with Christ was given, so that no further resurrection was to be expected. In scholarly debate 2 Tim 2.18 ('They say that the resurrection has already taken place') has often been adduced. This passage is then regarded as evidence of an attitude which prevailed in Corinth already in Paul's days. Now, given that Romans was written from Corinth, could the existence of such an ideology in Corinth explain why in Rom 6.3 Paul does not allow the parallelism between Christ and the person baptised to be complete? Certainly the baptisands die with Christ in baptism, but it is not actually said that they are raised with him; Paul speaks of the new life only in the future tense or as a purpose ('in order that'). On the other hand, the assumption goes on, Paul's disciple who wrote Col 3.11 represents a more original tradition, whereby the person baptised is also raised with Christ in baptism.

It is difficult to arrive at any certainty in a case like this, but the conviction that baptism had already given the life expected would link up well with other Corinthian phenomena with which Paul struggles in his letters to the community. Thus there are people who deny a future resurrection, at least according to Paul (1 Cor 15.12).[22] Furthermore, their high esteem of ecstatic glossolalia (1 Cor 12–14) may be at home in this context. Do the 'spiritual ones' call it 'the language of the angels' (1 Cor 13.1)?[23] An excessive belief in the power of baptism may also underlie the custom of which we otherwise know very little, namely that Christians had

[19] On top of the fact that the designation 'Hellenistic', as used in a cultural sense, cannot rightly be opposed to 'Semitic', 'Palestinian' or anything similar.

[20] Thus Schnelle 1983, 78, is rather cautious in his judgments, and largely the same holds true of Wedderburn 1987, 90–163. See also Betz 1995.

[21] See the survey of the scholarly discussion in Wedderburn 1987, 6–22.

[22] See G. Barth 1981, 86f, 96f; Schnelle 1983, 80, 210 (+ literature).

[23] Cf. *Test. Job* 48.3 on Job's daughter who fell into ecstasy: 'She got another heart and spoke the language of the angels'.

themselves baptised on behalf of the dead (1 Cor 15.29). These people would then be of the opinion that baptism was so concretely life-giving that it could mediate life to the dead.[24] There are certain parallels to this idea. On the one hand, 2 Macc 12.43f presupposes the possibility of sin-offerings and prayers for the dead. On the other hand, Plato refers to rites of purification prescribed by the followers of Orpheus, which were also performed for the dead.[25] Paul mentions the practice without criticising the massive 'sacramentalism', because he needs it as an argument in his main issue, that is, to prove that there is a resurrection of the dead.

A similar excessive belief in the objective effect of the rite may lie behind the admonitions in 1 Cor 10.1–13.[26] (Note the epithet 'excessive'; that baptism is an objectively effective sign is a Pauline thought.) In 1 Cor 8–10 Paul discusses how freely Christians may behave when it comes to attending pagan cults and the festivities which could take place afterwards. But it might also occur that meat was served at ordinary meals in the homes, which had been bought at the market and had originally been offered to an idol. To Paul's mind some Corinthians have gone too far in their freedom. He seems to assume that their practice derives from the idea that baptism (and the eucharist) have conferred a divine life with a sovereign liberty which is not disturbed by what a Christian does with his or her body, in this case feasting at pagan sacrificial meals. A similar attitude may also very well explain why some thought that they were at liberty to frequent the Corinthian brothels (1 Cor 6.9–20).

When Paul turns to these problems, he uses some motifs borrowed from the stories of the exodus. He reads these stories as warning examples, mixing the 'then' of the narrative with the 'now' of the Corinthians. The feeding with manna (Exod 16) and the water from the rock (Exod 17.6; Num 20.7–13) become types of the eucharist, and the passage through the Red Sea under the cloud (Exod 13–14) is taken as prefiguring baptism. So we also hear the echo of the abbreviated baptismal formula in 10.2: 'They were all baptised into Moses'. This double-exposure reading serves to demonstrate that, although the fathers participated in these 'sacraments', they did not escape the wrath of God when sinning: they were 'over-thrown', they 'fell' and 'were destroyed' (vv. 5, 8ff). In light of the fate of

---

[24] See Rissi 1962; also G. Barth 1981, 88–92; Murphy-O'Connor 1981; Wedderburn 1987, 288ff.

[25] *Republic* II 364E–365A.

[26] See G. Barth 1981, 81–84; Conzelmann 1981, 202–208; Lang 1986, 122–126; Wedderburn 1987, 241–248; Horn 1992, 176–179.

the fathers Paul maintains to the seemingly secure: 'Thus, the one who thinks that he stands must take care that he does not fall' (10.12).[27]

It is now time to return to the group of motifs which, according to my reconstruction, were connected with baptismal practice in the beginning. We cannot assume that the pre-Pauline and not-only-Pauline traditions which we have surmised in Paul's letters constitute one coherent baptismal thinking. Nevertheless it is worth while to ask how these primitive motifs are represented in them.

Thus here too baptism stands at the border between the new conditions and the old, on which Christians have turned their back. This *conversion* motif is expressed in 1 Cor 6.11, which also stresses the necessity that this conversion be continued as a 'sanctified' life. There we also surmise that the step from the old to the new brought the *remission* of sins ('You were washed ... you were justified'). The same tradition also refers to the idea that the Spirit was given and/or was effective at baptism – in so far that we assume that this phrase is traditional. Indirectly, Gal 4.6 (probably also traditional) together with Gal 3.26 represents a similar view, in that there baptism as the 'sacrament' of faith[28] gives Christians their status as the sons of God and they have the Spirit because they are God's sons.

As a *rite de passage*, baptism leads into something new, and this is also stressed in some of the not-only-Pauline material in Paul's letters. The new communion which the neophytes entered reduced the importance of, indeed questioned, the validity of the social, economic, and religious patterns of ordinary life (Gal 3.28; 1 Cor 12.13). Its members shared a supra-individual identity, which also meant that they were spiritually united, and this unity was supposed to have a counterpart in Christians' relationships in everyday life.

Baptism is clearly related to *Christ* also in this not-only-Pauline material. 'In' his 'name' Christians had left the old and entered the new; thus 1 Cor 6.11, according to which remission of sins and sanctification depended on him and his work. Romans 6 hints at the presence in Rome

---

[27] 1 Cor 10.1–13 has also been understood as saying that some Corinthians believed that when they received the Spirit in baptism this also brought this divine gift of life. Then reference has been made to 10.3f, where Paul mentions 'spiritual' food and drink. But, irrespective of how to understand 'spiritual' (πνευματικός) in this context (cf. Wedderburn 1987, 241–248), the adjective is not used together with the imagery employed for baptism. Accordingly, I prefer not to draw any conclusions from this passage concerning the baptism–Spirit relationship.

[28] If we should not, with Betz (1979, 181), assume that Paul added 'through faith' to the tradition.

of theologians who held a similar opinion on what Jesus and his work meant; in this case his death and resurrection are crucial for remission. For the tradition used presupposes that the Jesus-baptism not only mediated the blessed fruits of Jesus' death 'for you/us' (1 Cor 1.13), but also enabled the baptised person to die 'with' Christ and afterwards share a new life 'with' him. This description of a baptism 'into the name of the Lord Jesus' (or the like) could be understood by the Romans against the background of ideas held in other contemporary religions.

Thus Romans 6 also seems to presuppose a belief that baptism meant a share in a new life marked by Christ. The not-only-Pauline fragments refer to these new conditions in several ways: Christians are described as being 'in Christ',[29] furthermore, as being God's sons (Gal 3.26) and as belonging to Christ or to God (1 Cor 6.11; 2 Cor 1.22). The different turns of phrase stress different aspects of the new conditions in the Christ-communion, but all of them signify that the new life-conditions are determined by divine energy and stand under divine protection, everything depending on the heavenly *kurios*.

In 1 Corinthians 10 and 15 we surmised another approach to what it meant to be carried by divine energy or by the Spirit in the new Christ–communion. It seems that some Christians believed that this energy was given very concretely in baptism and the eucharist. Ecstatic phenomena such as glossolalia demonstrated ownership thereof, and some people appear to have been convinced that this divine energy was so strong and holy that their personal immorality did not matter. Others concluded that they could mediate the energy to people who were already dead by being baptised in their place.

Finally, we see very little of *the eschatological perspective* in these fragments. Of course this does not mean that it was absent when people in these circles reflected on baptism. However, Rom 6.3–8 suggests that there were theologians other than Paul who maintained that the one baptised died, was buried and was raised with the risen Christ, or at least received some sort of eschatological life with him. But such a belief is something else than concluding from Jesus' resurrection that the end is near (a thought inherent in the primitive eschatological perspective, as suggested above).

The pneumatics in Corinth may indirectly testify to the conviction that baptism takes place in an eschatological perspective. But they seem to have

[29] Schnelle 1983, 109–122, deals with the phrase in pre-Pauline tradition.

advanced one step further. Among them the hope of an eschatological consummation may have faded and the idea of an approaching judgment may have disappeared. Instead this group may have thought that they already possessed the full eschatological divine life.

6

The school of Paul

Already in his lifetime Paul gathered a circle of disciples and collaborators. After his death they passed on his heritage and even had disciples of their own who continued the work of the school.[1] This school adapted the Pauline heritage to new situations. The literary medium which was used for this purpose, and to which we still have access, is the letters produced by writers of the school, to whom it was natural to write in Paul's name. Many exegetical scholars – and the writer of these lines is one of them – are of the opinion that Ephesians, Colossians, 2 Thessalonians and the Pastoral Letters are such letters.

6.1. The Letter to the Colossians

The author of Colossians stands very close to Paul, whether he writes in Paul's life-time (maybe even by his commission)[2] or after his death. His relationship to the undisputed letters of Paul is somewhat peculiar;[3] he obviously knows them well, and turns of phrase from them often appear in Colossians. But on the other hand, he reinterprets his loans by giving them a slightly different meaning from that found in their original context.[4]

Like his master, the author of Colossians deals with baptism when arguing about other matters.[5] The 'other matter' of Colossians is the main purpose of the letter, to warn the addressees of a certain 'philosophy'. The writer uses the term 'philosophy' in a sense typical of the time, as referring to an ideology or a reasoned attitude to life. The ideology in question is represented by Christians who, *inter alia*, maintain that certain 'elements

---

[1] Conzelmann 1965/66, 233; Schenke 1974/75. For the baptismal theology of the school, see Weiss 1973.

[2] Thus Schweizer 1976, 26f.

[3] E. P. Sanders 1966.

[4] See Col 1.24f (Rom 12.5; 1 Cor 12.37; 2 Cor 1.5f; 4.10); 2.8, 20 (Gal 4.3, 9); 2.11 (Phil 3.3); 2.12, 20 (Rom 6.2–11); 3.11 (1 Cor 7.19f; Gal 3.28; 5.6); 3.12 (Gal 5.22f).

[5] His baptismal theology is thoroughly discussed by Halter (1977, 190–204). See also Larsson 1962, 188–223.

of the world' call for respect and also demand various ascetic practices (see 2.16, 18, 21, 23). Presumably the 'philosophers' revered Christ, but in addition seem to have respected these authorities more, or at least as much. The scholarly debate on the details of the 'philosophy' has been lively, but there is no need to enter upon it here.

In Col 2.8 the writer explicitly warns his readers of the 'philosophy': 'See to it that nobody takes you captive through the philosophy ...'. Beginning in 2.9 he presents his reasons, which are based on the importance of Christ. He emphasises his divine majesty: in him alone is encountered 'the fullness of deity'. 'Fullness' was used by contemporary thinkers to refer to the Absolute Being.[6] So, in Christ, our writer claims, we meet this 'Fullness' in an exclusive manner. Indeed, Christ is 'the head' of every power, viz. also of the authorities to whom the 'philosophers' are so respectful. In other words, Christ is their superior. His death and resurrection brought him to this exalted position and meant a triumph over the authorities (v. 15).[7]

This triumph really concerns the addressees, and plays an important role with regard to the goal of the argument, that is, to convince the Colossians that they need not pay respect to the cosmic authorities. In other words, the author would ally the addressees with Christ, who has demonstrated his superiority over the authorities. So it happens that baptism is brought into the discussion. It is first mentioned in 2.11 under the image of the Christ-circumcision.[8] Silently the author associates baptism with circumcision and uses the fact that a piece of skin is removed in that rite. So he can claim that the Christ-circumcision signified 'putting off the body of flesh', that is, we put away the old, all-too-human ways of being human and of forming our lives, which were also characterised by a

---

[6] E.g. Philo, *De vita Mosis* 2.238; *De somniis* 1.62.

[7] The passage is full of linguistic and exegetical problems. A somewhat literal translation says: 'For in him the whole fullness of deity dwells bodily, and you are filled in him, he who is the head of every principality and power, in whom you also were circumcised with a circumcision without hands in the putting off of the body of flesh, in the circumcision of Christ, buried with him in baptism, in which you were also co-raised through the faith in God's power, his who raised him from the dead. And you who were dead through your transgressions and the foreskin of your flesh, he made you alive with him, when he forgave us the transgressions, blotted out the bond (which concerned our duties) over against the rulings (and which was) against us. He set it aside when he nailed it to the cross. Having disarmed the principalities and the powers he put them to shame and triumphed over them in him.'

[8] Literally: 'Christ's circumcision', where, in principle, Christ could be the object of the circumcision. This interpretation has no advocates nowadays, and commentators rightly reject it.

propensity for moral weakness and sin.[9] Then the author presents another picture, which may be inspired by Rom 6.4: 'You were buried with him in baptism, in which you were also raised with (him) through faith in God's power who raised him from the dead' (2.12). The imagery of burial repeats what was said through the picture of circumcision, that the old conditions were eliminated. In both images something is discarded, a foreskin and a corpse, respectively. Both of them also have a positive aspect, even though this is less evident in the case of circumcision. Burial and death are followed by resurrection, and the image of circumcision presupposes that the rite was the sign of entrance into the people of God. The author also has both pictures tell something about Christ. For burial and resurrection in baptism take place 'with Christ', and the circumcision is said to be a 'Christ-circumcision'. Finally, one further element is common to the two images, namely that God is active. The circumcision-image only hints at this: it is characterised as 'not hand-made' (ἀχειροποίητος), i.e., non-human, divine power is at work.[10] In the latter picture the divine activity is more evident : 'you were raised' (v. 12), he 'made you alive' (v. 13), i.e., the passive voice refers to a divine activity. So both images also underline that God is at work in baptism.

Thus, in Col 2.12, the author argues in the same way as does Paul in Romans 6. The re-enactment of the work of Jesus in baptism is here represented as suffering 'with' Christ through the decisive phase of his saving work, viz. death and resurrection. But, in contrast to Romans 6, our author explicitly maintains that we are also raised with Christ in baptism, not only that we shall share the 'counterpart of his resurrection' (Rom 6.5).

In Col 2.13–14 the author makes that which he has just said more specific; he maintains that in baptism the addressees are made alive. The death from which they thus were saved depicts their previous situation, i.e. their pagan past. They did not then belong to God's people, and according to both Jewish and Jewish-Christian opinion a pagan equalled a sinner. For the Gentiles did not know God and his will, and thus went astray. When the text equates such a situation with death,[11] this may be interpreted as meaning that the human identity of people leading such a life is dissolved and that they have no possibility of a true relationship either to God or to

---

[9] Here probably the author reworks what Paul wrote in Rom 6.6: 'Our old man was co-crucified in order that the body of sin might be destroyed so that we no longer serve sin'.

[10] See Mark 14.58; Dan 2.44f; cf. Exod 30.6.

[11] Here the writer uses the image of death in another way from when he speaks of the death with Christ.

their fellow men. This is explained in detail when the writer continues, 'and you who were dead through your trespasses and through the foreskin of your flesh, he made alive with him, when he forgave us all our trespasses' (2.13). (As we see, the circumcision motifs are used once more.) In 2.14 the motif of remission is further developed, in that the author declares invalid the demands which the principalities and powers made on the addressees via the 'philosophy'. We need not embark on a detailed discussion of the exceptionally complicated imagery, nor of the equally complicated language, of this verse.[12] Instead it suffices to say that the death of Christ is presented as a decisive event. In different ways it put the authorities of the 'philosophy' to shame: on the one hand, the author maintains, their claims were crucified, crucifixion being the most shameful capital punishment of all;[13] on the other, in v. 15 we glimpse a general, who compels his prisoners of war to march in a triumphal procession. So the powers were put to shame, defeated by Christ. In v. 16, the author arrives at his conclusion, which is formulated with reference to the situation at Colossae: 'Thus, let no one judge you concerning food and drink . . .'. This application continues through v. 23, and simultaneously the weaknesses of the 'philosophy' are described.

Accordingly the addressees must not pay attention to the propaganda of the 'philosophy' because they, being baptised, have a share in Christ's superiority over its authorities: 'If you died with Christ from the elements of the world, why do you submit to regulations as if you lived in the world?' (2.20). The author has adopted Paul's idea of delivery from the power of the sin and applied it to the receivers: they are not subject to 'the elements of the world'.[14] 'This-worldly' principles (and those pursued by the 'philosophy' are such!) no longer pertain to the addressees, since they do not live in the world but are raised with Christ. This may sound radical, but the writer does not go so far as those theologians who are attacked in 2 Tim 2.18 and who

---

[12] Cf. the literal translation in footnote 7, above.

[13] They being the authorities behind *cheirographon* and *dogmata*: so also, among others, Schweizer 1976, 116; P. Müller 1988, 123f.

[14] Almost all commentators regard this expression as tantamount to a technical term of the 'philosophy' and try to find a referent for it in the culture and religion of the Roman period. More recent contributions to the debate include Schweizer 1988. After a review of the textual material, Schweizer finds the expression to refer to humanity's being enslaved 'in the ceaseless rotation of the four elements'. Rusam (1992) has had access to more material and advocates a similar understanding: 'The elements of the world' refers to the four (five) elements. But his example from Sextus Empiricus (*Pyrrhoniae hypotyposes* 3.152) indicates to my mind the possibility of a meaning like that I suggest above (the numbers, οἱ ἀριθμοί, are the cosmic fundamentals).

claim, 'The resurrection has already taken place'. He has no overoptimistic thoughts of his addressees' elevation above greater or smaller vices and sins; this is seen from his admonitions in what follows. Certainly the life they have received from Christ and now lead with him is a real life, but it is 'hidden with Christ in God' (3.3). But as eagerly as his master Paul, the author maintains that they are obliged to live out this life, and, indeed, the whole section 3.1–4.6 is based on the fact that the addressees have changed their living conditions by baptism; their whole existence is now governed by a new life-giving pattern. So the baptismal motifs resound again and again: 'If you were raised with Christ ..., seek that which is above' (3.1); 'for you died' (3.3); 'therefore kill your earthly members' (3.5); 'you have put off the old man ... and put on the new one,[15] where there is no longer Greek nor Jew, circumcision and foreskin, barbarian, Scythian, slave, free' (3.9–11);[16] 'thus, put on ... compassion, kindness' (3.12).

We have now seen how the author of Colossians uses baptism as the objective basis of his argument that the addressees must not be coaxed into accepting the 'philosophy's' claims. Instead they must live according to the pattern of the new man. The text contains several echoes from Paul, and if we consider the recipients' side of the communication, it is a fair assumption that they recognised the echoes; if this is correct, it reinforced the polemics against the 'philosophy'. For the echoes are not only Pauline – they are also not-only-Pauline, and we recognise several details from the material treated in the chapter on baptismal thinking before Paul and 'not-only-Pauline' baptismal thinking.

When considering the baptismal thinking in Colossians, as it can be surmised from the warnings and arguments, I shall at the same time keep an eye on the so-called primitive motifs, which I suggested lay behind the earliest baptismal practice. Beginning with the *eschatological perspective*, we have, on the one hand, seen how the author is of the opinion that already in the present one of the classical elements of eschatological expectation has come true in baptism, namely that of resurrection. There are good reasons to believe that he has baptism in mind also in 1.13 when writing that God 'transferred us into the kingdom of his beloved Son';[17] i.e. in this passage too we perceive a realised eschatology. On the other hand, the ethical admonitions, based on baptism, are obviously directed towards the

---

[15] Cf. Rom 6.8; Gal 3.27.
[16] Cf. Gal 3.28; 1 Cor 12.13.
[17] E.g. Käsemann 1960a; Halter 1977, 183–190, 598–604 (where further literature is cited); Lohse 1977, 74; Gnilka 1980, 48.

future.[18] Because the addressees 'were raised with Christ', they shall 'seek the things above' (3.1); this may be characterised as an eschatology in spatial rather than in temporal categories, but the baptismal death, which brought a hidden life with Christ in God (3.3), also looks forward to a time when Christ will 'appear' and the Christians will 'appear with him in glory' (3.4). In other words, the 'with Christ' which was given in baptism is a present reality and must be realised in everyday life, but it also anticipates a future 'with Christ'. The idea that the Lord will 'appear' or 'be revealed' occurs in texts by Paul (1 Cor 1.7) and by authors in the Pauline school (2 Thess 1.7; 2.8; 1 Tim 6.14).[19] But there is no point in trying to determine exactly what sort of eschatological scenario the writer has in mind, if any. He is fully traditional, however, when voicing his negative admonitions, the theological basis of which is also baptism: the addressees died with Christ, and for this reason must put to death immorality, impurity, etc.; if they do not, they are threatened by 'the wrath of God' (3.6).

Conversion and baptism have obviously not taken place in a perspective of imminent eschatological crisis. But the new conditions of life into which the Christians were baptised have an eschatological framework. Indeed they are, on the one hand, an *eschaton* lived in the present, but, on the other, those who remain faithful and steadfast can expect their full realisation one day.

In the previous paragraph *conversion* was mentioned. In Colossians baptism is never explicitly connected with conversion, nor is it presented as a consequence of a preaching with such an aim. But in the baptismal contexts similar ideas appear. Thus baptism stands, in the same way as conversion, at the boundary between past and present. The conditions of the past are painted in dark colours: the Colossians were dead (2.13), they were Gentiles (2.13; 'foreskin'), and thus unrighteous (2.13; 3.5–9), they lived in the body of flesh (2.11) and their life was that of 'the old man and his practices' (3.9). On the other side of the boundary they are now raised from death (2.12; 3.1), made alive (2.13), forgiven (2.13), and have put on the new man (3.10). So all of the dark details have received bright counterparts. The importance of the motif of the new man should not be underestimated. Indeed, it is a basic principle underlying the paraenesis of the context; with an appropriate comparison Gnilka calls it a Christ-programme.[20]

In a sense, that which was said about conversion in the preceding paragraph also relates baptism to *faith*. For when a person takes the step

---

[18] See e.g. P. Müller 1988, 123.
[19] See also 1 Pet 1.7, 13; 4.13.
[20] Gnilka 1980, 187.

from the old to the new, he or she finds a new basis for existence, Christ (2.5), or God and his power (2.12). In 2.12 the writer combines baptism and faith in a way reminiscent of Gal 3.26f: 'You were buried with him in baptism, in which you were also raised with (him) through faith in God's power who raised him from the dead'. Of course we should not imagine a division, so that baptism has the former effect and faith the latter. Rather baptism is the exterior counterpart to belief, albeit an exterior counterpart in which God is active. To some extent the argument of the passage depends on the belief by the addressees that baptism has effected a death 'with Christ', away from the authorities of the world (2.20). But, on the other hand, faith in God (who is at work in baptism) confers a share in Christ's life.[21]

Baptism's *connection with Christ* is evident in Colossians and is the basis for the author's use of baptismal notions for his argument against the 'philosophy'. The argument depends on the idea that the Colossians died and were raised with Christ and therefore, because of their unity with him, are free from the worldly powers. Or in other words: they are liberated, because in faith and through baptism they have received a real share of the new living conditions which belong to the people to whom the new man model applies. There is more to it than faith in a promise of future benefit, for Christ's victory is real, and the Christians participate in it. This is so because what God performed in the past (which is also reported in 2.14f) becomes a present reality for them in baptism. They could adapt the wording in Exod 13.8, 'This the Lord did for me when I came out of Egypt', saying instead: 'This God made for me when I was buried and raised with Christ in baptism'.

But this life with Christ must be realised in the present, and in a way which befits those who are delivered from Christ's adversaries. (They correspond to the power of sin in Paul's theology.) The old man, i.e., the old, purely human, only mundane conditions, have been put off in baptism, and renewed surrender to these powers means denial of self. Nevertheless, the writer has to admonish his addressees: 'put to death the members that are on the earth' (3.5), i.e. oppose such ways of life as are according to the old, the things which you have put off, and work instead to realise the new life you have received.

Finally, we have seen that the baptismal 'with Christ' also envisaged a 'with Christ' 'in glory' (3.4).

---

[21] Gnilka 1980, 131.

The saving work is described in 2.13f in a compact mixture of associations; its centre is Christ's death on the cross, and on this death also depends *the forgiveness of sins* which is an essential element of the passage into the new life. For Christ's death meant that the bond which also contained the obligations to the elementary powers was set aside. Furthermore, the addressees, being raised with Christ, left behind the transgressions and unrighteousness of their Gentile past (see also 1.14).

The church plays a certain role in Colossians (1.18, 24; 2.19), but is only indirectly related to baptism. The Colossians have put on the new man (or entered the new humanity) where there is no Greek nor Jew etc. (3.10f), and this 'model' stands for basic conditions of life which ensue from baptism. In the context the author mainly thinks of the ethics of the addressees, but in his way of thinking this new humanity is throughout determined by Christ, who is 'all and in all' (3.11). The concept of his kingdom – to which 'we' have been transferred (1.13), is closely related, and so is the notion that he is the head of the body, the church (1.18).[22] So exegetes commonly suggest that 1.13 be understood in light of the author's ideas concerning baptism. Thus this author's baptismal thinking has an ecclesiological aspect, but thereby it also has cosmic dimensions, which relate to his high Christology. So the saved people are saved from the power of darkness and from the demands of cosmic powers, rather than from a future wrath (cf. 1 Thess 1.10).

The Spirit, finally, is not mentioned in Colossians. Consequently, it is not mentioned either as something that is received on entry into the new life. Certainly the author can speak of being filled by Christ, in whom dwells the fullness of deity (2.9f); moreover, he writes that the Colossians have been made alive with Christ (2.13) and that they have a life hidden with him in God (3.3) – all phenomena that other early Christian theologians can connect with the Spirit. But our author did not follow the traditional way of speaking of the Spirit as the gift of the time of salvation or of the new covenant.

6.2. The Letter to the Ephesians

On the one hand, on the textual surface of Ephesians baptism plays a minor role; it is mentioned only once (4.5), although the author probably refers to it again in 5.26. In neither case is it a topic in its own right, but only an element among others in the running presentation. On the other hand,

[22] Pokorný 1987, 144.

Ephesians is so thoroughly permeated by thoughts which easily could be associated with baptism that it has even been regarded as a baptismal homily or as containing parts of a baptismal liturgy.[23] Without going so far we can nevertheless state that the letter takes into account that the addressees are ex-Gentiles who are now Christians. To them the writer stresses the divine favour which they thereby enjoy and the duties which this involves. In other words, the letter moves in the thematic sphere of the readers' transition into the church, a transition in which baptism was certainly decisive.

However, discussing the place of baptism in Ephesians presents us with a methodological problem. The letter belongs to the same Pauline tradition as Colossians and also makes use of much material from this letter. In some cases this material is clearly related to baptism in its context in Colossians. But when the material appears in Ephesians, no mention is made of baptism. It is not wholly unlikely that these borrowed phrases hint at the baptismal thinking of the writer of Ephesians, although he gives no indications to this effect. But he may also be less loyal, so to speak, to his predecessors, and may consciously exclude baptism from the borrowings. Moreover, what about the readers? Did they perhaps perceive a reference to baptism in these passages? In other words, could they fill in the text with associations from Colossians or from elsewhere, e.g. from baptismal instruction or from a baptismal liturgy?

The best thing to do seems to be to concentrate on those passages which clearly or probably deal with baptism. The Colossian echoes which in Ephesians do not clearly deal with baptism are adduced only when we find support for baptismal references in the clear passages.

The first baptismal passage to be discussed is Eph 4.3–6:

> Be eager to maintain the unity of the Spirit through (or: in) the bond of peace, (4) one body and one Spirit, just as you also were called to the one hope of your call, (5) one Lord, one faith, one baptism, (6) one God and Father of all, who is above all, though all and in all.

These lines occur in the beginning of the letter's admonitory section. They are preceded by an exhortation which is the starting-point of what follows, enjoining the addressees to lead a life worthy of their calling (4.1), in other words, worthy of the fact that, ultimately at God's instigation, they have become Christians. To do so means to live in humility, meekness and mutual love (4.2). Then, in 4.3–6, follow – not without a certain stylistic elegance – the seven factors that comprise unity. Commentators

---

[23] Schille 1960. Cf. G. Barth 1981, 129f; Schnackenburg 1982, 18f.

often suggest that these represent fragments of baptismal instruction and/ or baptismal confessions.[24]

However we assess the origin of the list of the seven factors or of certain elements therein, the fact remains that the letter and its readers stand in the Pauline tradition. So we have a wider ideological context, represented by the Corpus Paulinum, which helps us to reconstruct the significance of these factors of unity in relationship to each other. The admonition to maintain 'the unity of the Spirit' (4.3) holds pride of place, introducing as it does the theme of unity. The unity of the Spirit is presumably effected by or constituted by the one Spirit of God. Paul deals with the topic at length in 1 Cor 12–14, and there (in chapter 12) also uses the imagery of the body when developing the idea of unity. He writes, *inter alia*, 'By one Spirit we were all baptised into one body . . . and were all made to drink of one Spirit' (1 Cor 12.13).[25] It is reasonable to assume that this belief was known in Pauline communities.

Turning now to the heptad, we also take into account that the writer has the beginning of the Christian life of the addressees in mind; thus, in 4.1–6 he speaks several times of their 'calling'. So we may link the seven elements to each other as follows: When the addressees became Christians, the one God 'called' them, and their answer was *faith*, in which they submitted to the one *Lord*, Christ. So they are also addressed in the letter opening, namely as 'the faithful in Christ Jesus' (1.1). This entrance into the Christian community had a ritual side, *baptism*, and both the context and the Pauline background indicate the writer's belief that this baptism was a baptism into the one *body* of Christ, in which the one *Spirit* is at work. The unity of the baptism thus seems to depend on the fact that it is a baptism into the one Christ; if this is so, the text does not refer to a situation in which people consider being re-baptised. The people who are unified by these factors also have a common *hope*, which is the eschatological goal of the call, but of which the Spirit is also a bond. Finally, in this whole process the one *God* is at work, who is above all and through all and in all. Thus all the factors of unity are ultimately founded on the unity of God and are placed in the same wide, theocentric perspective which surrounds salvation according to 1.3–14; 2.4–10; 3.14–21.[26]

---

[24] E.g. Schnackenburg 1982, 162. I myself am somewhat doubtful about the suggestion, as it is wholly possible that the heptad simply has its origin in a wish to begin a new section with rhetorical elegance.

[25] Or 'all of us had the one Spirit poured over us'; see above, chapter 4.5.

[26] Schnackenburg 1982, 169.

Eph 5.26 is the second passage which explicitly mentions baptism. It belongs to the part of the so-called household-code which deals with husband and wife. Their relationship is compared to that between Christ and the church:

> (25) ... Christ loved the church and gave himself up for her, (26) that he might sanctify her, cleansing (or: having cleansed) her by the bath of water through a word, (27) that he might present (or: bring up: παραστήσῃ) the church to himself, glorious, without spot or wrinkle or any such thing, but instead being holy and without blemish.

Using the symbolism of a wedding (cf. 2 Cor 11.2), the author presents the death of Christ as being 'for' the church. Earlier in his letter (1.7), he maintained that 'we' are redeemed and forgiven through this death and, furthermore, that God, who raised Christ (1.20), saved 'us' when he raised 'us' with Christ and even enthroned 'us' with him in heaven (2.5f). The addressees, being ex-Gentiles and therefore at that time 'far off' from God, are now 'brought near' through the blood of Christ (2.13), that is, through his sacrificial death. When the readers/listeners arrive at our passage, these things should colour their understanding when they read that Christ's death took place out of his love and that it was 'for' the church – we recognise the old 'for the sake of' (ὑπέρ) formula.

If now baptism is in view in 5.26 (and there are good reasons for thinking this[27]) one may wonder why the author brings it in at all. In the admonitory context husbands are ordered to love their wives as Christ loved the church and gave himself up for her. Without trying to penetrate the author's deepest intentions, it seems natural to assume that to him, as to his master Paul, baptism was the visible and effective sign which made Christ's death relevant to the one baptised. In the present context he establishes a further connection between his address to married people and baptism by alluding to the custom of the bridal bath. Moreover, through referring to baptism, the author succeeds in making Christ's example more urgent; it is not only a past event, but the addressees themselves presently enjoy the fruits of it.

Normally it is individuals who undergo baptism, but here, in a somewhat astonishing way, it is performed on the church. The idea is probably that when individuals are continuously 'cleansed' in baptism, they become

---

[27] The passage was probably inspired by Col 1.22, which refers to the circumstance that the addressees were formerly strangers to and enemies of God but are now reconciled through the death of Christ: that is, it has to do with their becoming Christians. The writer of Ephesians has the same things in mind but adds the reference to baptism.

members of the church, the body of Christ (5.30). The upshot is a church of cleansed people. The cleansing realises the saving work of Christ, which is described as his self-surrender (5.25). The associations are not only to the bridal bath (cf. Ezek 16.18–14) but also to cultic purifications.[28] The latter association derives from the reported aim of the cleansing, that the church be 'holy and without blemish' (cf. 1.4; Col 1.22).[29] But in both cases the application of the imagery is that the sins of the past were forgiven when the salvific event was applied to the baptisand in baptism (2.5). But in this context sanctification also involves an ethical duty to live according to sanctity, to the consecration to God or to the Lord, or the submission to him (cf. 1 Cor 6.11). Thus the individual Christians are called to live in accordance with the sanctity of the Christ-body.

The expression 'through a word' (ἐν ῥήματι) is strange,[30] and several solutions of the riddle have been suggested; does it, for example, refer to a baptismal formula,[31] or to a proclamation or a homily at the baptism?[32] In any case, Christ is the agent: he gave himself up, he sanctifies, he cleanses. 'Through a word' is a modifier of the latter verb, telling how Christ cleanses. In other words, the author does not draw attention only to the water rite; he also lets an utterance (a 'word') indicate how Christ cleanses through the bath. In the choice between the different possibilities mentioned above, I tend to prefer that whereby the expression refers to an announcement. In that case the 'word' would relate the rite to Christ who is active behind it and in it. This activity is not only the cleansing; as the sentence is construed,[33] the latter is but a specification of the sanctification, which, in its turn, is the purpose of Christ's self-surrender (ἵνα).

So we turn again to our 'primitive motifs'. Baptism's *connection with Christ* is evident. He cleanses the people who are baptised into the church so that she becomes a holy bride for him. But the basis of this cleansing is his submission to death for her sake (cf. 5.2). Both his death and the cleansing demonstrate his love. The image of the wedding also indicates that the baptised persons are put under Christ's protection and power as, according to contemporary social conventions, the wife and the other members of the household stood under the protection of the husband. In

---

[28] Sampley 1971, 48f; M. Barth 1974, 629; Dahl 1982, 148f.

[29] Cf. e.g. the usage of ἄμωμος in Exod 29.39; Lev 1.3, 10, etc. concerning sacrifices.

[30] See further Sampley 1971, 134–139.

[31] Schlier 1963, 257f; Gnilka 1971, 282; Mussner 1982, 158.

[32] Dibelius 1953, 94f; von Campenhausen 1971, 4; G. Barth 1981, 110.

[33] The cleansing is expressed in a circumstantial participle, specifying the activity of the main verb (to sanctify).

4.4ff too (the one) faith and (the one) baptism were closely related to the (one) Lord. Thus his saving work is made present and relevant in baptism. In 2.1–6 the author seems to use terms from Colossians which are there connected with baptism, in order to speak of the same salvation: the addressees were made alive together with Christ. To this a comment is added: 'By grace you are saved' (2.5). The form of the verb (perfect passive) indicates that this salvation is already in their possession – which is different from Paul, to whom salvation is an eschatological concept referring to something yet to come. Indeed, as we have observed, in Ephesians the Christians are already enthroned with Christ in heaven (2.6), which may be understood as another way of saying that they belong to his all-encompassing sway, a church regarded from a cosmic perspective.

The cleansing in baptism envisaged, according to 5.26, that the church was to be holy and blameless. Probably this cleansing included that *the sins of the past were forgiven*. The turn of phrase 'gave himself up for' in 5.25 supports such an understanding, and in 2.5 we glimpse a similar view behind the words that in the past 'we' were dead 'because of our transgressions' but, by God's grace, we were made alive together with Christ. Thus the gift of life should at least also mean the forgiveness of transgressions. Nevertheless, in 5.26 the accent is on the duty of Christians to manifest in their lives the sanctity they have received.

The relation to Christ is connected with the *church*. In Eph 4.4f and in 5.30 the writer mentions the body of Christ, and within the circle of associations of this concept we should also reckon that the believer is baptised into this body (cf. 1 Cor 12.13). This church is here not a group of people waiting for final salvation with Christ, but rather a powerful life-sphere of cosmic dimensions,[34] 'the fullness of him who fills all in all' (1.23). In other words, the eschatological aspect of the church (if we should use the concept of eschatology at all in this verse) *here* means making her a cosmic realm rather than giving her a direction in time. But the church is thereby also a sphere of life of direct relevance for the addressees: when they were baptised, Christ's love was applied to them, and in the church they are still the subject of his loving care (5.29f).

The Spirit and *faith* are both listed among the seven factors of unity in 4.4ff, but are not explicitly connected with baptism. In 1.13, however, the writer refers to both of them when dealing with entrance into the people of

---

[34] Merklein 1981a, 48–62.

God.[35] Thus he mentions how the addressees heard the gospel of salvation, believed in it, and were sealed with the Holy Spirit of promise, which is the guarantee of the coming heritage (cf. 4.30). But, although *conversion* and stations on the way into the church are mentioned, nothing is said of baptism. On the other hand, 4.4ff and 5.25ff seem to represent a view according to which baptism is a matter of course, so it is difficult to assume that the writer left it out on purpose in 1.13. When he prays that God will give the Spirit to the addressees, he defines it as a spirit of wisdom and revelation, which informs them of the hope conferred when they became Christians (at their 'calling', 1.17f). This hope implies that the gift of the Spirit has *eschatological* connotations. The classical expectations for the new covenant, e.g. in Ezek 36.26f, included that Gentiles would join God's people. This has a counterpart in Eph 2.14–21 (cf. e.g. Isa 60). We also encounter other traces of traditional eschatological expectations. The Christians have received the seal of the Spirit with regard to 'the day of redemption' (4.30), and in the household code slaves are reminded that all, slaves and freemen, will be held accountable for their deeds before the Lord (6.8f). But the eschatology has become more spatial than temporal; the eschatological perspective tends to lend a transcendent dimension to the life of the church rather than to cause anxiety or provide hope and comfort in a situation which is on the verge of dissolution. So also the connection between baptism and traditional eschatology has been weakened: the intention of the baptism/bridal bath to 'present' a holy bride does not refer to the longed-for heavenly marriage (as e.g. in the Book of Revelation) but to the occasion when the addressees became Christians.

6.3. The Pastoral Letters

The Pastoral Letters should be treated together. The style, the topic, and the ecclesiastical situation which they presuppose, all speak in favour of such an approach. Although baptism is mentioned only once, in Tit 3.4–7, we can use all of them to shed light on this text.

In the context the writer orders 'Titus' to remind the Christians to live meekly and to be submissive to the authorities (3.1f). Such a life is said to be completely different from 'our' earlier life, when we were 'enslaved by

---

[35] Schnackenburg (1982, 64) and others assume that the passage contains echoes from baptismal instruction. In addition, the image of the seal which is used here may have something to do with baptism. This is denied, however, by Schnackenburg, who is of the opinion that this usage of the image is later. Cf. above, in chapter 4, on 2 Cor 1.22.

various passions and pleasures, living in wickedness and envy ...' (3.3). In 3.4 he returns to the present and directs the readers' attention to the basic reason why 'those who believe in God' should excel in good deeds (3.8):

(4) But when the goodness and kindness of God our Saviour appeared, (5) he saved us, not because of deeds in righteousness which we had done, but according to his mercy, by a bath of regeneration and renewal in the Holy Spirit, (6) which he poured out upon us richly through Jesus Christ, our Saviour, (7) in order that we, justified by his grace, might become heirs of eternal life, as we hope.

Thus the addressees were saved on the occasion of their baptism. But this writer does not think along the same lines as his colleague who wrote Ephesians, according to whom Jesus won his bride, the church, giving himself up for her and cleansing her in the bath. Instead his outlook is more traditional and also, if we may say so, less celestial. Moreover, the baptismal salvation is not particularly bound to Jesus' work. Instead it was performed by God and depends on his mercy. So also elsewhere in the Pastorals the writer holds God to be the Saviour; he is the Saviour of all (1 Tim 4.10) and wants all to be saved (1 Tim 2.3f). When salvation is said to be given because of God's mercy, not because of meritorious righteous works, the writer of course follows Paul. But to Paul the problem was particularly whether Gentile Christians were obliged to obey the Mosaic law, the Torah, in order to be accepted as members of God's people. Our author is not involved in such a discussion, but is inclined to speak of 'the law' in a manner reminiscent of later Christian terminology, according to which 'the law' almost denotes 'God's will'. Thus he does not speak of works 'of the law' (i.e. works demanded by the Torah, e.g. in terms of food-laws; Rom 3.20 etc.), but of works of 'righteousness', i.e. good and righteous deeds in accordance with the will of God.[36] On the other hand, we should note that these deeds of righteousness are contrasted with 'our' earlier life, which is described in terms of gross vices. We may paraphrase the author's message as follows: 'We went astray and were enslaved by various passions, ... so certainly God did not save us because of any righteous deeds on our part, but ...'.

Thus baptism became a station on the border between the old and the new, and there regeneration and renewal took place. This is the first time we encounter the term regeneration in our baptismal texts.[37] The picture was

---

[36] Hasler 1978, 96.
[37] Cf. 1 Pet 1.3, 23; John 3.3, 7.

used in several religious contexts in antiquity.[38] Here it acquires the meaning that in baptism a completely new human existence has its beginning.

But the author further specifies how God, through this bath, delivered Christians into their new existence, namely through the Holy Spirit.[39] The saving factor was not the bath alone, nor only something that God worked through the Spirit, but a divine work performed through the external sign of the water baptism. When the author says that the Holy Spirit was 'poured out', he uses traditional language (Rom 5.5; Acts 2.17f quoting Joel 2.28). But he does not seem to refer to ecstatic or charismatic phenomena which appeared among the addressees in general. Rather, as in other instances,[40] he uses Spirit-categories to describe God's present work in the church. When God saved in baptism, he did so by the renewing activity of the Spirit therein.

God poured out the Spirit 'richly, through Jesus Christ, our Saviour' (3.6). Here we find the reference to Christ which we missed in 3.4f. But his work is, so to speak, subservient to God's. Like God, he is called a Saviour.[41] In Tit 2.13f the writer further defines the salvific work of Christ: 'Our great God and Saviour Christ Jesus, who gave himself for us to deliver us from all iniquity and to cleanse for himself a peculiar people who are zealous for good deeds.' We recognise the old 'for us' formula. But in other places in the Pastorals God's salvation and the saving work of Jesus are brought together. Thus 1 Tim 2.3–7 speaks of 'God our Saviour' who wants all to be saved, but also of 'the only mediator between God and men', 'who gave himself as a ransom for all', something which is now proclaimed. Apparently this is how this salvation will take effect – people must hear of it. Similarly in 2 Tim 1.9–11: 'The power of God ... who saved us ... not according to our works, but according to ... his grace, which was given to us ages ago in Christ Jesus ... but which has now been

---

[38] Thus Jews could compare a proselyte to a newborn child (for examples see Jeremias 1958, 39f). The Stoics spoke of the regeneration of the whole world after the final catastrophe they expected (for material see Büchsel 1933, 686f). Other philosophers could speak of the regeneration of individuals or of the soul, thus also Philo (see ibid.).

[39] The Greek says literally: 'Through a bath of regeneration and of renewal of holy Spirit', where all the 'of'-phrases are in the genitive. The last one, 'of holy Spirit', should be understood as expressing who is active behind the regeneration and renewal (thus G. Holtz 1972, 234) or who is their cause (thus Haufe 1976, 563).

[40] The author regards himself as Paul's ghost-writer and in 1 Tim 4.1 reports how the Spirit predicts apostasy in the last days, i.e., he ascribes a prophetic spirit to Paul (Hasler 1978, 33f; Roloff 1988, 219f).

[41] God is the Saviour according to 1 Tim 1.1; 2.3; 4.10; Tit 1.3; 2.10; 3.4. Christ is the Saviour according to 2 Tim 1.10; Tit 1.4; 2.13; 3.6. God saves in 1 Tim 2.4; 2 Tim 1.9; Tit 3.5. In 2 Tim 2.10 we read of salvation 'in Christ'.

manifest through the revelation of our Saviour Christ Jesus, who abolished death and brought life and immortality to light through the gospel, for which I was appointed a preacher ...'.[42] So in the Pastorals the work of Christ becomes the salvation brought about by God in the present, through the proclamation of the Gospel.

Does the author hold that the same is true of baptism? Or, to put it more succinctly: is Christ's salvific work in any way related to the baptism in which God saves? One reason for a positive answer is the way in which 'Jesus Christ, our Saviour' is introduced in Tit 3.6. For the phrase may be understood as signifying that when the renewal was effected in baptism through the Spirit, and this Spirit was 'poured out' 'through Jesus, our Saviour', then the salvific work of Christ was the earthly basis or starting point for God's salvation that was performed in baptism by the Spirit. But even though in such a case baptism may be called a Jesus-baptism, both Paul and the other representatives of the Pauline school whom we encountered above must be regarded as being far clearer than the Pastorals in their ideas of how the saving death and resurrection of Jesus are made relevant in baptism.

In this context it is noteworthy that the author represents a phase in the early development of Christian theology, in which the theologians are moving towards a deeper reflection on the problems which are later treated in doctrines of the Holy Trinity. Applying terms of later times to our text, we could say: here God the Father is the First Principle, in the world of time and space Jesus Christ has performed the saving work of God, which is made actual and effective among mankind through the Spirit, *inter alia*, in baptism. But the whole is worked by God.

Before the author turns his attention to the eschatological goal in Tit 3.7b, he summarises his remarks on salvation through baptism in 3.4–6, using the short formula 'justified ($\delta\iota\varkappa\alpha\iota\omega\theta\acute{\epsilon}\nu\tau\epsilon\varsigma$) by his (i.e. God's[43]) grace'. This is of course the classical Pauline expression,[44] but here the literary and ecclesiastical contexts are different. Justification is now deliverance by grace from the old, sinful life into a new existence, in which God's power carries the believers. Therefore they must also apply themselves to good deeds (3.8; let us not forget that our baptismal text belongs to a paraenetic context).

We may ask why the author has incorporated these lines on baptism

---

[42] Some interpreters suggest that the passage contains fragments of a baptismal liturgy; thus Beasley-Murray 1962, 207; Schille 1965, 60ff. Cf. Brox 1969, 230 and G. Barth 1981, 130. Similar suggestions have been made for Tit 2.13, which we touched upon above; thus Schille, ibid. Rightly Barth, ibid., is doubtful.

[43] The pronoun used is $\grave{\epsilon}\varkappa\epsilon\tilde{\iota}\nu o\varsigma$, which in the context should refer to God.

[44] Cf. e.g. Rom 3.24; 5.1, 9.

into his argument. The answer is probably that, in his view, in baptism God saved 'us' from the sinful conditions under which 'we' formerly lived, so that we may now be careful to live in accordance with the new conditions received in baptism. Thus although the author's reflection is shallower than that of his master, he is not far from the principal attitude held by Paul in Romans 6.

In Tit 3.7b the goal of God's salvation is introduced: 'We will, as we hope, become heirs of eternal life'. The author uses Old Testament Jewish traditions, but these traditions have obviously been filtered through Paul. As he can characterise the Christians as God's own people (Tit 2.14),[45] he can here ascribe to them a hope which is based on their being 'heirs' of eternal life.[46]

When we now return to the so-called primitive motifs, we can be relatively brief. We have seen that to this author, too, baptism is a rite of decisive importance; there, by grace, God is at work as saviour through the Spirit. In the Pastorals too, baptism is related to *Christ*, but it is not exactly clear how. It is possible, but no more, that the same holds true of baptism as holds true of the proclamation of the Gospel, in other words, that God saves in the present when the proclamation actualises Jesus' work, which he accomplished when he gave himself up and brought life and immortality to light (2 Tim 1.9–11).

In 2 Tim 2.11 the author uses an expression which we recognise from Rom 6.8, 'If we died with (Christ), we will also live with (him)'. Nothing in the text indicates that this refers to a baptismal death with Christ,[47] and in the context it forms part of an ideology of martyrdom.[48] It says that (the fictive) Paul suffered in his service to the Gospel, and this is characterised as a death with Christ. What in Romans 6 was the existential realisation or re-

---

[45] Cf. Exod 19.5; 2 Cor 6.16.

[46] Cf. Rom 8.17; Gal 3.18, 29; Col 1.12; Eph 1.11.

[47] It is not even self-evident that the text deals with dying precisely with Christ. Thus Hasler (1978, 64ff) reads instead: 'When we already together have gone into death . . .'. But the context seems to favor the reading 'with Christ', not to mention the weight of the Pauline heritage. Polycarp (*Phil.* 5.2) understood the passage in a similar manner. Dibelius 1966, 81, and G. Holtz 1972, 167, assume that 2 Tim 2.11–13 is a liturgical hymn. Holtz interprets the passage on the assumption that its original 'Sitz im Leben' was baptism and the Lord's supper. Even if this were a correct assumption, the only conclusion which can be drawn as to our task now is that the Pauline statement has become a fixed element of the theological vocabulary. But its particular contents are hardly to be discerned. Accordingly the passage is of little use when it comes to the question of whether or not the Pauline baptismal theology has been changed.

[48] E.g. Hasler 1978, 65f; Jeremias 1981, 44.

enactment in baptism of Christ's suffering has become a community of fate between martyrs.

The line of thought in Tit 3.1–6 implies (but no more!) that in the Pastorals too baptism is associated with *conversion* and *remission of sins*. In more cautious terms: the author makes use of a pattern which is often found in texts by Paul and his disciples, namely that the pagan life is painted in very dark colours; it consists only of vices and wretchedness. This past is contrasted with the new, Christian life that opens up beyond conversion and baptism, which is a life in forgiveness and purity.[49] Titus 3.8 is joined to 3.1–7, in which the ethics are based on the 'baptism of renewal', and so 'those who have believed in God' (3.8) may well be the same people as those who were delivered by baptism to righteousness and hope according to 3.4–7 (cf. 1 Tim 1.16; 4.10). Thus this author also would connect baptism with *faith*.[50]

Titus 3.4–7, the only passage in the Pastorals which indisputably deals with baptism, does not mention the *church*. But most probably the author holds that those who, according to Tit 3.4–8, have been saved in baptism from the old vices and who must now be careful to apply themselves to good deeds, are the same as those who have been saved from all iniquity and purified to be Christ's own people (thus Tit 2.14).[51]

According to our author, the *Spirit* is at work in baptism. This Spirit is not said to bring charismatic experiences. Rather, talking of the Spirit seems to be the mode of reference to the divine power with which God saves in baptism, so providing new life conditions. Without regarding the Spirit as a guarantee of eternal life (2 Cor 1.22; 5.5), the writer nevertheless believes that the work of the Spirit in baptism gives the Christian the hope of eternal life (Tit 3.7).[52] Thus baptism is regarded within *an eschatological perspective*, but this perspective is not characterised as a crisis[53] nor as an intensive longing for liberation. Rather, the eschatological perspective involves a goal beyond the earthly life. At the same time this eschatological hope constitutes a framework around the exhortations, both those in the context of the passage on baptism and those elsewhere in the Pastorals (2 Tim 4.1–8; Tit 2.12f).

---

[49] Cf. Rom 6.17–22; 1 Cor 6.9–11; Col 3.7f; Eph 2.2–10; 4.17–24.
[50] Regardless of what the author means by 'faith'; see e.g. Roloff 1988, 6, 70, 104.
[51] Cf. Exod 19.5; Deut 14.2. And see note 41 above.
[52] Cf. Rom 8.16f; Gal 3.29; 4.7; Eph 1.14.
[53] Cf. Trummer 1978, 227ff; Towner 1986.

7

The First Letter of Peter

'So put away all wickedness and all insincerity ... and long for the pure spiritual milk like new-born babies' (1 Pet 2.1f). These clauses from the First Letter of Peter have prompted several interpreters to assume that much in this letter directly or indirectly refers to baptism or to ideas thereon held by the writer and his readers.[1] As in the case of Ephesians, it has also been suggested that the letter contains long or short sections of a baptismal liturgy, or that it is a baptismal homily which has been reshaped into a letter and then addressed to a wider audience.[2] In our days the enthusiasm for proposing such hypotheses has diminished, but it remains relatively certain that when the author explains what a Christian way of life means, not least that it also involves suffering,[3] he uses thoughts and motifs which are connected with baptism.[4]

Be that as it may, baptism is explicitly mentioned only once in 1 Pet (3.20–22). In a somewhat rough translation the passage says:

> ... in the days when Noah built the ark, into which a few, i.e. eight souls, were rescued through water, (21) as also now baptism in a corresponding way rescues you; it is not a removal of the dirt of the flesh, but the pledge of a good conscience to God, (it rescues you) through the resurrection of Jesus Christ, (22) who has gone into heaven and is at the right hand of God, after angels, authorities, and powers have been subdued under him.

The Greek at the beginning of 3.21 is somewhat awkward, but relatively clear. But the words on the good conscience can be understood in more than one sense. They can also be rendered 'a prayer to God for a

---

[1] Goppelt 1978, 86, 117f and passim; Brox 1979, 22; Kosala 1985.
[2] See the surveys in Goppelt 1978, 38ff, and Brox 1979, 19ff.
[3] See 1.6f; 4.12–16; 5.10.
[4] In Knoch 1990, 105f, there is a concentrated but instructive excursus on baptism in 1 Pet.

good conscience' or 'the prayer of a good conscience to God'.[5] Without being too definite, I prefer to read the text in the manner indicated by my translation above. It is compatible with the author's opinion, expressed elsewhere in the letter, that becoming a Christian means to be called to a life of obedience and holiness (1.2, 14ff, 22; 3.9).

The author's style is somewhat peculiar.[6] It is certainly not primitive, although clauses are heaped on top of each other rather than interwoven in a web of main and subordinated clauses. The writer does not forge chains of thought comprised of assertions and arguments, and often it is not clear how different ideas are related to each other in the running text, nor how comparisons and imagery should be understood.

The context of the quoted passage contains admonitions which relate to the circumstance that the addressees have been subjected to sufferings and can expect to encounter more of the same (3.13 and onwards). In 3.18 the outlook is widened through a reference to the fact that Jesus also suffered, although he was innocent ('he suffered, righteous for the unrighteous'). This motif and the blessed consequences of Jesus' suffering are developed in the following clauses. The style becomes solemn and rhythmic, and parts of the phraseology may very well be traditional.[7] The passage leads up to the statement that Christ, 'made alive in the spirit', 'preached to the spirits in prison' (3.19). The next verse explains that these spirits were those who once were punished at the Flood. The motifs of the Flood narrative, including descriptions of the fate of the fallen angels, were widely developed in the Judaism of those days; this is attested by several intertestamental writings, not least by the *Enoch* literature, and the author seems to presuppose that his readers know enough about these motifs to be able to follow him. The second half of 3.20 then seems to add some slightly looser associations: at the Flood Noah was rescued through water, and to the author this becomes a picture of the salvation of the addressees. After this digression he returns in 4.1 to the line of thought he left in 3.17 and continues to admonish his readers.

Thus in our brief baptismal passage the writer makes use of several features of the Noah story. As only 'a few' persons, i.e. Noah's family, were

[5] The latter possibility is chosen by Schelkle (1961, 109) and Kosala (1985, 42f). Brox (1979, 178f) follows the same path as I do. Goppelt (1978, 259): 'Eine(r) Bitte, die den Bittenden verpflichtet'. There are no other instances where ἐπερώτημα means 'prayer', but the verb ἐπερωτάω, which is formed from the same stem, may mean 'pray', 'ask', etc. (see Matt 16.4).
[6] Goppelt 1978, 45f.
[7] Bultmann 1967; Kosala 1985, 77–102.

116

THE FIRST LETTER OF PETER

rescued, so the Christians are few in number. Two other details are, however, more important: water is the means of salvation and a 'salvation' has taken place.

One may ask at what time the author would place the salvation he mentions in verse 21. Actually he writes 'saves now'. Does he refer to an event in progress now, in which the addressees are involved? The answer may be, 'Yes and no'. 'Now' is the time to which Noah's rescue pointed as a 'type', i.e. as a sign of what was to come. According to 1.10f the prophets searched for and inquired about this salvation and about the time of its occurrence. The Spirit within them had predicted that Christ, the Messiah, would suffer and then be glorified. Thus, on the one hand, salvation/rescue is now present and now given. But, on the other hand, it is stressed that the Christians look forward to their salvation. They expect the outcome of their faith, 'the salvation of (their) souls' (1.9). The resurrection of Jesus has 'borne (them) anew to a living hope' and to an imperishable inheritance in heaven (1.3f). God guards them through their faith 'for the salvation which is ready to be revealed in the last time' (1.5). The remaining time is short: 'The end of all things is at hand' (4.7; see also 4.13; 5.1). Certainly this temporal perspective is also that of 3.20f, our passage on baptism. So, the salvation which is 'now' given through baptism looks forward to a fulfilment soon.

It may be valuable to ask what our author means by the word 'salvation'.[8] According to 1.10ff, salvation had a prehistory: the prophets predicted the sufferings and glorification of Jesus. Thus the fate which befell Jesus relates to salvation, but in what respect? Probably one essential aspect of the author's thoughts consists of a pattern whereby sufferings are followed by exaltation. The same pattern then also holds true for those who are saved, the Christians, who follow the same path. This pattern is also visible in 4.13: 'Rejoice to the extent that you share Christ's sufferings, that you may also rejoice when his glory is revealed'.

In 1 Pet 1.18ff the author uses another word for 'save' which belongs to the same semantic field, to 'ransom' or 'release' (λυτροῦν). Here too it is said that salvation is predicted, which implies that it is contained in a divine plan (1.20). Furthermore, it is a salvation 'from the useless ways (of living) inherited from your fathers' (1.18). It is brought to pass 'not with silver or gold' but 'with the precious blood of Christ, of the lamb without spot or blemish' (1.18bf). Thus the sacrificial death of Christ is the means

[8] Cf. for the following paragraphs Kosala 1985, 172–185.

117

whereby he saved his adherents from the old conditions of life that were determined by sin. But in this passage the resurrection/glorification of Christ is also emphasised, because the circumstance that God has raised Jesus and given him glory is the reason why the addressees can have faith and hope in God (1.21). Thus we again encounter the connection between suffering and glorification that seems to be so important with regard to the situation of the addressees.

According to 1.3 and 1.23 the salvation from the old conditions into the new meant a new birth (see also 2.2). The image stands for the entry into a new mode of human existence.[9] Judging from 1.23 ('not of perishable seed'), God himself is the source of these new life conditions. They are available to the addressees through the gospel, the word of God (1.23–25).

In 1 Pet 1.3–5 too the fate of Jesus is related to the salvation of the Christians. They are 'born anew' so that they have a hope which includes a heavenly inheritance, because Christ has gone before them from death through resurrection. So salvation means release *from* the present 'various trials' *to* 'glory and honour' (1.6c–7).

Finally, we can note that salvation may also mean exemption from the judgment which is to come upon those who do not obey the gospel of God (4.17; also 1.17).

We have now gathered material from 1 Peter which can fill the gaps between words and clauses in its short passage on baptism. In the context of the passage we have recognised the Christ pattern: he 'also' suffered (3.18) and was brought to life. When the same sentence says that Christ suffered[10] vicariously 'for sins' (also 2.25), the contents are similar to what we read in 1.19, 'not with silver or gold'. The result is that he 'brings you to God' (3.18). Thus here again we see a salvation from something to something.

When, in 1 Pet 3.21, the author claims that baptism 'saves', we can now determine the meaning of the concept more precisely. We shall also see that other motifs of the text originate in the Noah narrative. Thus we can now discern a fuller answer to the question of what the Christian is saved from. The divine judgment in the Noah story and the unrighteous and unrepentant people, who are Noah's opposites in the Flood story (Gen 6.5), apparently have a counterpart in those evils from which the Christian

---

[9] See further, Schelkle 1961, 28–31; Goppelt 1978, 92ff.

[10] p[72], S, A give good manuscript support to the reading 'he died' instead of 'he suffered'. The choice is difficult, but is of minor importance to our issue.

addressees are saved: the old, pagan, meaningless life style, the judgment which awaits those who disobey the gospel, the pattern of sin and wickedness, and sufferings. Christians are also saved *to* something. As Noah's family was saved from death to life, so Christians are saved to a hope, to an inheritance, to healing (2.24), to life and to glory. In a way they already possess salvation, but its final realisation is still to come. As so often in 1 Peter,[11] in 3.21 Christ's resurrection is the foundation of salvation. It makes his death into more than a mere death and points to a life beyond it.

In 1 Pet 3.21b the author mentions the effect of baptism: 'It is not a removal of the dirt of the flesh, but the pledge of a good conscience to God.' Regrettably our survey of the salvation motif in 1 Peter does not help us to understand what the writer actually means by this statement. Is the clause about a pledge of a good conscience to God, a prayer *of* a good conscience, or a prayer *for* a good conscience? I prefer the first suggestion, as there is no clear evidence that it denotes 'prayer'. We should not, however, be too quick to assume that 'a good conscience' means 'without being conscious of any guilt'. Rather, a translation like 'with a sincere heart', or something similar, would be more apt. The significance would then be that baptism means that the believer sincerely turns to God, away from old realities and the pagan past.[12] This implies the acceptance of a life of obedience, righteousness, and holiness (1.2, 14f, 22; 2.24; 3.9).

So we may return to our primitive motifs. Thus there can be no doubt that in 1 Peter baptism is regarded from an *eschatological perspective*. 'Now' is the time when the prophecies about the coming age of salvation are fulfilled, and this salvation is given in baptism (3.21). Believers already receive this eschatological salvation, but it is emphasised that it still awaits its consummation in glory, when Jesus will be 'revealed' (1.4–9, 13; 4.13; 5.10).

Baptism is essential for the reception of salvation, but other elements in the transition from the old to the new have also appeared. So 3.21b, odd as it is, may refer to *conversion*, at least as I have understood it; the 'pledge of a good conscience' signified a sincere turning to God, away from old realities and from the pagan past. Elsewhere the author refers to the transition to Christianity in terms of rejection of the old aberrations (2.25) and of the earlier life-style that was lived under pagan presuppositions (1.14, 18; 4.3).

[11] 1.3, 21; 3.18; 4.13; 5.1, 10.
[12] Similarly, Brox 1979, 178.

Furthermore, the *proclamation* of the gospel and its *reception* are part of this transition into the new (1.12, 25; 4.17); 1 Pet 2.9 refers to the same transition using the image of a summons out of darkness.

The author calls Christians the faithful or believers (1.7, 21; 2.7). But he presents their acceptance of the proclamation as an act of obedience, the intention of which was that they alter the basic conditions and norms of their life (1.2, 14, 22; cf. 2.8; 3.1; 4.17). (He does not use the concept of *faith* in this context. In his usage, faith often has a connotation of faithfulness and hope, as e.g. 1.5, 9. There the individual is 'saved' not through becoming a believer, but through being faithful and holding steadfastly to the Christian hope.[13])

Although not all of the mentioned elements of the transition from old to new are explicitly connected with baptism, the author certainly regards them as belonging to the process of which baptism is one element. It seems fair to say that, like so many other theologians of the first Christian generations, he is of the opinion that baptism is the external, effective sign, whereby other aspects of the way into the church are ritually represented.

Moreover, our short passage provides clear evidence of the view that baptism is the step into the small rescued flock which is gathered in expectation of the final salvation. This is seen from the comparison with the eight persons rescued in the ark. In 2.9f the author uses the traditional, biblical designation of *the people of God*, into which those who believe have been called. They are 'a chosen (cf. 1.1) race, a royal priesthood, a holy nation, God's own people' (cf. Exod 19.6; Isa 43.21).

In 1 Pet 3.20f baptism is related to *Christ:* it 'saves through' his resurrection. In the letter as a whole we find several aspects of this salvation, and of course it would be an oversimplification to assume that we should think of baptism every time the text mentions salvation. But, on the one hand, baptism is a sounding-board underlying much of the letter, and, on the other, salvation is mentioned mostly in contexts which deal with aspects of the transition into the new life. So it seems justified to think of the different aspects of the entrance into the Christian flock as parts of the same process, in which baptism is a sign which gathers and expresses what is done both by the convert and by God. It is, moreover, an effective sign. Therefore we can maintain that when 3.21 says that baptism saves, this refers to the same salvation to which the author refers in 1.3ff. There, the resurrection of Christ (cf. 3.21c) is claimed to provide the faithful with

[13] See Goppelt 1978, 100f, 115.

the hope that, with Christ, they will share the inheritance, i.e. the coming glory. His death and resurrection are also the pattern of suffering and glorification which is applied to Christians. But when his death and resurrection brought about this salvation (1.11f), they were also vicarious acts which conferred liberation from the old, meaningless life (1.18–22), as well as from *sins* (2.24; 3.18).

Thus, even though not all of the 'primitive motifs' are explicitly associated with baptism in 1 Peter,[14] they are clearly linked up with the author's remarks on salvation. This salvation, including the hope of the addressees, is received by them in their baptism.

---

[14] If 1.2 alludes to baptism, then 1 Peter also connects the Spirit with baptism. There the letter is addressed 'to the colonists ... who are chosen and destined by God our Father and sanctified by the Spirit to be obedient to Jesus Christ and to be sprinkled with his blood'. How the addressees have been 'chosen' is described in the immediately following words. As in some passages we have discussed earlier, this verse also represents a primitive form of Trinitarian theology: the will of the Father is realised in the work of Christ, and on the basis thereof, the addressees are now sanctified, in other words, dedicated to God, through the Spirit. They are obliged to live according to this sanctity after they have pledged themselves to obedience. The words on obedience and sprinkling with the blood of Christ allude to the rites whereby the covenant between God and Israel was made and which are described in Exod 24.3–8. (Thus the sprinkling with blood should not be taken as a mixture of two images, one of rinsing with water, one of sacrifice. This is, however, the case in Rev 7.14.) The same Spirit is at work in the proclamation of salvation (1.12), and is also said to 'rest' upon the Christians (4.14). In my opinion, the use of the term 'sprinkling' (ῥαντισμός) is the strongest argument for a reading of the text with baptism in mind. But as the sprinkling in this case is not so clearly a cleansing water rite but a sacrificial one, I feel hesitant as to whether there are enough reasons to regard 1.2 as a baptismal text. Accordingly, I see no certain evidence that the Spirit is clearly associated with baptism in 1 Peter.

8

The Letter to the Hebrews

Hebrews was apparently written by a rhetorically conscious author[1] who wanted to persuade his readers/listeners not to surrender their Christian faith but steadily remain with the Lord whom they had professed. The massive theological argument is subservient to this admonitory purpose.[2] So in chapters 3–10 the author demonstrates that Christ is the high priest of the covenant who has offered the sacrifice which once and for all brought about reconciliation between God and man. In consequence, Christians must not behave as if this were not true by leaving the Christian group. To prove his point the writer adduces a host of arguments based on biblical interpretation.

Before the author begins the final admonitions in chapter 11, he completes, in 10.19–39, the presentation of Jesus, the high priest, by drawing conclusions concerning some basic features of a Christian attitude. The effect of the conclusion is strengthened by the incorporation of several echoes from the preceding argument. Most probably 10.22 alludes to baptism, but in order to comprehend the verse we must also take its context into account. In the following, relatively literal, translation of 10.19–25, the echoes from earlier passages are indicated within parentheses.

> (19) Brethren, since we have confidence to enter (cf. 3.6; 4.16) the sanctuary through the blood of Jesus, (20) – he made a new and living way for us through the curtain (cf. 9.7f), that is, through his flesh – (21) and have a great priest over the house of God (cf. 3.6; 4.14), (22) let us draw near (cf. 4.16; 7.25) with a true heart in full assurance of faith, with our hearts sprinkled (cf. 9.13) (clean) from an evil conscience (cf. 9.14) and with our bodies washed with pure water. (23) Let us hold fast the confession (cf. 4.14) of our hope (cf. 3.6), for he who promised (cf. 4.1; 6.12; 9.15) is faithful. (24) And let us observe one another in order to stir up one another to love and good works, (25) not neglecting our

---

[1] See Nissilä 1979; Übelacker 1989.
[2] This is particularly stressed by Übelacker (1989).

gatherings as is the habit of some, but encouraging one another, and all the more as you see the day drawing near (cf. 3.13).

There is a general consensus among its interpreters that verse 22 alludes to baptism.[3] The author applies to the Christians the rite of sprinkling which, according to biblical ordinances (Exod 29.4; Lev 8.30), served as some kind of consecration of the priests. Probably he understands this rite in the same way as when, in 9.13f, he interprets the purification through water and the ashes of a red heifer (Num 19.9, 17), saying: 'How much more will the blood of Christ ... purify our conscience from dead works (i.e. works which lead to death) to serve the living God.'

Thus, according to Heb 9.14, Christ's purifying sacrificial death is an objective fact, independent of 'us'. In 10.19–22 the author does not say how 'we' have taken it to ourselves nor how it purifies precisely 'our' conscience. In the letter as a whole, this personal application of the objective reconciliation is described in several ways. Thus Christians are 'called' and will receive the inheritance (9.15), which, of course, is another reference to their acceptance of the gospel. The author alludes to the same process when he says that one 'repents from dead works' (i.e. from one's earlier, mortal way of living; 6.1; cf. 9.14), accepts the message in 'faith' (4.2f; cf. 2.2f), and professes oneself an adherent of this high priest (3.1; 4.14; 10.23).

But here in Heb 10.19–22, it is baptism that makes Jesus' sacrifice relevant and applies it to Christians. It has brought about a purification from their sins. The writer uses the expression that the heart (let us say, the centre of the personality) is clean from an evil conscience. In light of 9.14 this means that in baptism the earlier sinful mode of life was forgiven, the one which led to spiritual death.[4]

In the following verse (23), the author admonishes his readers/listeners to hold fast to the confession that imparts hope. This confession may have been an element in the baptismal rite, i.e. the baptised person may have explicitly confessed his/her faith in Jesus. This, however, must remain a guess.

In verse 24f, the writer directs his readers' attention to the Christian community, which the author is so anxious the addressees should not leave. Within it they should spur on each other to love and to good works, and 'encourage' one another, so that fellow-Christians do not give up their

---

[3] Thus Michel 1966, 346f; Braun 1984, 310; Attridge 1989, 289; Weiss 1991, 530.
[4] See also e.g. 10.17: in the new covenant God will 'no longer remember sins'.

faith or slowly drift away from it. Earlier in the letter, this community has been represented as the people of the new covenant, established through the sacrifice of Christ (9.15). Participation in the gatherings of the Christians is a demonstration of fidelity to the Lord and to one's confession, which becomes more important as the ultimate crisis, the 'day', approaches (10.25; cf. 10.37).

Thus the Christians have a good and just relationship to God, because in the new covenant they live under conditions determined by the consequences of the once-for-all sacrifice which Christ has made. But they can break this relationship to God. Confronting this possibility, the writer resorts to harsh and threatening terms: 'If we sin deliberately after receiving the knowledge of the truth, there no longer remains a sacrifice for sins' (10.26; RSV). The sacrifice mentioned is that which is made relevant or applied in baptism.

Likewise, in 6.4–6, the author maintains concerning those who have 'been enlightened and have tasted the heavenly gift and become partakers of the Holy Spirit, and have tasted the goodness of the word of God and the powers of the age to come, and then commit apostasy', that 'it is impossible to bring them to repentance again'.[5] Later on in the early church, 'enlightenment' could denote baptism,[6] but this hardly suffices to support an identification of enlightenment with baptism in Hebrews.[7] On the other hand, the experiences mentioned in 6.4ff all apparently belong to entrance into the Christian community,[8] and we have seen that our author takes baptism into account as a self-evident element of this process. Thus baptism probably belongs to the field of associations of 6.4ff.[9]

Both of the Hebrews passages on the impossibility of a renewed repentance place entrance into the church into an eschatological perspective. This entrance meant wonderful gifts for Christians, and more were still to come. If they, however, rejected the salvation which they had taken to themselves, the same eschatological framework became threatening and dangerous.

In the preceding brief deliberations on baptism in Hebrews, we have encountered most of our so-called primitive motifs. Thus baptism is closely related to *Christ*, and of course linked up with the high priest Christology

---

[5] Trans. RSV.
[6] Justin, *Apology* 1.61.12f; 65.1.
[7] Grässer 1990, 348; cf. Braun 1984, 165.
[8] Hegermann 1988, 132; Grässer 1990, 348.
[9] Weiss 1991, 342ff.

of the letter: his once-for-all sacrifice is made relevant in baptism. *The remission of sins* depends on this sacrifice and is clearly connected with baptism. The same holds true of the idea of *the people of the new covenant* (constituted through Christ's sacrifice). The *proclamation* of the gospel, *conversion* and faith are mentioned as self-evident elements when the context touches upon the addressees' membership in this people.

Baptism has an *eschatological* horizon in the following senses. Together with other phases of entrance into the church, it means that neophytes are taken into the new covenant. This is already a decisive eschatological framework, which comprises life and hope for those who stand fast. This is expressed in several ways in the letter: the Christians await the sabbath rest (4.1–11) and the inheritance (6.12–17; 9.15), they have a hope (6.18f) and a goal 'behind the curtain' (6.19f), in the sanctuary (10.19); they expect salvation (9.28), that which is promised (10.36; 11.40, etc.), and the coming city (13.14). On the other hand, the eschatological perspective threatens those who commit apostasy, and this is why the author paints the consequences of complete apostasy in such horrifying colours.

Strictly speaking, the gift of *the Holy Spirit* is also an aspect of the eschatological perspective. It is explicitly mentioned in 6.4, and there it belongs to the experiences that occur at entrance into the church. According to the same passage (6.5), the addressees then also 'tasted the powers of the coming age'. In 2.4 the author also refers to the occasion when his audience received the Christian message and he says that God then confirmed the *proclamation* 'with signs and wonders and various powerful acts and with the distribution of Holy Spirit according to his will'. The language is strongly coloured by the Bible, but it nevertheless implies that some charismatic phenomena have occurred.

Thus in Hebrews baptism is connected with all of the primitive motifs, although an explicit, close connection only exists for a couple of them, the relation to Christ and the forgiveness of sins. But the others also belong to the process whereby new believers join the people of the new covenant.

9

The Acts of the Apostles

9.1. Introduction

Luke has certain objects in view when writing Acts,[1] and in this respect there is no difference between him and other historiographers of his days. It belonged to the cultural conventions for historians to write with one purpose or another.[2] When looking for the particular Lukan purpose, we should take seriously the circumstance that Acts is the second part of a two-volume work. In other words, when Luke introduces his Gospel, he actually introduces this whole work – at least this ensued once both parts of it had been published. Thus in the beginning of the Gospel Luke states that he will give an orderly account of 'the things which have been accomplished among us', so that the reader may understand how reliably he has been instructed. The 'things' which are reported in Acts concern the way in which the testimony about Jesus spread from Jerusalem in wider and wider circles. In the long run it is to reach 'the end of the world' (Acts 1.8). Luke and his readers stood in the midst of this development and accordingly knew that even more distant goals were set for it. In addition, the account contains a few secondary emphases. So probably Luke also wishes to remind his Gentile-Christian readers of the noble offspring of the community to which they belong, and the narratives concerning the fellowship of the first Christians, how they cared for each other, devoted themselves to the apostolic teaching, etc., are certainly meant to paint an ideal which should inspire the faithful readers of Luke's day.

When reading Acts, we should be aware that as an historian Luke follows certain literary conventions. To fulfil his purpose, he chooses and arranges his material. The literary conventions also required that persons and events be presented in a credible manner so that the main actors and their actions appeared as was proper to their roles, and they behaved as the

[1] Maddox 1982; Pesch 1986 1, 29–34; D. Peterson 1993.
[2] Hengel 1979, 11–61.

readers expected them to do.[3] This means that even with a limited scope such as ours, we are confronted with a number of uncertainties when we ask questions concerning the history of the early church: what actually happened? With this is associated the problem of how far Luke is using sources.

One simple example of these difficulties is the following. In chapter three we discussed the different baptismal formulae which occur in Acts: 'into the name of the Lord Jesus', 'in the name of Jesus Christ', and 'because of the name of Jesus Christ'. In that context it was mentioned that Luke lets Jewish Christians use the last two expressions, which have a more biblical ring (2.38; 10.48), whereas the 'into' formula is natural for himself.[4] Now, is 'in the name of N.' Jewish-Christian tradition or is it an example of Luke's skill as an author? Chapter five mentioned the possibility that 1 Cor 6.11 with its 'in the name'-phrase goes back to Jewish-Christian tradition. If this is so, we are not confronted by an either/or, but by a both/ and, because in that case Luke both uses tradition and meets certain stylistic demands on a good historiographer.

In what follows, the questions concerning tradition–history will be more or less disregarded. Instead we shall concentrate on the question of what Luke's text is likely to have told its readers. We let Peter and other Jewish Christians be the characters whom Luke presents. In the textual world which Luke constructs, the baptismal formulae represent two slightly different approaches to Jesus who gave baptism its meaning, one focusing on Jesus, the heavenly *kurios*, the other on Jesus, the Messiah. In what follows, I shall touch upon the question of how this textual world is related to the world of history only as something which, in this connection, is of secondary importance.

Baptism is mentioned as a matter of course when Luke reports that people join the church after having accepted the testimony about Jesus. He devotes little if any attention to theological reflections on baptism. Consequently, we should be careful when studying baptism in isolation. I shall assume that Luke has a coherent view on baptism and that he is of the opinion that the main actors in his narrative share his attitude in this matter. But nevertheless the material seems to contain some tensions. Thus the relation of the Spirit to baptism is presented in different ways, and, as already noted, there are three baptismal formulae. I have proposed an

---

[3] Plümacher 1972, 39; van Unnik 1979, 59; Hemer 1989, chapter 3; Gempf 1993.
[4] Hartman 1985.

approach to the latter phenomenon and shall soon discuss the passages in which the Spirit plays a somewhat surprising role.

Since in Acts the brief references to baptism appear as notices in the running narrative, it is not necessary to deal with all of the particular passages separately. Instead I shall discuss a few texts in which baptism is allowed somewhat greater scope or is somehow problematic. When, towards the end of this chapter, I return to the question of the primitive motifs, I shall also cite other passages which refer to baptism.

9.2. Baptism on the day of Pentecost

Our first text is Acts 2.37–42, which reports on the effects of Peter's sermon on the day of Pentecost:[5]

> When they heard this, they were cut to the heart, and said to Peter and the other apostles: 'Brethren, what shall we do?' (38) Peter said to them: 'Repent, and may every one of you be baptised in the name of Jesus Christ unto the remission of your sins, and you shall receive the gift of the Holy Spirit. (39) For the promise is for you and your children and all those far off, whom the Lord our God calls. (40) And he testified with many other words and exhorted them: 'Be saved from this generation of crookedness!' (41) Those who received his words were baptised, and there were added that day about three thousand souls. (42) And they kept to the teaching of the apostles and the fellowship, to the breaking of bread and the prayers.

The entrance of three thousand into the church is the culmination of the story. Before that step takes place, its background and meaning are described, and afterwards its consequences are related. Thus the action taken by the three thousand is a response to the speech which Peter gives when the Spirit has fallen on the apostles. The account begins by explaining the gift of the Spirit, that God's promise in the prophecy of Joel is thus fulfilled (Joel 2.18–32a). Luke modifies Joel's text to fit his understanding of the situation; in Joel the outpouring of the Spirit will take place 'thereafter', but Luke writes 'in the last days'. On the one hand, this represents early Christian tradition which, in its turn, has inherited the Old Testament-Jewish idea that God would give his Spirit in the expected

---

[5] This sermon, like other speeches in Acts, is a manifestation of the literary convention mentioned above concerning how to write history. Such an assumption does not necessarily involve denial that missionary preaching took place, nor that these speeches to some extent represent topics of importance in such preaching. See Wilckens 1974.

age of salvation. (We touched upon these ideas in chapter one.) On the other hand, Luke also has his own view of the Spirit and its work. Thus he is of the opinion that the age of the salvation has begun with the work of Christ, and that therefore in this time God saves people through the mission of the church; but the actual power in and behind this mission 'in the last days' is the Spirit. Yet the end is not imminent, nor does it behoove people to speculate on its date (Acts 1.7). This is the 'eschatological' perspective in which the testimony about Jesus is first presented in Acts 2 and in which the Spirit is seen to be at work.

Towards the end of his speech Peter accuses the Jews of having crucified Jesus. That this action was a crime is demonstrated by God's raising him and making him both Lord and Messiah (2.36). This leads to pangs of conscience on the part of the audience, who show themselves ready for conversion.

Peter's answer to the penitents contains several aspects of baptism which recur elsewhere in Acts. Thus baptism belongs to a larger whole involving abandonment of the old, outdated or sinful situation and entrance into new conditions by joining the apostolic community gathered by the Spirit around the witness of the heavenly Lord. The starting point is the apostolic message and its reception. There the steps into the church begin. Individuals repent and turn away, here from the 'crooked generation' (v. 40; cf. Deut 32.5) which has rejected its Messiah, thus sinning against God (cf. 3.19). Instead of saying that people 'receive' (v. 41) the message, Luke can in other passages say that they 'believe' (e.g. 8.12; 16.31; 18.8). In 2.41 this reception is expressed in that the converts are baptised. The passive mood has two dimensions. One is that people take the step of submission to baptism; baptism becomes, so to speak, the external side of their acceptance of the message and of its impact. The other dimension pertains precisely to the passive voice as such:[6] the external sign is something which is performed on the person by someone else; something is given to the person who accepts it.

Here baptism is a sign mediating God's forgiveness, first of the sin of which Peter has just accused his audience, that is, of having rejected him whom God had sent (cf. 22.16, on Paul's baptism). But in Luke's audience the motif of the remission of sins almost certainly had another referent. Among his readers it would rather refer to a general aversion to God; when the audience consisted of Gentile Christians, such an aversion would have

---

[6] See G. Barth 1981, 38ff.

been manifested by a way of living which was defiled by particular pagan sins (cf. 26.18). The referent the motif would have for a Jewish-Christian audience is somewhat unclear; we could perhaps surmise that they would be forgiven for their solidarity with those who did not accept Jesus, the Messiah. This may be supported by the fact that according to Acts it is through him that God grants forgiveness of sins (5.31; 13.38).

In the Pentecost narrative, baptism is said to be performed 'in the name of Jesus Christ'. As long as there are no indications to the contrary, it is fair to assume that the phrase is meaningful to Luke and his readers. So what does it signify here? The Joel quotation in Peter's speech says that 'whoever calls on the name of the Lord shall be saved' (Acts 2.21; Joel 2.32a). In this context, 'the Lord' should most probably be understood as referring to the Lord Jesus, and thus he is the one on whom they should call. In its position at the beginning of the events to be narrated in Acts, this Joel-quotation becomes programmatic; it is a prophecy concerning that which happens in the narrative when individuals repent and are baptised, in other words, they 'call on the name of the Lord' and are 'saved'. Thus Jesus Christ becomes the fundamental referent of the rite that marks the culmination of the conversion of the three thousand.

But the role of Jesus calls for further discussion. The subject is treated in Luke 24.44–49. In this passage, Jesus speaks generally of what will happen in the time of the church. The eleven and some others are told that repentance unto the remission of sins shall be preached in the name of Christ to all nations (v. 47). The fundamental presupposition of this work of preaching is that according to the scriptures the Messiah would suffer in order then to rise (v. 46). Indeed, Luke maintains that not only the suffering and the resurrection are predicted in scripture, but also the preaching of repentance and forgiveness; in other words, they also belong to God's plan of how the world will be saved.[7] Such a way of viewing the mission, the testimony about Jesus (Acts 1.8), implies that, because the readers of Luke have also heard this preaching, they too are included in the same divine plan.

When we compare Luke 24 and Acts 2 the following picture emerges. In the former text we hear of a preaching of repentance unto the remission of sins in the name of Christ, whereas in the latter baptism is performed in the name of Jesus Christ unto remission, and the baptism follows upon a preaching leading to repentance. Apparently both texts refer to the same

---

[7] See Goppelt 1976, 607ff.

kind of process.[8] Again, then, what is the role of Jesus Christ? In Acts 2, the remission of sins is not related to Christ. Luke does not say there that it is given because Jesus has suffered and died for sinners, nor does he say this anywhere else.[9] Instead, the death of Jesus is the path the Messiah must walk in order to enter his glory (e.g. Luke 17.24f; 24.26). So when in Luke 24 repentance/conversion and forgiveness take place 'in his name', this may rather mean turning to the exalted and gracious Lord (Acts 15.11), who received sinners already when living on earth.[10] In the words of the Joel quotation, the repentant converts 'call upon the name of the Lord'.

Thus forgiveness and conversion are somehow linked to Jesus. But this is even more true of baptism. Although the phrase 'in (into) the name of' is vague, Luke is apparently of the opinion that baptism takes its meaning from the Jesus in whom Luke and his readers believe. He is the Jesus who is described in the Gospel of Luke, the Jesus who had to enter his glory through suffering (Luke 24.26); he is the Messiah whom the Jews had rejected, who is now the subject of the testimony of the church, who graciously forgives sins, and who now saves those who call on him.

According to the programme for the mission of the church in Luke 24.47–49, the same Jesus also sends the Spirit, whom the Father has promised to give (v. 49). In Acts 2.38f, the converts receive the same gift when they enter the Christian community, an entrance which comprises conversion, faith, baptism, and forgiveness, all of which are closely interconnected. In 2.39 Peter mentions the reason why the audience will receive the Spirit: God's promise is for them, more specifically the promise contained in the Joel quotation concerning the Spirit and salvation for those who call on the name of the Lord. Presumably it does not involve distorting 2.39 if the verse is taken to mean that the promise belongs to 'you' for two reasons: first, because 'now' is the time of the fulfilment of the promises (cf. also 2.16f), and secondly, precisely because the audience 'call on the name of the Lord'. Others too will 'call on the Lord', 'all that are far off, whom the Lord our God calls'. Actually the latter verse contains an

---

[8] See also the following passages: Luke 1.77 (knowledge of salvation through the remission of sins); Acts 5.31 (Jesus was exalted in order that Israel might receive remission of sins through his name); 13.38 (through him remission of sins is preached); 26.18 (the Gentiles will repent and be forgiven through faith in Jesus).

[9] Moreover interpretations of the death of Jesus similar to that cited are on the whole missing in Luke–Acts. One exception is Luke 22.19, where Luke quotes liturgical tradition, and another is Acts 20.28, which is also traditional (see Roloff 1981, 306). I would suggest that in the last case Luke tries to make his Paul sound Pauline!

[10] Schweizer 1982, 225.

echo from the continuation of the Joel passage: 'Among the survivors shall be those whom the Lord calls' (Joel 2.32). Thus when humans 'call on' the Lord, he 'calls' them. In other words, when they receive the preaching and so call on the Lord, this means that God calls them.[11]

In the world of the text, the gift of the Spirit is expressed in phenomena of a markedly charismatic nature. As a matter of fact, however, Luke does not explicitly mention that the newly converted received the Spirit, and he tells us even less about, e.g., their speaking in tongues. But the Spirit is also the power behind the mission of the church. To Luke's audience the report on the ecstatic phenomena recalls what tradition presumably told about the first period of early Christianity. It is however doubtful whether Luke wants the readers to strive for something similar. Probably they should rather think that among them the Spirit is at work under less spectacular forms. If this is so, the manner in which the first Christians, i.e. those of the narrative, are an example to Luke's readers, is rather to be found in the conclusion of the narrative. There the three thousand do not fall into ecstasy but keep to the teaching of the apostles, to the Christian community, and to the common worship.[12] These were features which Luke meant should be typical of the people of God in whom the promises concerning the last age were being fulfilled; humans entered it through baptism after having received the testimony of Christ and after having repented.

9.3. The Cornelius story

The narrative on the conversion of Cornelius and his household is one of those in Luke's book on the first Christians which have been considered to be problematic.[13] At the end of the story Peter addresses those who have gathered in Cornelius' home. He starts by emphasising that God does not show any partiality – Cornelius is a Gentile, as we know from the beginning of the account, even though he is also a so-called God-fearer[14] – but, says Peter, 'in every nation anyone who fears him and does what is

[11] Roloff 1981, 63.
[12] Weiser 1981–85, 95f.
[13] See Roloff 1981, 135, 174. It also raises rather complicated problems concerning the history of traditions; for a condensed survey, see Weiser 1981–85, 258ff.
[14] For the term and the discussion of the problems, see Cohen 1989 and Hemer 1989, 444–447.

right is acceptable to him' (10.34f). Then follows the 'testimony', that is, the apostolic preaching about Jesus, who was killed but raised from the dead, whom God has ordained to be judge of living and dead (10.37–42); the testimony also refers to the listeners, for Peter is reported to proclaim that according to the prophets 'every one who believes in him receives forgiveness of sins through his name' (10.43; RSV).

When the Jesus testimony has thus reached a stage at which Cornelius and the other presumptive converts can be involved, the story takes a new turn, in that something supernatural occurs: the Spirit falls on the audience. This astonishes the Jewish Christians present, but Peter draws the conclusion: 'Can any one withhold water for baptising these who have received the Holy Spirit just as we have?' (10.47). So he commands that they be 'baptised in the name of Jesus Christ' (10.48).

In the following scene the Christian Jews of Jerusalem call Peter to account for his action; then, *inter alia*, he retells the vision which Cornelius had according to the beginning of the narrative (10.3–6): an angel told him that Peter was to 'speak words to you (to Cornelius) by which you will be saved, you and all your household' (11.14). Peter also slightly twists his earlier reply concerning withholding water from baptism; now it becomes: 'Who was I that I could hinder God?' (11.17). The reason why he raises this question is, according to the preceding verses, that he realises that the Gentiles have received the Spirit just as, according to the Lord's promise, he himself and the others did 'at the beginning', when they were 'baptised in (or: with, Greek ἐν) Holy Spirit' in contrast to John's water baptism. Finally, the Christian Jews who had been critical at the outset interpret the whole event: 'Then God has granted repentance unto life to the Gentiles too' (11.18).

This somewhat circumstantial account may help us to discern how Luke presents baptism here. It belongs to a series of events which is described with different terms: it is labelled 'repentance unto life' (11.18), 'to be saved' (11.14), 'to be received by God' (10.35). It comprises several phases: a proclamation of the testimony (10.37–43), the reception of the word of God (11.1), belief in Jesus who grants forgiveness of sins (10.14), God's gift of the Spirit (10.46), baptism in the name of Jesus Christ (10.48). Most of the actions in the narrative are performed by humans, but they are driven thereto by God or the Spirit. This holds true of Cornelius' summoning of Peter and of Peter's coming and speech (it is 'commanded by the Lord', 10.33). God alone, however, is responsible for the gift of the Spirit. The mention of 'the beginning' (11.15) makes this event a new

Pentecost at which God launches a new phase in his salvific plan.[15] The reference to the word of the Lord concerning the apostles' baptism with the Holy Spirit in contrast to John's water baptism (11.16; cf. 1.5) may be understood as reinforcing the same feature of a second Pentecost in the progression of the testimony to the wider world. Furthermore, it emphasises that this time too, as at the first Pentecost, God takes the initiative. Possibly the reiteration of the saying of Jesus implies that the first Pentecost did not definitively fulfil the promise, but now the fulfilment is accomplished.[16]

But what about baptism in this division of events among the various actors? According to 10.47 no one should stop anyone from baptising Cornelius and his household; but according to 11.17 Peter should not prevent God. From what? From giving the Spirit which he had already given? Rather, he could not prevent God from fulfilling his reception of these new, Gentile, Christians (10.35: 'anyone who fears him ... is acceptable to him'), and from giving them life (11.18: he has 'granted them repentance unto life'). They would, as it were, be deprived of both of these divine gifts if humans prevented them from being baptised.[17]

The sequence of the reported events, the bestowal of the Spirit followed by baptism, has opened this passage to dispute. We recall that in 2.38 the sequence is reversed. Is one or the other sequence 'normal'? The discussion of the preceding paragraphs indirectly sheds some light on the question: God's own initiative breaks in to demonstrate the necessity of taking the step into the Gentile world.[18] But the narrative also indicates that the process of passing into the group of 'those who believed' (4.32) was looked on as an integral one, although it was composed of several elements and aspects. This means that, even to Luke, the gift of the Spirit is not simply to be identified with charisms but is also an active agent in the whole process (Acts 6.10; 9.31; 10.19; 15.8 etc.).

Finally, we should briefly recall that here Luke reports that a 'house', i.e. a whole family, possibly including slaves, believe, receive the Spirit, and are baptised (similarly also in 16.14f and 18.8). Paul also testifies to the same phenomenon when he notes in 1 Cor 1.16 that he baptised 'the household of Stephanas'. This is due to the fact that religion was not a private affair to

---

[15] Roloff 1981, 176.
[16] Thus G. Schneider 1980–82 2, 83.
[17] Roloff 1981, 176.
[18] Roloff 1981, 135, 174; Weiser 1981–85, 270; Lüdemann 1989, 130 (quoting Dibelius).

the same extent as is the case in modern Western society. The social and economic kernel of the society was the family, which in religious matters too functioned as a unit. This collective was represented by the head of the household, as a rule the father of the family. (But in 16.14 a tradeswoman takes her household with her into the new religion.[19])

On the other hand, already in New Testament times we also hear that individual members of a household became Christians without the others taking the same step; this is the case according to 1 Cor 7.12f; 1 Pet 3.1; 1 Tim 6.1f[20] In the martyr legends of later times it is a common motif, emphasising the steadfastness or the courage of the Christians who were harassed, threatened, or tortured even by family members because of their Christian faith.

9.4. Spirit and baptism in the Samaria mission

Acts 8.14–17 has also been counted among the texts which raise questions as to the relationship between baptism and the gift of the Spirit. According to the context, Philip preached the gospel in Samaria and baptised those who believed (8.12, 16). They, however, did not receive the Spirit 'but had only been baptised into the name of the Lord Jesus' (8.16). Peter and John are sent thither; they pray for the converts that they may receive the Spirit and lay their hands on them, whereupon they do receive the Spirit (8.17).

When dealing with such a text it is important to distinguish between the history of the underlying tradition and the meaning of the present composition. Thus it is entirely probable that vv. 14–17 come directly from Luke's hand, whereas both the preceding and the following pieces derive from traditions about Philip and Peter respectively.[21] As Luke's account now stands before us, however, it expresses a wish on Luke's part to link the growing Samaritan church with Jerusalem, which is the origin of the testimony. This is all the more important in this case, as the

---

[19] Something similar was the case in Corinth according to 1 Cor 1.11; maybe also in Colossae, according to Col 4.15, depending on how one assesses the variae lectiones.

[20] Passages according to which households have been baptised have been used in discussions on infant baptism. Their argumentative value is however doubtful, not primarily because in these cases (small) children would not have been counted among the household, but because the view of antiquity that the family constituted a unity in religious matters hardly exists in the (mostly Western) circles in which these debates proceed in our day. In other words, what seems to have been one of the basic ideological-sociological presuppositions in New Testament times for a baptism of the whole household is hardly present now. Thus arguments for infant baptism should be drawn from elsewhere.

[21] Weiser 1981–85, 200.

movement into Samaria is particularly marked out as a significant stage when Luke describes the way of the gospel in Acts 1.8: 'You will receive power when the Holy Spirit comes upon you, and you will be my witnesses in Jerusalem and in all Judea and Samaria . . .'. For some reason or another, it was essential to emphasise the inclusion of the semi-Jewish or 'heretical' Samaritans in God's people. So 8.14–17 brings out how, although the Samaria mission was initiated by others, it was incorporated into the mission with which the risen Christ charged his apostles.[22]

9.5. The case of the 'disciples' at Ephesus

Acts 19.1–7 is another text which raises problems as to the relationship between Christian baptism and the gift of the Spirit. Here is the text:

> It occurred when Apollos was at Corinth that Paul passed through the upper country and came to Ephesus, and found some disciples, (2) and said to them: 'Did you receive the Holy Spirit when you believed?' They answered: 'But we have not even heard that there is a Holy Spirit.' (3) He said: 'Into what, then, were you baptised?'. They said: 'Into John's baptism.' (4) Paul said: 'John baptised with the baptism of repentance, telling the people that they were to believe in him who was to come after him, that is, Jesus.' (5) When they heard this, they were baptised into the name of the Lord Jesus. (6) And when Paul laid his hands on them, the Holy Spirit came on them, and they spoke with tongues and prophesied. (7) And they were about twelve men in all.

Luke's words go straight to the point so that the twelve men, somewhat astonishingly, are called 'disciples', and Paul's question on the Spirit is abruptly introduced. Their answer may not be astonishing within its context, but from a historical point of view we may wonder whether there truly were 'disciples', meaning 'Christians', of such an awkward sort.[23] On the other hand, Luke suggests that they were not real disciples = Christians[24] but instead followers of John the Baptist. But their knowledge

---

[22] Jervell 1972, 126; Roloff 1981, 135; Weiser 1981–85, 204. Thus it is inadvisable to assume that the passage contains traces of two rites, different from each other, a baptism in water and a laying on of hands mediating the gift of the Spirit; thus Quesnel 1985, 177, 194. This is not to deny that Luke may very well reflect a ritual practice of prayer and laying on of hands at baptism; see also 19.6, 17.

[23] Pesch 1986 2, 165, suggests that the term reflects the way the disciples of John designated themselves.

[24] Weiser claims that they should be understood as people 'in the immediate preliminary stage before Christian belief' (1981–85, 515). Käsemann (1964) claims that they were Christians, although of a less orthodox bent, who according to Luke in this story are properly connected to the *una sancta*. Beasley-Murray (1962, 111), Roloff (1981, 281f) and Weiser (ibid.) suggest that they constituted a marginal group.

of their master's message seems to be somewhat meagre, assuming the accuracy of the traditions which tell us that he proclaimed that the coming, Strong One would baptise in Holy Spirit (whatever John may have meant thereby).[25]

Again, it seems wise to distinguish between (a) the historical questions, (b) the history of tradition and redaction, and (c) the text as it now stands within the present double work of the Gospel of Luke and the Book of Acts. As regards the historical question, the account reflects the probability that not least in Western Asia Minor, the Christian church encountered Jews who revered the Baptist and so had to determine her own identity vis-à-vis them; we may recall the prominence of the Baptist and his followers in John's Gospel, which may reflect a similar state of affairs there.[26] Apparently the critical points were the position of Jesus, the Christian Jesus-baptism as differentiated from that of John, and the gift of the Spirit.[27]

The history of tradition and redaction is difficult to assess. The Lukan Paul's reference to John's message of course goes back to tradition, but is nonetheless edited by Luke.[28] Certainly the baptismal formula, 'into the name of', is traditional too, but does not necessarily have the same source as the other traditions. The rest of vv. 2–7 also bears witness to Luke's hand. Weiser even thinks that Luke has reworked a tradition that in Ephesus Paul had instructed some disciples of John and baptised them with the Christian baptism.[29]

However, what really matters with regard to our present task is the Lukan text's comments on baptism. The elements of the somewhat rough and sketchy first part of the narrative point to deficiencies on the part of the twelve men. They were not really 'disciples', although they are called so. Their faith, if any, was not in Jesus. They did not even know of the Spirit, still less possess it, and they were not baptised with the Christian baptism. The structure of the account makes the gift of the Spirit its focal point. It is the object of Paul's first question which triggers the following dialogue, and its final bestowal solves the initial problem. But the route between the two poles is instructive. First, Paul presupposes that becoming a 'believer' implies that one has received the Spirit. Then the information

[25] See Weiser 1981–85, 516.
[26] Pesch 1986 2, 166.
[27] So Roloff (1981, 281) suggests that the story describes a pattern for the Christian encounter with the disciples of the Baptist.
[28] Weiser 1981–85, 513.
[29] Weiser 1981–85, 512.

that the men had not even heard that there was a Spirit is not countered with a question concerning their faith but with one on their baptism. This places Luke (or, rather, the Lukan Paul) among other New Testament theologians to whom baptism is the sacrament of faith.[30] As he builds the story, it becomes clear that a defective belief (not connected with the gift of the Spirit) must be coupled with a defective baptism. The somewhat strange questions concerning 'into' which baptism the 'disciples' had been baptised should be understood in light of the solution to which the narrative leads, the baptism 'into the name of the Lord Jesus'. (John's position in Luke's eyes is such that his baptism cannot be described as one 'into' his name.[31])

Thus as in vv. 2f Luke went in Paul's questions from faith to baptism, so he now travels the same route: John the Baptist here refers to Jesus as the Coming One in whom all should believe; he then implies that the men accepted this claim: they 'heard', and so they were baptised, but now with the 'real' baptism. Thus the necessary preconditions for receiving the Spirit should exist, and in a sense they do, but the actual bestowal is linked to the laying on of hands, which should be understood as a ceremony joined with the principal rite, the baptism.[32]

Thus in this passage Luke has, on the one hand, demonstrated how the different elements of entrance into the church belong together: hearing of Jesus, accepting this message – belief, baptism, gift of the Spirit, all forming a unit with several aspects. If we consider the passage in this light, we shall not be too bewildered by the fact that in the account Paul seemingly first connects the gift of the Spirit with becoming a believer, then vaguely with baptism, and finally with the laying on of hands.

9.6. Traces of ritual details?

Luke's narrative of the first Christians may reflect a few details of how baptism was administered.[33] Thus Acts 8.15–17 and 19.6 may indicate

---

[30] See John 3.15; Gal 3.26 etc.; also Mark 16.16.

[31] Conzelmann 1972, 119.

[32] To Pesch (1986 2, 166) the laying on of hands symbolises the 'ecclesiastical–apostolic binding of the sacrament'. As to the possibility that its appearance here represents a trace of an actual early liturgical element, see below.

[33] Although the following detail is not particularly connected with Luke–Acts, this might be the place to refer to Stommel 1959, where some material is gathered which sheds light on how ritual 'baths', rinsings, etc. were performed. It is particularly interesting that the 'baptisand' took his place in the water and had water poured or sprinkled over him.

that prayer and laying on of hands belonged to the rite. Furthermore, Cullmann has suggested that 8.36, 10.47, and 11.17 represent traces of the feature that at baptism the question was posed whether anything 'prevented' the candidate's being baptised.[34] Here we may surmise a detail of the baptismal rite used in Luke's ecclesiastical environment,[35] but we can hardly draw any conclusions concerning an older tradition.

In some manuscripts there is a longer reading of Acts 8.37 to the effect that Philip says to the eunuch: 'If you believe of all your heart, it can be done. He answered: I believe that Jesus Christ is the Son of God.' The reading does not represent the original, but it certainly comes from the baptismal rite of the church to which the scribe who brought the reading into Luke's text belonged.[36]

Furthermore, Acts 22.16 may reflect another ritual detail: 'Rise and be baptised and wash away your sins, calling on his name' (see also 2.21: 'Call on the name of the Lord'). Did the candidate mention Jesus' name or call upon him? Was this done in such a way as to mark that the baptism was performed 'into the name of the Lord Jesus'?[37] The answer to these questions must be hesitant, but in all probability the rite was accompanied with such interpreting prayers or allocutions or proclamations that it was clear to those who took part and those who assisted that it was naturally called a baptism into the name of the Lord Jesus.

Moreover, it is very likely that those who were baptised confessed that they 'believed'.[38] Such a detail could then explain why different early Christian traditions all use the term 'believer' as the normal designation of the Christians. The person who performed the baptism may for example have asked (not unlike what we encounter with Hippolytus): 'Do you believe in the Lord Jesus?' The answer would be 'I believe' (which, of course, is equal to the English 'I do'). (Cf. also the longer reading in 8.37, referred to above.)

---

[34] Cullmann 1958, 65ff. This question appears in the Pseudo-Clementine *Homilies* 13.5.1 and 11.2. Also Matt 19.14 par. has been adduced in this context; one should not 'prevent' children from coming to Jesus, that is from being baptised. Such an understanding is rightly rejected by, among others, Pesch (1976–77 2, 132) and Gnilka (1986–88 2, 81).

[35] Weiser 1981–85, 211.

[36] G. Barth 1981, 131.

[37] See Beasley-Murray 1962, 100f and cf. Kramer 1963, 73ff. According to Jas 2.7 a name has been proclaimed 'over' the addressees. In chapter 3 above (footnote 52), I assessed (somewhat critically) the suggestion that the phrase reflects an element in the baptismal rite.

[38] Cf. Kramer 1963, 60 (on the *pistis*-formula).

One further question arises concerning the liturgical practice. In all the narratives of Acts on baptism and conversion, the steps are taken at great speed.[39] The most salient example is in the account of the jailer at Philippi, in which the whole sequence from the first acquaintance to baptism, which also includes his household, occurs within a few hours of the night (16.30–34). Did Luke also mean that the conversion of the three thousand at Pentecost was an event covering only a few hours? I am not asking what really happened on this or that occasion (if anything at all happened) but two other questions: on the one hand, did Luke have access to a tradition to the effect that in the first days of the church baptism followed very quickly, and, on the other: what was the practice in the ecclesiastical situation of Luke and in that of his readers? We remember that, when we discussed 1 Cor 1.12–17, this passage made us assume that in Corinth baptism was preceded by a period of instruction.

It is not easy to answer these questions. But we should take into account that Luke may allow himself to shorten the perspective, to reduce and to simplify. Furthermore, we may assume that the reports concerning the swift success of the testimony underline how forcefully the power of the Holy Spirit (Luke 24.29; Acts 1.8) broke through, and how great and convincing was the message. In other words, we should perceive the same tendency behind these reports as we see behind the notices of the large numbers of converts in 2.41, 47; 4.4; 5.14; 11.21; 14.1.[40]

So far, then, we have seen that the rapid succession from listening to the apostolic message and onwards to baptism could be regarded as reflecting Lukan ideology rather than historical realities. But one point suggests the existence of some historical facts behind these features in Luke's narrative, the heritage from John the Baptist and Judaism. John, like the first Christian preachers, turned to fellow Jews, and preacher and audience shared a common basis on which the preaching of repentance could build. The audience knew the God to whom they must return and were familiar with the moral demands inherent in the covenant. They knew enough of Jewish eschatological expectations to be able to comprehend a message concerning a Messiah, maybe even a crucified and risen Messiah.[41] In the case of John there is no reason to assume that people had to spend some time as catechumens before being baptised; nor is there for the Jews who became Christians in the earliest phase of Christianity. The fellowship in

[39] See on the following, G. Barth 1981, 127f.
[40] As to this understanding of the figures, see Weiser 1981–85, 96f.
[41] For the latter details, see Jeremias 1958, 36.

the Christian community that ensued could provide them with more knowledge of the Jesus, into whose name they had been baptised.

When, however, Christian mission advanced to non-Jewish circles, it became natural and necessary to develop forms whereby new converts were initiated into the Christian faith and morality. In the beginning the instruction was probably informal, but gradually it would acquire settled forms. Already in the narrative of the jailer in Philippi, Paul and Silas deliver a very brief introduction to the Christian faith, in that they answer the jailer's question about what to do to be saved: 'Believe in the Lord Jesus, and you and your household will be saved'; they then immediately speak 'the word of the Lord to him and to all of his household' (16.31f).

Nevertheless we know very little about the period of the first Christians. The hints in 1 Corinthians 1 concerning Corinthians gathering around their teachers may, however, be mentioned here. In the chapter on Paul, I remarked that commentators often assume that these teachers instructed the converts and also baptised their pupils. Furthermore, Heb 6.2 refers to doctrinal elements, and these may belong to such an introduction. Finally, scholars of the form-critical and traditio-historical school have, not without success, suggested that fragments or large sections of baptismal confessions, exhortations or liturgies can be distilled out of the New Testament letters.[42] Although optimism as to the possibilities of reconstructions of this kind has been somewhat tempered,[43] these results do help to indicate that in Luke's time, indeed earlier, baptism was preceded by a period of deep contact with and instruction on Christian faith and ethics. When we arrive at the time of the *Didache* (the beginning of the second century) we encounter the ethical admonitions of 'the Two Ways' (*Did.* 1–6), which represent baptismal instruction. The same *Didache* also prescribes that the one who is to be baptised, as well as the one who baptises, fast for one or two days beforehand (*Did.* 7.4). A few decades later, Justin the Martyr explicitly tells how the candidates are prepared (*Apology* 1.61), and not many years later we find the same injunction in Hippolytus (*Apostolic tradition* 20) and Tertullian (*De baptismo*).

9.7. The primitive motifs

Again it is time to ask about the possible role of the so-called primitive motifs. Thus in so far as, according to Acts 2, baptism belongs to the

[42] See Vielhauer 1975, 39f.
[43] G. Barth 1981, 129–134.

salvation of 'the last days', this apparently sets baptism in an *eschatological* context. But the eschatology is understood in a particularly Lukan manner. When addressed to Gentiles, the preaching of the necessity of repentance and faith may refer to the future judgment to be conducted by Christ (10.42; 17.31). Nevertheless the threat of an approaching crisis does not cast its shadow over the preaching and the call for conversion. Rather they are borne up by the idea that the salvific eschatological gifts are given now because of the work of Jesus and because of his exaltation.

The *Spirit* is among the gifts mentioned (2.38, 8.14–17; 10.44ff; 19.1–6). It is closely connected with baptism, but it is less clear how it is connected. Probably the differences of later centuries between churches of a more catholic type (including Anglicans/Episcopalians and Lutherans) and those following a more nonconformistic line have resulted in an undue expectation of precision on Luke's part. Thus the question has been asked: does baptism as a performed rite *(ex opere operato)* confer the Spirit, or are repentance and faith the basis for God's gift thereof?[44] But Luke holds it all together in a way which seems self-evident to him; moreover here we should again remember that in Luke's view the Spirit is active in the totality of the process of mission, preaching, and entrance into the saved community, as well as in that very community. In Luke's day, however, this work of the Spirit in the community is presumably regarded as the power which is active in Christians when they 'keep to' the teaching of the apostles, to the church fellowship and to the worship (2.42), rather than as the cause of extraordinary phenomena.[45]

Modern Christians have sometimes contrasted baptism in water with baptism in the Spirit.[46] It is advisable then to note that the phrase 'baptise in the Spirit' appears only twice in Acts, in 1.5 and 11.15f. In 1.5 the risen Christ tells his disciples: 'John baptised with water, but in few days you will be baptised with Holy Spirit'. In 11.16 Peter refers to this saying of Jesus, quoting it verbatim (except for the temporal adverb). In other words, the difference between the two baptisms is not between a Christian baptism in water and a Christian baptism in the Spirit. Instead, the gift of the Spirit to the church is contrasted to the mere water-baptism of John. The reason why the contrast in these two cases is between two baptisms is of course the tradition that John opposed his water-baptism with a baptism in the Spirit

---

[44] See Beasley-Murray 1962, 266–279.
[45] Weiser 1981–85, 101.
[46] M. Barth (1951) and K. Barth (1967, 2–44) contrast the two sharply. See further Dunn 1970, 58–102; Pesch 1986 1, 281–285. To the following, see G. Barth 1981, 62ff.

(and fire) to be performed by the Strong One who would follow after him (Mark 1.8; Matt 3.11; Luke 3.16). Thus, although it may appear only as a difference of nuance, the problematic issue is the relationship between baptism and Spirit; this issue was treated above in the deliberations on the 'problematic' passages.

We may continue along the same lines, asking whether the apostles had been baptised with water in order subsequently to receive a baptism in the Spirit. Luke does not say what he thinks in the matter. In this case too it is commendable to distinguish between the historical question and that concerning the meaning of the text. Above, I suggested a short answer to the second query when discussing 1.5 and 11.15f. The historical question is probably to be answered in this manner: no, probably the apostles were not baptised with the Christian water-baptism, but some of them had undergone John's baptism. Luke gives us no explanation of why they were not baptised. Possible answers must be hypothetical, e.g. they had lived with Jesus until he was 'taken up' (1.21f), and this physical presence 'with him' gave them a particular position,[47] in so far as there was no need that Jesus Christ and his work should be proclaimed and made relevant to those who had accompanied him during his ministry; so their own experiences of Jesus as his disciples did not need to be complemented with a baptism into his name.

It is evident that in Acts baptism is connected to *missionary preaching*,[48] *repentance*[49] and *faith*. The preaching is of course the testimony of the risen Christ. Repentance means that Gentiles turn away from the darkness of paganism (11.18; 13.48f), Samaritans from their mode of Judaism, represented by the magic of Simon (8.10–13), and Jews from their hostility to Jesus, the Messiah.[50]

The converts entered the *church*, the saved flock of the last days,[51] which according to 2.42 kept to the teaching of the apostles, the breaking of bread, etc. Entering this community was also connected with the *forgiveness of sins*, which ensued from acceptance of the preaching,[52] or, in other words, from belief.[53] According to a few passages, remission is attached to

---

[47] Beasley-Murray (1962, 87) takes this line.
[48] E.g. 2.38; 3.19; 8.22; 17.39; 26.20.
[49] E.g. 8.12f; 9.42; 10.43; 14.23; 16.31.
[50] On Luke's attitude to Jews and Judaism, see Jervell 1972, 41–74; P.-G. Müller 1979; Maddox, 1982, 31–65; J. T. Sanders 1987; O'Toole 1993.
[51] 2.40ff; 11.18; 13.48.
[52] 3.19; 5.31; 13.38.
[53] 10.43; 26.18.

baptism. This is the case both in 2.38 and in 22.16, where the former persecutor Paul is ordered: 'Be baptised and wash away your sins'. As in other instances, we should also here – in fairness to Luke – beware of isolating the different elements of the initiation from each other. They form a unity, and baptism is the gathering, visible, effective sign around which the others can be grouped. Acts 22.16 renders it a 'sacramental' function, but it should not be regarded in isolation from the other elements.

Finally, baptism is related to *Christ*. According to 2.38, Peter's audience must be baptised 'in the name of Jesus Christ'. Luke's readers/listeners encountered this Christ in Luke's gospel, although he now is also *their* Messiah and *their* exalted Lord. In these capacities he is the fundamental referent of the whole process of which baptism is a part. Thus salvation is given only in his name (4.12), preaching about him leads to acceptance of the message, i.e., to faith,[54] and in his name repentance unto[55] the remission of sins is preached to all nations (Luke 24.47).

Thus we can state that in Acts all the so-called primitive motifs are well represented, although in a form which is integral to Luke's vision of how that which was accomplished 'among us' (Luke 1.1) is now made known in the time of fulfilment; this message is accepted by more and more people 'to the end of the earth' (Acts 1.8). The goal is not yet reached, but Luke looks forward to it. However, he does not seem to be distressed either by the fact that it may be close or by the possibility that it may be far distant.

[54] 4.4; 8.12ff; 9.42; 11.1; 13.48; 14.1; 17.11.
[55] Or with other good manuscripts: repentance *and* remission.

10

The Gospel of Matthew

In the above chapter on John the Baptist we caught a glimpse of how the evangelist of the First Gospel had edited the narrative on the baptism of Jesus (Matt 3.13–17). In his account Matthew not only tells his readers about Jesus and about the secret of his person, but also presents Jesus as an example: as they themselves have been baptised, so has Jesus. Moreover, when the readers arrive at the end of the Gospel, they realise that the fact that they have been baptised is in accordance with the command of Jesus, as it is included in his commission to the disciples (28.17–20):

> And when they saw him they worshipped him; but some doubted. (18) And Jesus came and spoke to them: 'All authority in heaven and on earth has been given to me. (19) Go therefore and make disciples of all the nations, baptising them into the name of the Father and of the Son and of the Holy Spirit, (20) teaching them to observe all that I have commanded you. And lo, I am with you all days to the end of the age.'

The words of Jesus in this passage are hardly authentic in the sense that they were uttered by the historical Jesus; this is a common opinion among biblical scholars, as was mentioned in the chapter on the origin of the Christian baptism. From a historical point of view Jesus' words may rather be regarded as reflecting the conviction of the evangelist and of his church that their baptismal practice was in accordance with the will of the risen Jesus.[1] Thus it is probable that the baptismal formula of Matt 28.19 belongs to the ecclesiastical milieu of Matthew; it would be strange if their baptismal rite deviated from what the Gospel presented as the command of Jesus.

Traditio-historical analyses of the ending of Matthew indicate that the

---

[1] Schweizer 1959, 399; G. Barth 1981, 16f; Roloff 1981, 62.

passage contains several distinct traces of the pen of the evangelist but also traditional elements, not least the baptismal formula.[2] The suggestion that these verses are later additions to the Gospel[3] seems to go too far, and the evidence adduced in support is rather flimsy.[4]

That the risen Jesus possesses an overwhelming authority is a fundamental feature in the passage and determines several of its details. This is obvious already from the way the disciples salute him, as genuflection or prostration (which is what 'worshipped' stands for here) is a sign of the reverence which befits very high human potentates or persons of divine dignity. Jesus' authority is explicitly mentioned at the beginning of his words: he has 'all authority in heaven and on earth'. Earlier in the Gospel Jesus also appeared with an authority (7.29; 8.6ff; 21.23–27) which is demonstrated in his teaching, in his forgiveness of sins, and in his mighty works; thus the evangelist emphasises that Jesus was authorised by God to perform his work. Indeed, he had come into being in his mother's womb through God's Spirit, which indicates that his future activity would take place in God's power (1.18).

But here, in Matt 28.19, Jesus' power and authority become universal.[5] The contents of the sentence 'all authority in heaven and on earth has been given to me' are similar to the statement in Phil 2.9, 'Therefore God has exalted him and given to him the name which is above every name'. The name 'which is above every name' is God's name. Of course the phrase does not denote a simple change of name; rather, the name refers to the position or character of the exalted one. Now the passive form in Matthew, 'has been given', is equal to the active 'God has given'. Furthermore, 'all authority in heaven and on earth' actually belongs to God. Certainly there are differences between Phil 2.9 and Matt 28.17–20, but both passages signify that when Jesus had performed his work on earth, God invested him with his own divine power. As time passed, this idea gave rise to much theological deliberation and, for that matter, to much theological dispute. The theological problem is, how can one hold on to a fundamental monotheism and confess at the same time that Jesus has a divine nature? In the theological milieu of Matthew, Psalm 110 (quoted in Matt 22.44) certainly contributed to the establishment of concepts: 'The Lord said to my Lord: sit at my right

---

[2] G. Barth 1981, 13f; Gnilka 1986–88 2, 504.

[3] Conybeare 1901; see the discussion in Trilling 1964, 35.

[4] Nepper-Christensen 1985, 203 (+ literature).

[5] Lange (1973, 25–95) discusses at length the concept of power and its importance in the text.

hand'.[6] In Matthew, however, the picture is not one of enthronement, as in Psalm 110;[7] this is true notwithstanding that the passage incorporates echoes from Dan 7.13, according to which the Son of Man is brought to the Ancient of Days and receives 'dominion, and glory and kingdom, and all peoples, nations, and languages must serve him'.[8]

In Matthew 28 the risen Christ has, as it were, the position of God's viceroy with cosmic authority. One may speculate whether Matthew thinks that Jesus had less authority during his earthly ministry, e.g. when he forgave sins (Matt 9.2). Be that as it may, it is beyond dispute that here the realm over which he holds sway is immensely larger than when e.g. he explained that he was sent only to the lost sheep of Israel (15.24). Nonetheless the evangelist and his church were definitely serious when they confessed: 'Hear, O Israel, the Lord, our God, is one' (Deut 6.4), the beginning of the Shema confession which almost certainly the Matthean Jewish Christians regularly prayed, as did other pious Jews.[9] Surely they were not of the opinion that God, the Father, had abdicated and given all power to the Son. Rather, the Gospel reflects the belief that once the Son has performed his work on earth, God's reign is definitely marked by his communication with humans in and through that which Jesus of Nazareth did, said, and was.[10]

In its position at the end of Matthew's narrative, the commandment of Matt 28.18ff has as its point of departure the person of Jesus and his work, including his teaching, of which the Gospel has informed the readers. Since the power of the risen Lord is so far-reaching, his work is extended to 'all nations', which in this context, means 'to Jews as well as to Gentiles'. The crux of the commission is that people shall be made disciples. It has been pointed out that this manner of exerting power is typically different from what we encounter in Dan 7.14: 'to him (i.e. the Son of Man) was given

---

[6] The quotation plays a role also in Acts 2:34ff (on resurrection and exaltation), in Rom 8.34 (Christ, the risen one, now intercedes for us), in 1 Cor 15.25 (the resurrected and exalted one now reigns until everything is subjected to him, who will then submit to the Father), in Eph 1.20–23 (the risen one is superior to everything, including all powers), Col 3.1 (the risen Christ is at God's right hand), and Heb 1.3, 13; 8.1; 10.12 (when the Son has performed a purification from the sins, he sits at the right hand of the Majesty, more exalted than the angels), and Heb 12.2 (he is enthroned after his suffering). On the use of Psalm 110 in the early church see Lindars 1961, 45–51, and particularly Hay 1973.

[7] Emphasised by Lange (1973, 242–245).

[8] Lange (1973, 218–246) discusses the combination at length.

[9] Jeremias 1966, 78ff. In several works Gerhardsson comments on the importance of this confession for the evangelist behind the First Gospel, e.g. Gerhardsson 1967/68.

[10] Felderer 1959, 554–560.

dominion and glory and kingdom, and all peoples, nations, and languages must serve him.' As stated above, this Danielic passage influenced our Matthean text, but making people disciples involves respect for their own free will, a feature which hardly is to be imagined behind Daniel 7.[11]

Moreover, in Matthew to be or to become a disciple has particular connotations. Thus discipleship means submission to the divine authority represented by the risen Lord (cf. 4.18–22); it means learning the secrets of the kingdom (13.1f) but also 'following' Jesus, i.e., living as he lived and taught, being prepared to suffer (16.24f); but it also means to be 'with' him 'all days' (28.20).

According to the Great Commission, making people into disciples involves teaching them all the commandments of Jesus. In the context of Matthew, these commandments are of course those which Jesus has given according to this Gospel, including the slight Jewish-Christian colour of the understanding of the Torah and of ethics which is so typical of Matthew.[12] Such commandments are found particularly in the Sermon on the Mount (5–7), in the commissioning of the Twelve (10), and in the rules regarding the community (18).

When the missionaries make people into disciples they also baptise them into the name of the Triune God.[13] Matt 18.20 ('gather into my name') demonstrates that the evangelist, as well as his church, knew the 'into the name' formula and to use it in the almost technical sense we discussed in the chapter 'Into the Name of the Lord Jesus'. The name indicated the fundamental referent of the rite. Here the name is not that of the Lord Jesus or of Jesus Christ (or: Jesus, the Messiah) but that of the Triune God. This does not mean that Jesus is not regarded as Lord or Messiah; this is evident already from the introduction of our passage, and Jesus' Messiahship is apparently crucial to the Gospel of Matthew as a whole. But the whole of the Gospel, at the close of which we encounter this narrative, also fills the triune 'name' with significance. Thus what God is and means according to Matthew's presentation of Jesus and of his work is the fundamental referent of baptism. For the work of Jesus is God's work. Above, we saw another early Christian theologian doing something similar

---

[11] Grundmann 1972, 578. Grundmann (ibid.) also answers the implicit question: how does a nation become disciples, or how do you baptise a nation? Disciples are always individuals, but these individuals represent the nation to which they belong.

[12] E.g. Luz 1985–90 1, 62–72.

[13] Among the older texts this formula is also found in *Didache* 7.1, 3; Justin, *Apology* 1.61; Ireneus, *Adversus haereses* (lat.) 3.17.1; Tertullian, *De baptismo* 13, *De praescriptione haereticorum* 7.20.

in Tit 3.4–7.[14] One reason for this development toward Trinitarian language is certainly a current theological and Christological reflection. This reflection was probably inspired not least by the new living conditions of the church; on the one hand, it now found itself among 'all the nations', where the belief in the one God was no longer the self-evident foundation undergirding confession of Jesus and baptism into his name. On the other hand, and this holds true particularly of Matthew, although the church had taken the step beyond Judaism, it was still involved in debates with Jews. In such a debate it was essential to the Christians to maintain that they had a monotheistic belief in the One God. Simultaneously they had, however, to defend their belief in the Father's Son, who nonetheless was not a second god. When they also claimed that the Spirit of God had been at work in the Son and in his deeds (3.13–17; 4.1; 12.15–37),[15] this idea helped them to hold on to their monotheism.

Thus the baptismal formula of Matthew is loaded with such contents as the reader encountered when reading the whole Gospel. Behind baptism stands the God whom Jesus called his father.[16] This Father is he who has created the universe and sustains his creation (6.26; 10.29); he has sent the Son and given him his commission (11.27; 26.42, etc.); he has history in his hand and is the ultimate measure of what is good and righteous.[17]

The Son is precisely Son: in our passage no other Christological titles occur, neither 'Son of Man' nor 'Lord' nor 'Christ'. The Son-title implies that in obedience to the will of the Father Jesus has performed the task entrusted to him, thus putting the Father's plan of salvation into action.[18]

From the beginning the Spirit is at work in the person of Jesus (3.13–4.1) and in his deeds (12.15–37). Probably the evangelist was of the opinion that the work which the Son had accomplished as commissioned by the Father, was now continued by the same Spirit, the Spirit of the present and active God.[19] Another expression of this way of thinking is to be found in the last words of our passage, 'Lo, I am with you all the days'.

What remains to be said about these verses can be introduced by asking to what extent we encounter the motifs which seem to have been linked with baptism from a very early stage. Thus baptism is obviously here a

---

[14] See also Eph 1–2.

[15] Schweizer 1973, 187f, 349. Accordingly the evangelist seems to imply that the Jews in his milieu sinned against the Spirit when they refused to accept this idea.

[16] 7.21; 10.32; 26.42, etc.

[17] 6.1, 10, 15; 7.21; 18.14; 24.36; 25.34.

[18] 4.3, 6; 16.16ff; 21.37ff; 26.36, 46.

[19] Cf. 10.20. See Schweizer 1959, 399ff.

consequence of a *missionary preaching* by those entrusted with the task of making disciples. While the terms *repentance/conversion* and *faith* do not appear in Matt 28.17ff, there can be no doubt that they represent what Matthew expects will be the response to the mission.[20] From 18.6 it can be surmised that in the Matthean church, too, those who had become the disciples of Jesus were called 'the believers', 'the faithful', etc.

The relationship of baptism to *Christ* depends on the all-embracing power of the Risen One. When people become his disciples and are baptised, this power is realised. One may ask what role his death and resurrection play in this context. According to Matthew, Jesus' death is 'for many' (20.28), and his death belonged to the commission which the Father had given to the Son (26.36–46). Through his resurrection it led to the power which is now to be realised in the mission of the disciples. The evangelist does not, however, connect the death and resurrection of Jesus with baptism; instead, they become stages on his way to the dominion into which people are to be incorporated through becoming disciples, a process which, *inter alia*, includes being baptised.

In the discussion of the baptism of John it was noted that, in the Gospel of Matthew, this baptism was not characterised as one for the *forgiveness of sins*. Instead, *Jesus* was to 'save his people from their sins' (1.21). When he forgave sins (9.2–8), this derived from his task of establishing the kingdom of heaven. His blood was shed 'for many for the forgiveness of sins', which is re-enacted or made relevant in the eucharist (26.28). According to 18.15–20, after his life on earth the sins which are loosed in the church are loosed also in heaven. So evidently sins were forgiven, so to speak, in the name of Jesus (18.15–20), but there are no distinct signs that in Matthean thinking forgiveness was given in baptism. Nevertheless it is reasonable to assume that this was the case. For when people were received into the new covenant (26.28) or into the dominion which had been established through the divine salvation, it would be natural to believe that they were purified from the sins of the past.[21] Furthermore, in so far as Christian baptism was compared with that of John and the gift of forgiveness was not ascribed to the latter, it is natural to infer that such forgiveness was connected with the Christian rite. But the question must remain open.

From the baptismal formula it is obvious that *the Spirit* is linked with baptism. But the evangelist is hardly of the opinion that the Spirit confers ecstatic gifts. Rather the passage presupposes a conviction that the Spirit, in

[20] 4.17; 8.10; 11.20f; 18.6, etc.
[21] Trilling 1964, 32–35.

other words, God as present and active, makes relevant that which the Son as commissioned by the Father has performed. This is suggested by the passages in Matthew which deal with the Spirit (1.18ff; 3.15–4.1; 12.15–37).

In the section above concerning the baptism of John, I touched upon Matt 3.11: 'He will baptise you with the Holy Spirit and with fire'. It is a fair assumption that the passage enlightens us on how the evangelist and his readers regarded their baptism. Matt 28.17–20 suggests that the words of the Baptist be understood as follows: Jesus had once worked in the power of the Spirit (3.16 etc.), and he also collaborated 'with' the missionaries in the accomplishment of his work when people were made his disciples, so being brought under his cosmic dominion; baptism was one decisive step in this procedure, and it is likely that here the Spirit, God being active among humans, was regarded as being at work. So the same Spirit is also present in the church, not least during persecution or other forms of opposition (10.10; 12.31f).[22]

The church has been mentioned indirectly several times in our discussion of Matthew 28. Obviously baptism has an ecclesiastical aspect, for when the evangelist presupposes that Christ's dominion will include more and more disciples, those who are so gathered form 'his' church (Matt 16.18). It is a people of God, made up of disciples from all nations (1.21; 2.6; 21.43), i.e. of disciples in the Matthean sense of the word.[23]

Finally, mission and baptism take place in an *eschatological perspective*. Baptism is performed in the presence of Christ 'all days to the end of the age'. Another kind of eschatological perspective comprises the conviction of the evangelist and of his church that the Messiah has appeared and is now endowed with 'all authority in heaven and on earth'. Baptism is one expression of how this power is manifested, for it is an element in people's becoming disciples. Thus, in a sense, we may speak of a realised eschatology, of an age of salvation already begun, of a kingdom already somehow realised. But in this eschatological present the disciples also look forward to a further, coming realisation, not however in the sense that everything develops in a positive direction, step by step, day by day. Instead an ultimate crisis is to be expected. But for the same disciples, the evangelist has composed the eschatological discourse in chapters 24–25, one essential message of which is: 'Be ready, for the Son of Man will come at an hour you do not expect' (24.44).

[22] See Luz 1985–90 2, 266f.
[23] Carlston 1992, 1294f (further lit. 1283).

11

The Gospel of John[1]

Our present Gospel of John has gone through a history of revisions, additions and editing. This is indicated already by such strikingly harsh transitions in the text as those in 14.31 and 20.31. Here John 3.1–21 will be treated,[2] a passage considered in attempts to reconstruct the tradition-history of the Gospel, including suggestions of various sources.[3] Thus it has been claimed that, in an earlier phase, the Gospel of John represented a Christianity which did not know of – or even want to know of – baptism, eucharist, or structured ministry. In that phase of the prehistory of John our text is assumed not to have contained the words 'born of water and Spirit' (3.5) but only 'born of the Spirit' (Wellhausen, Bultmann[4]). At the final stage a redactor is assumed to have made the Gospel more acceptable from an ecclesiastical point of view by adding 'water and'.[5]

Even if there would be some truth in the suggestion that an ecclesiastical redactor has been at work, which is somewhat doubtful, it is a legitimate and important task to ask for the meaning of the text which resulted from the redaction process. So we shall deal with 3.1–21 as the text now stands. Such a concentration on the present shape of the text need not mean ignoring the situation in which the Gospel was written. The

[1] I do not take 1 John into consideration. Baptism is not mentioned in this letter, but there are expressions which may reflect ideas on baptism. Indeed, in this case also, the letter has been assumed to be a baptismal homily or a baptismal ritual or to contain echoes from baptismal paraenesis (Brown 1982, 242ff, 319ff etc.). The passages adduced to support such claims are 5.7f (the three witnesses), 2.29 (on being born of God; cf. John 3.3, 5), 2.12 (forgiveness of sins in his name), 2.20 (anointment from the Holy One).

[2] Accordingly I shall not deal with 13.8–10 (the washing of the disciples' feet), nor with 19.34 (blood and water). It is a matter of dispute whether any of these passages refers to baptism, and even if this were the case, it would not give us any essential information beyond what we find in 3.1–21.

[3] See Becker 1979–81, 32–38, 112–120.

[4] Bultmann 1968b, 98.

[5] A sober discussion of the tradition-history of the passage occurs in Becker 1979–81, 129–147.

Johannine letters testify that this situation contained tensions and was dramatic. But when it comes to reconstructing precise details of the ecclesiastical situation, it soon becomes evident that we have at our disposal only vague indications that are susceptible to several interpretations.[6] A few features are however discernible. Thus, theologians of opinions differing from those of the author have obviously appeared within the group behind the Gospel (e.g. 1 John 4.1; 2.18f, cf. John 6.60, 66);[7] their beliefs may have been 'gnostic' in some sense of the word, and they seem to have had other ideas about the person of Christ;[8] these theological differences also implied differences in terms of ethics (1 John 3.7).

John 3.1–21 naturally falls into three parts, 3.1–3, 4–8, 9–21. Each part is introduced by a statement or a question of Nicodemus, which receives an answer from Jesus. Each time these answers become longer. In every one of them we encounter the solemn formula 'truly, truly, I say to you', which underlines the weight of what is said. The three parts should be taken as a whole, and the author does not finish the treatment of his theme until he arrives at the end of the third part.

In the first part (3.1–3) Nicodemus opens the discussion by praising Jesus for his miracles and his teaching. In a somewhat astonishing manner Jesus answers by seemingly talking about something else: one 'cannot see the kingdom of God' unless one is 'born from above' (or: 'again'). Indirectly, this becomes a subtle criticism of the position which may be surmised behind the words of Nicodemus, a belief in Jesus' authority as a teacher because of his miracles. The criticism, then, would be that such a position comes from below and does not lead into the kingdom of God.[9] Arrival there is only given from above, from God (cf. 1.13).

As yet Jesus' answer at the end of the first part is only an assertion. In addition, the double meaning of *anothen*, 'from above' or 'again' keeps the reader in suspense. The new question of Nicodemus, which begins the second part, presupposes the meaning 'again', but represents at the same time a gross misunderstanding of a kind which is common in John.[10] It is the point of departure for v. 5: 'Unless one is born of water and Spirit, he cannot enter the kingdom of God'. Through the question of Nicodemus the meaning of 'to be born' has become 'to be born again'. A birth by water

---

[6] See the attempts in Brown 1979, and Olsson 1987.
[7] See Brown 1979 and Hengel 1989, chapter 3.
[8] 1 John 2.22; 4.3, 15; 5.1, 5, 13; cf. John 20.31.
[9] Becker 1979–81, 133.
[10] See also 2.19–22; 4.10f, 31ff; 6.41f, 51f; 7.33–36; 8.21f, 31ff, 56ff; 13.9ff; 14.4f.

can hardly refer to anything but baptism. Taken by itself, the phrase may be understood as suggesting a massive sacramental belief, one not unlike that which we surmised behind 1 Corinthians. It is possible that the statement indirectly echoes such a position in the ecclesiastical world of the evangelist.[11] If this is the case, the evangelist contradicts it in the following verses.[12] Be this as it may, we should note that in Jesus' answer it is not the water baptism that is emphasized but the circumstance that the entrance into the kingdom of God is brought about by the Spirit of God.

Here, as elsewhere in the New Testament, the image of birth stands for God's gift of a new life, a new identity and an existence under new conditions.[13] These conditions are determined by new presuppositions which are not 'carnal', i.e. human and worldly. Above, we met other New Testament authors who paint the previous life of the new Christians in dark colours. Here, the dark background is neither a pagan past (as with Paul's addressees) nor a Judaism with a negative attitude to Jesus (sometimes in Acts) but human nature in its weakness, limitation and mortality. Such weakness is also inherent in the faith of those who only revere Jesus in Nicodemus' way, as well as in the position (if we assume for a moment that there was such a position) of those who concentrate so much on baptism as an outward act that they forget that the new, divine life is given only through the Spirit of God. The believer controls the new life as little as he controls the wind. Nor can people who are worldly and carnally minded grasp whence those who are born again and from above have received their divine life, nor can they understand where the latter are going, i.e. that they are following Jesus to his Father and their Father (cf. 3.13; 16.28).

The third part of the narrative begins with the question of Nicodemus in verse 9, which causes Jesus to explain how 'this' can be done, the birth from above which is brought about by the unrestrainable Spirit of God. The answer is that it is possible because the Son of Man is 'lifted up'. This is the first time we encounter this ambiguous Johannine expression, which recurs later in John's Gospel (e.g. 8.28; 12.32). On the one hand, it means that Jesus is physically lifted up on the cross, on the other that he ascends to the Father. This being lifted up enables those who believe (3.15a) to have this life from God. Verses 16–18 then indirectly interpret the meaning of 'lifted up', that God 'gives' his Son. The narrative then explains

[11] Becker 1979–81, 225f; cf. Schnelle 1987, 202.
[12] Barrett 1978, 209.
[13] See John 1.13; 1 Cor 4.15; Tit 3.5; 1 Pet 1.3, 23; 1 John 3.9.

('because', γάϱ) why the Son was 'given', and thus also indicates why, ultimately, people can 'see (enter) the kingdom of God', as the words portray in vv. 3 and 5; it is feasible because God so loved the world. At the same time it becomes evident that to the evangelist the traditional term 'kingdom of God' is equal to 'eternal life'.[14]

Indeed, the concept of eternal life is important in the passage, as it is in the whole of John's Gospel. Here it appears in the first extended speech given by the main character of the book. God bestows eternal life on those who believe; this means a new human existence with a fundamentally new framework of life, new immanent and transcendent relationships, a new goal and a new direction of life. This is all guaranteed and determined by God, not by what is immanent. 'Eternal life' is replaced by another expression in 3.17, where it is stated that the aim of God's sending the Son was to 'save' the world. People partake in this salvation through belief in the Son (3.15f), for the believer already has 'eternal life' and is not subject to the divine judgment (3.18). On the other hand, those who do not believe perish and are condemned, indeed, they condemn themselves through their attitude to the Son (3.18–21).

When 3.1–22 is read as a unit, it becomes evident how much is actually linked up with God's 'giving birth' and with the Spirit's life-giving. Thus the circle of ideas also encompasses belief in the Son, acceptance of his word (in the Johannine environment, the Johannine understanding of Jesus) and living by this word (5.24; 8.51f). Baptism is part of this life-giving work. On the one hand, the strong accents on the divine initiative ('from above') and on divine activity (the Spirit) tend to emphasise the 'sacramental' aspect of baptism: here life is really given, and here God is truly at work. On the other hand, baptism is still the 'sacrament' of faith, because it is stressed that life is given to those who believe (3.15).

Several of our 'primitive motifs' appear in this text, but all with typically Johannine nuances. Thus the fundamental answers of Jesus refer to a question asked from an *eschatological perspective*: how can one enter the kingdom of God? This question is rephrased in the more Johannine expression, how can one have eternal life? Although a futuristic eschatology

[14] The three expressions in 3.3, 5, and 15 are semantically parallel:

3.3	unless one is	born from above	he cannot see
3.5	unless one is	born of water and Spirit	he cannot enter
3.15	whoever believes ...		has
3.3	the kingdom of God		
3.5	the kingdom of God		
3.15	eternal life		

is not wholly absent from our text,[15] what matters is the divine life which is given in the present and not affected by death (11.25).

This life is given to the one who *believes*. The promise does not appear until we reach the third phase of the text, which is introduced by the question how 'this' can be, i.e. the new birth from the Spirit. But the presupposition of faith is that the Son of Man is lifted up (which, in its turn, results from the Father's sending the Son out of his love). Thus, as regarded from a human point of view, in order to have the new life one must take the step of becoming a believer. As seen in a wider perspective, both faith and the life which it gives are the work of God's Spirit (see also 6.44: the Father 'draws').

So the traditional linkage between baptism and *Spirit* is also encountered in John. But it has been transformed, so that the role of the Spirit is particularly connected with man's rebirth in baptism by God, from 'above'. At the same time the interest concentrates on the Spirit's mediation of divine life. This agrees with other passages in John, according to which the Spirit is at work, giving divine life, when the work of Jesus is continued and actualised in the church.[16] This outlook should also dictate the interpretation of the traditional saying in John that Jesus will baptise in Holy Spirit (1.33): Jesus' work becomes a source of divine life. No ecstatic phenomena can be discerned on John's horizon.[17]

Finally, in John baptism is evidently related to *Christ*. Here too we find that the death of Jesus is interpreted as being for sins (1.29; cf. 11.50f), but this aspect is not connected to baptism. Nevertheless, the 'lifting up' of the Son of Man is the place on earth where the divine life, now given by the Spirit through faith and baptism, enters the world. The work of the Son, including his ascension to the Father, is the basis of God's life-giving self-communication in the time of the church (4.34; 5.36; 19.30). Baptism is the visible sign and medium of God's giving birth to human beings into this new life. They receive this life through the agency of God's Spirit, but the same Spirit is also active behind their belief and their continuous participation in this life. Ultimately, however, it springs from God's loving will to save humans, which is realised in the work of the Son.

[15] At this point we need not enter upon the question how far the Johannine tradition in one phase or another has disregarded a so-called traditional eschatology (as e.g. Bultmann thought). See Becker 1979–81, 244ff.

[16] 7.39; 14.17, 26; 15.26f; 16.7–11. See also Schnelle 1987, 205f. I disregard the discussion of how the Paraclete is related to the Spirit; the excursus in Becker 1979–81, 470–475 is a good survey.

[17] See Schnackenburg 1964–84 1, 304; Klos 1970, 71ff.

12

Mark 16.9–20

Opinions differ on whether the evangelist behind the Gospel of Mark really finished his book with the words of 16.8, 'for they were afraid', or whether this verse was originally followed by a further section, now lost, which gave a less abrupt ending. But there is no doubt that 16.9–20 is a later addition. It is usually assumed that the passage was composed in the second century, as Tatian and Ireneus, both then living, know about it. But it does not occur in any Greek Bible manuscript before the fifth century.[1] The text consists of material from the resurrection narratives of the other Gospels and from episodes in Acts. This passage comprises a commissioning of the disciples by the risen Lord (16.15–16):

> Go to the whole world and proclaim the gospel to the whole creation. He who believes and is baptised will be saved; but he who does not believe will be condemned. And these signs will accompany those who believe: in my name they will cast out demons, they will speak in new tongues, and they will pick up snakes (with their hands),[2] and if they drink any deadly thing, it will not hurt them; on the sick they will lay their hands, and they will recover.

Among our 'primitive motifs' we here find the *preaching* of the gospel, which is met by either *belief* or unbelief. To the author baptism and faith are obviously connected.[3] Baptism and faith look forward to the future salvation, i.e. *the eschatological perspective* still prevails. Forgiveness of sins is not mentioned, nor is the Spirit nor the church. But the miracles which according to 16.17f will be experienced by those who believe (and are baptised) are such as Acts explicitly connects with the pouring out of the Spirit. Here they are called 'signs', events through which God confirms

---

[1] In Codex W. See Pesch 1976–77 1, 40–47, 2, 544–548; Gnilka 1978–79 2, 356f.

[2] The bracketed words are missing in some manuscripts.

[3] The passage has sometimes been used as an argument against infant baptism. This, however, is already a questionable undertaking for the simple reason that it was written at a time when it seems that infant baptism was practised in the church. See the material from Origen and Tertullian in Jeremias 1962.

that the preachers do his work; thus also the converts are affected by God's own activity (see also 16.20).

We should hardly regard these verses as a direct testimony to how a theologian of the middle of the second century thought of baptism. But they indicate what the writer thought would be a fitting ending of the Gospel of Mark, and according to such an idea he selects items and motifs from the original texts. Apparently, it is natural to him to emphasise mission: had it not been for the mission, neither he nor his audience would have been Christians, and faith and baptism are natural consequences. It is surely no exaggeration to say that to him also baptism is the sacrament of faith.

One may ask what the function of the eschatological perspective is. The words on judgment and salvation reflect traditional turns of phrase. This need not mean that they are void of content, but the preaching is nevertheless not endowed with a fervour that springs from eschatological yearning, nor does it determine the recruitment of neophytes to faith and baptism. Concerning the miracles to which the text refers (under some inspiration from Acts) we may venture the opinion that they were not such as the author and his fellow-Christians normally expected to confirm the belief that divine powers were at work with them. Such an opinion is supported by some features of Montanism, which appeared in the middle of the second century, the representatives of which accused the church of lacking the spiritual gifts of the first generation.[4]

[4] See Aland 1960.

13

At the end of the road through the New Testament

13.1. Looking back

We have now reviewed all of the New Testament texts which deal with baptism in one way or another, and it may be worth while to glance at the distance covered. We have travelled through a changing landscape and the impressions left from the journey are diverse.

On the one hand, the texts represent a variety of modes of thinking about baptism, a variety which in some cases was wider than was acceptable to some New Testament authors. Not only have we noted differences between the 'orthodox' authors, e.g. between Paul and Luke, but we have also seen traces of other early Christian groups such as the enthusiasts in Corinth or the 'philosophy' in Colossae.

On the other hand, it is hard to avoid the perception of a certain unanimity between the different modes of dealing with baptism. Such an impression may depend on the circumstance that after the discussion of every author or group of texts we considered the extent and ways in which the so-called primitive motifs were represented in the passages under consideration. I hope that this approach has not meant that an alien pattern has been forced on to the texts, but that the question has proven meaningful. If this is the case, the impression of a certain unity is not fallacious, but the primitive motifs represent a basic structure beneath the different ways of reflecting and writing on baptism which we meet with the different authors.

Of our 'primitive motifs', the Christ-relation of baptism plays a decisive role in all our material. This is also why this book is called 'Into the Name of the Lord Jesus'. At the outset I reached the conclusion that this formula brought us back to the earliest phase of the history of Christianity. In that context I also tried to demonstrate that the formula indicated that the Lord Jesus, his person and his work, were a fundamental referent of the christianised baptism of John. They were the source of the gifts which were mediated by the rite.

Thus the formula 'into the name of the Lord Jesus' is older than the earliest of the New Testament texts dealt with above. It seems to suggest that Jesus was very early regarded as being a living, heavenly authority who made the baptismal rite meaningful. The cultic reverence for him, the dead and risen one, and the conviction that he and his work are directly relevant to mankind, formed the foundation of the rite.

The formula 'in the name of Jesus the Messiah' seems to have implied other nuances in the Christological thinking behind baptism. It pre-supposes a belief in Jesus as the Messiah, which it would seem natural to locate in a Judaeo-Christian milieu, and which would indicate a conviction that in Jesus were fulfilled the divine promises which gave rise to the expectations of a saviour sent by God in the age of salvation. To be baptised in his name should mean taking the step into the community which gathered around this Messiah. Converts already tasted some of the fruits of the kingdom of God and would partake in the salvation which had been inaugurated by him and which would soon reach its fulfilment. As was the case with the other formula, probably here also his death and resurrection were important, for it was the conviction that he was not dead that started the development of the cultic assembly in which baptism was practised.

Paul uses almost organic terms when dealing with this Christ-relation. The Christian is 'in Christ', which has decisive consequences for the way in which baptised persons should live the life they received when entering the Christ-communion. Both Paul and other theologians in his Christian milieu seem to have regarded baptism as a cultic actualisation of the salvific work of Jesus. Thus according to Romans 6, those who were baptised died 'with Christ' in baptism, and 'with' him they also received a life which they now should live 'for God', but which also had a future, a definitive life 'with' Christ.

Some Pauline disciples developed this idea in a manner which was different from Paul's. Thus the author of Colossians maintains that baptism actualises Christ's victory over all cosmic powers so that the person baptised can share his victory and need not respect those defeated potentates. In Ephesians, the writer makes a similar claim, that Christians live in a realm of cosmic power dominated by Christ. The image used is that of enthronement with Christ in heaven. The disciple of Paul who wrote the Pastoral Letters is somewhat vaguer in this respect, in that he does not focus as sharply on Christ as his colleagues in the Pauline school do. Certainly one may also in his case speak of an actualisation of the salvific work which was performed in the past, but when the writer speaks of 'salvation', to him God is the one who saves, although he does so through the work of Christ, the saviour.

Not surprisingly, the writer of Hebrews refracts his ideas concerning the meaning of baptism through the lens of his representation of the death and resurrection of Christ in images from the temple service of the high priest. In baptism the Christian was allowed to share the blessed fruits of this sacrificial service.

In Luke, too, baptism is bound to Christ, but via the preaching of the salvation brought about by Jesus. Thus baptism becomes the ritual point of intersection between that which is preached and its acceptance, i.e. faith.

In 1 Peter the hope of salvation is based on the resurrection of Christ. He suffered as the addressees are now suffering, but his resurrection means that he has also gone before them to the glory for which they now hope.

Moreover, when the Gospel of John deals with baptism, the reader's eye is directed to the exalted and glorified Lord, albeit in a particular manner. Jesus' way through passion to glory is as a whole labelled an 'exaltation', indeed the Son of Man's being 'exalted'/'lifted up' equals his hanging on the cross. This strange exaltation is, however, the prerequisite for humans to be born again (and/or from above, that is, by God) from water and Spirit. In other words, Christ's 'exaltation' enables them to receive a new human existence in an open and good relationship to God. This is how they can enter the kingdom of God – or, with a more Johannine wording, possess eternal life – which is impossible for that which is 'flesh' to do. But behind this 'exaltation' lies the fact that the Father loved the world and so gave his Son.

Matthew, too, links baptism with the exalted Lord. But here he is the risen one who has all authority in heaven and on earth. This position of his is the reason why his messengers must make disciples out of all nations, one aspect of which is that they are baptised. But to be a disciple also includes leading a life according to his precepts, of which the reader could be informed through the Gospel of Matthew. In this manner his power is demonstrated. Baptism was performed 'into the name of the Father and of the Son and of the Holy Spirit'. When Matthew quotes this formula from the ritual of his church, he hints at a reflection reminiscent of that in John's chain of thought in developing the idea of the new birth and also, in a sense, of what we found in the Pastorals. Thus the Father laid the foundation which is Christ and his work, and this is made relevant and effective through God's active presence on earth through the Spirit.

Among our 'primitive motifs' the eschatological perspective also plays a decisive role in most of the passages we have discussed. When, in the beginning of this book, we considered the Jewish religious soil in which baptism was rooted, we encountered some texts which expressed hopes and expectations concerning the age in which God would save his people. This was also the framework of the preaching and baptism of John the Baptist. The first Christians inherited his baptism and christianised it, interpreting the paschal events in eschatological terms. It is hard to determine what their eschatological imagery was like, but they obviously had a basic conviction that God had brought about a new situation in which salvation could be gained – whatever was meant by 'salvation'.

Thus in all our baptismal passages baptism has an eschatological framework, although it appears differently from author to author. With Paul baptismal purification and justification were contrasted with the dirt and unrighteousness of the past of his converts, which had prevented them from inheriting the kingdom of God; implicitly it is said: but now this is possible (1 Corinthians 6). In the process of entering the Christ-communion, baptism was an objective central factor. Already in the present age this entrance meant a share in divine life, which, however, at the same time looked forward to fulfilment. In the tension between this 'already' and this 'not yet' we encountered Paul's ethics which were determined by the demand 'Become what you are', and were to be realised in a present which hastened towards the moment of testing before Christ's judgment seat (2 Cor 5.10).

Indirectly, some details in Romans 6 show that other theologians in the early church also believed that in baptism God granted gifts which more or less meant a fulfilment of eschatological expectations. It effected that, with Christ, one died from the old and was raised to a new life of heavenly origin. It seems that in Corinth there were Christians who went so far as to abandon the outlook to the future which belonged to the heritage from the Old Testament and Judaism. Instead, they were convinced that they had already fully acquired this divine life.

In Colossians too baptism has an eschatological framework, but its author emphasises more than Paul does that already in the present time the baptised persons possess a life with Christ and share his victory over cosmic spiritual potentates. One may call this a spatial eschatology, but it is also coupled with the expectation of a coming 'revelation' of the Christians when Christ is 'revealed' (Col 3.4). Furthermore, according to Ephesians the Christians already possess a life 'with' the enthroned, heavenly Christ, and the motif plays an even more important role there than it does in Colossians.

Both in 1 Peter and in Hebrews, baptism has a natural context of eschatological hope and eschatological threat. Thus in 1 Peter salvation is not only a reality conferred now through baptism (3.21) but at the same time also the object of the Christian hope (1.9); furthermore, the comfort and admonitions of the letter are based on the fact that 'the end of all things is at hand' (4.7). In Hebrews, the whole letter turns to the readers/ listeners against the background that 'in these last days' God has spoken by his Son (1.2), and the earnest, even harsh warnings receive an additional sharpness because 'you see that the Day is drawing near' (10.26).

In the Gospel of John, the new birth from water is one of the preconditions for entry into the kingdom of God, or in more Johannine terms, for obtaining 'eternal life'. According to John, to know God and the one whom he sent is eternal life (17.3). In other words, there is certainly an eschatological context surrounding baptism in John's Gospel also, but this context is typically Johannine.

According to the programmatic Joel quotation in Acts 2.17 the testimony of the risen Lord and the preaching which calls people to repentance/conversion are dated to 'the last days'. But this preaching hardly takes place in the face of an imminent, ultimate crisis. Nevertheless the risen Lord bestows gifts which belong precisely to the eschatological age, particularly the Spirit, on those who accept the preaching, believe, and are baptised.

Finally, in the Gospel of Matthew, we surmised an eschatology which in a sense was already realised. For when 'disciples' are made from the nations, this expresses the realisation of the cosmic rule of the Messiah, whom God had sent when the promises concerning the age of salvation were fulfilled. On the other hand, this mission takes place with a view to the 'end of the age'. In the world of the evangelist this end of the age was so imminent *and* so distant that he felt obliged to exhort his readers: 'watch' (chapters 24–25).

Thus among our 'primitive motifs' the relationship to Christ and the eschatological framework are fundamental. The others evidently depend on them or are their corollaries. So in different ways baptism emerges as a decisive point in the process in which the believer abandons his or her past for a new life, whether the texts speak of repentance/conversion, of leaving pagan darkness behind, of putting off the old nature, of abandoning the power of sin, of possessing the remission of sins, or of becoming a disciple.

167

When the latter expression occurs in the Gospel of Matthew, its meaning is close to that of faith in other texts. Faith is a faith in the Christ who makes the rite meaningful, even though the different theologians – a Paul, a Luke, a writer of Colossians, a John – can speak of faith in somewhat different terms.

The remission of sins is also related to the two main primitive motifs. According to traditional thinking it was one of the gifts expected in the age of salvation, but it is also bound to Jesus and his work, as in those interpretations of his death which say that it was 'for our sins' or 'for us'.

The idea that the Spirit would be given in the age of salvation belonged to the heritage from the Old Testament and Judaism. So almost all of our texts somehow link baptism with the Spirit. But despite the general scholarly consensus that it was commonly held in the early church that the Spirit was bestowed in the rite of baptism, it is hard to find indisputable arguments in support of such an opinion. The New Testament writers differ considerably in their ways of regarding the Spirit. Thus with Luke the gift is demonstrated in extraordinary events and ecstatic experiences. But with the same Luke it is also, and not least, depicted as the divine force behind the mission and behind the fact that new converts join the saved people of God. The enthusiasts in Corinth valued above all glossolalia and ecstasy; Paul is somewhat doubtful about this view, but also in his opinion entrance into the Christ-communion, with its ritual focus in baptism, conferred divine charisms on the Christians. In Pauline thinking, however, the Spirit is also, and particularly, the divine power which builds the church and a pledge of the future eschatological liberation.

All our authors take baptism for granted. In different ways they represent a conviction that it means an encounter between the divine and the human. An earthly, concrete event mediates divine actions and conveys spiritual gifts. Such a view of rites is nothing peculiar as regarded in the perspective of phenomenology of religion. But over and over again it has also become evident that baptism and its meaning cannot be isolated from the combination of events, actions, attitudes, experiences and phenomena which together make up the transition from the past and its conditions to the new, Christian life. Baptism is the ritual focus of this cluster of events, and the close connection between baptism and the other elements may explain why our authors do not always clearly link baptism with repentance/conversion, forgiveness of sins, faith, justification, or the gift of the Spirit. To disregard the circumstance that baptism belongs to such a larger whole may have the result that it is unjustly focused upon, but also, paradoxically enough, that its importance is underestimated.

The differences between the authors we have studied and their multiple ways of using ideas on baptism point to a continuous reflection, which mirrors how early Christian theologians were confronted by new questions and new problems. The images which we found during our survey of the baptismal texts of the New Testament have shown that, on the one hand, a few elements appear to have been fundamental and, indeed, taken for granted. This is true especially of the relationship to Christ, the eschatological saviour. On the other hand, baptism and baptismal thinking have been integrated with every writer's theological views and thus have become part of the arsenal used when the authors discussed occasional issues. In such cases we also observed how formulae and established motifs were incorporated with the presentation, by theological giants such as Paul and John and also by their less renowned colleagues and followers.

13.2. Onward?

This chapter is entitled 'At the end of the road through the New Testament'. This does not necessarily mean the end of the road through the *early church*. This road can be regarded as being longer, and in that case we are now only at a halt. Thus a possible 'onward' is implied, and such an 'onward' has at least two aspects, one historical, the other ecclesiastico–hermeneutical.

First, the question may be asked from an historical point of view. The history of the church of which we surmise some features in the New Testament continues without any visible breaks, and there is no sharp division after what could be called New Testament times. Actually the oldest sources of the subsequent history of the church date from a time in which New Testament texts were still being written, or contain traditions rooted in those times. Thus it is reasonable to pursue the study of this diversified history into the second century, and the following chapter will do so. Certainly the 'apostolic' texts played an important role for several of the Christian writers of the second century, but life and thinking in the church developed continuously, not least in terms of baptism. Features of this development can be discerned in several texts from this century, e.g. in the Apostolic Fathers and the writings of St Justin. In the face of this material it would be of interest to ask: What happens to the rite and to the inherited ideas? What is taken over and what is left out? How is the choice made? How are elements from the past combined? Are there new elements? Do others disappear? In chapter fourteen below, I venture into this field with a study of baptism in the *Didache* and the *Shepherd of Hermas*. But of course there is much more to do.

The second aspect which may motivate a question-mark after the title above was labelled ecclesiastico–hermeneutical. The adjective 'hermeneutical' stands for general principles concerning the interpretation and understanding of linguistic signs. The element 'ecclesiastical' narrows this definition, because the use of New Testament baptismal texts in a church context involves more than dependence on the general conditions of interpretation and understanding of texts; the latter must be respected by the historically working exegete just as much as by other scholars. But both from an hermeneutical and from a theological point of view it is inadvisable to imagine that a question asked in a church context has been answered once an historical–exegetical investigation has been performed. Rather those who would interpret and understand these texts for application in the church today must reflect on the criteria of such a task. In our case already the variety of the views adopted by the New Testament authors calls for consideration. Which author or which theology, if any, is to dominate? It is unfair, both to New Testament authors and to theology or hermeneutics, to believe that New Testament texts on baptism can be applied in a church of later times by 'reading as it is written and doing as it is written', as the saying goes.

The investigations in this book do not approach the problems mentioned in the preceding paragraph. But we should not forget their existence and their importance. Which criteria can or should be applied to the use of the baptismal passages and of the results of historical–critical exegesis? And why should these criteria and not others be applied?[1] What importance has, for instance, the heritage of the church in terms of the practice and understanding of baptism and theology? Consequently, if investigations such as the present one are to play a role when it comes to Christian usage and application of the Bible, the results should be the point of departure, but not more, for further reflection.

---

[1] Schenk 1990 emphatically calls for such a reflection with regard to the document produced by the World Council of Churches, *Baptism, Eucharist and Ministry*.

14

Baptism in the *Didache* and in the *Shepherd of Hermas*[1]

In the previous chapter, which concluded the study of the New Testament baptismal texts, I intimated that it might be instructive to pursue the investigation into the Christian material of the second century. This cannot be done fully in this context, but I shall nevertheless finish these pages with a glance at two writings of the Apostolic Fathers in which baptism plays a major role, the *Didache* and the *Shepherd of Hermas*.

When a New Testament scholar takes up these two texts searching for their treatment of baptism, the question is soon likely to arise: Why have the New Testament texts on baptism not left more visible traces? So we must remember that at the time of these texts, the New Testament was only in the process of becoming canonical, in terms of both authority and extent. It belongs to the background, but does not *per se* constitute an authoritative basis of baptismal practice and theology.

Thus the texts we shall study seem to reflect a living undisputed tradition and, above all, an undisputed practice. This is not to say that there was no underlying baptismal theology, but this is often difficult to discern. One simple but important factor behind this phenomenon is that the literary genres of the two texts, more precisely a church order and an apocalypse with an ethical–pastoral aim, do not easily lend themselves to the expression of theology.

Both in the *Didache* and in the *Shepherd* baptism is not only self-evident but obviously obligatory. But if we do not assume that this was so because of a sheer ritual duty, there should be an underlying theological concept of baptism, which explains why the rite was necessary. Of course, I am not the first to seek an answer to this question.[2] But I shall do so against the background of the above investigations of baptism in the New

---

[1] This chapter is a revised version of Hartman 1994 that has been adapted to this new literary context.
[2] One basic investigation is Benoit 1953. Other contributions will be cited below.

Testament, and this background will make its mark on the last paragraphs of my discussions of the two books.

14.1. Didache

In *Didache*, the main passage on baptism is 7.1–4:

> Concerning baptism, baptise (imperative, 2nd pers. plur.) thus: after you have begun by saying (προειπόντες) all these things, baptise into (εἰς) the name of the Father, of the Son and of the Holy Spirit in living water. (2) But if you have no living water, baptise (imperative, 2nd pers. sing.) in other water. And if you cannot in cold, (then) in warm. (3) And if you do not have (enough of[3]) either, pour water three times on the head into the name of Father, Son and Holy Spirit.[4] (4) And before the baptism let the baptiser and the one who is baptised fast, and any others who are able (εἴ τινες ἄλλοι δύνανται). And you shall order the one who is baptised to fast one or two days before.

This is a ritual manual. Its counterpart concerning the eucharist (*Did.* 9–10) contains prayers which tell us something of the underlying eucharistic thought, but no such material is encountered here.

The passage quoted is immediately followed by some general rules on fasting (this is mandatory on Wednesday and Friday; 8.1) and on the Our Father; its wording is cited and it is to be said three times a day (8.2–3). Then 9.1 begins 'Concerning the eucharist'. It has been suggested that the place of the Lord's Prayer in 8.2 indicates that it was 'handed over' at baptism. This is possible, but hardly more than that. The general fasting rule of 8.1 is connected to the particular rule on fasting in 7.4 via a keyword association, and the ruling on the Our Father can be joined to that on fasting according to the same pattern of piety which also carries the composition of Matt 6.1–18 (alms-giving, prayer, fasting). On the other hand, chapter 8 stands out as a unit *within* the portion of the text on baptism, which begins in 7.1 with the heading 'Concerning baptism'. For the next heading of this kind follows immediately after chapter 8, in 9.1, 'Concerning the eucharist'.[5] But the composition *is* loose.

The rules on baptism are preceded by *Did.* 1–6, the admonitory treatise on 'the Two Ways'. It certainly has a tradition history of its own before being included here,[6] but for our present study it is important that it is

---

[3] Thus Rordorf 1972, 507, who refers to the Georgian version which has this reading.
[4] Here, both 'name' and the Persons lack the article. This has prompted many suggestions, see Noack 1982, 252.
[5] There is one more in 11.3, 'Concerning apostles and prophets'.
[6] See e.g. Vögtle 1936, 113ff, 196ff; Wibbing 1959, 33ff, 61ff.

explicitly connected with the rite of baptism: 'after you have begun by saying all these things'. Benoit has rightly mentioned the similarity to Jewish proselyte baptism,[7] at which some of the commandments were read aloud. Of course this practice did not mean that the proselyte had not been previously instructed in the *halakah*. Something similar probably holds true of baptism in the *Didache*.[8]

The somewhat surprisingly punctilious rulings on which kinds of water could be used for baptising can be taken as a sign of the importance and necessity that baptism really was performed.[9] But why was it so important? The instruction of the Two Ways is a suitable point of departure for our attempts to reconstruct some aspects of the principles of baptism. The inclusion of the Two Ways treatise in the rite underlines its initiatory function. The people initiated apparently no longer come from circles in which Jewish morals can be taken for granted. Instead a Gentile background of the converts necessitates a more thorough ethical instruction. At this transition into the new, the old, pagan conditions are depicted as the way of death: sterile, unfruitful, negative, ending in destruction and in separation from God. Certainly this attitude to the transition is well represented in the New Testament,[10] but it is significant that the catalogue of the Two Ways is here part of the baptismal rite. So it is no surprise to find that the mortal realm which the one baptised is leaving also contains idolatry, sorcery, and astrology (3.4; cf. 5.1).

The place in the ritual of the instruction on the way of death also indicates that it has a paraenetic function: do not return to it (cf. 6.1: 'See to it that no one leads you astray from this way', i.e., the one of life). We may, however, ponder the following facts: pre-Pauline tradition (1 Cor 6.11), Paul (Rom 6.1–14), and also the Pauline disciple responsible for Colossians (Col 2.6–23) are of the opinion that Christ has saved his adherents from this mortal, sinful environment. But the *Didache* does not seem to represent such a way of regarding the importance of Christ. Christ is not called saviour, nor is he explicitly said to 'save' (σῴζειν or ῥύεσθαι). But in 5.2, at the end of the description of the way of death, it says: 'May you be delivered (ῥυσθείητε), children, from all these'. No responsible actor is mentioned. But that which is said in 9.2 makes it

---

[7] Benoit 1953, 13–15.
[8] Benoit 1953, 7. Cf. Noack 1982, 260.
[9] Noack 1982, 252.
[10] E.g. Rom 6.17–22; 1 Cor 6.9ff; Gal 4.8f; Eph 2.1–10, 11–22; Col 3.5ff; 1 Pet 1.14ff.

reasonable to assume that the implied subject is God, through Christ: 'We praise you (εὐχαριστοῦμεν), our Father, for the life and knowledge (γνῶσις) which you made known to us through Jesus your servant (παῖς)'. And similarly in 10.2: 'We praise you ... for the knowledge and faith and immortality which you made known to us through Jesus, your servant'.

Without entering upon a discussion of the Christology of the *Didache*,[11] we can state that apparently Jesus is represented particularly as the revealer, sent by God. The life which he has made known is, at least to some extent, that described as the way of life, which has immortality as its goal.[12] Jesus' role as the mediator of life is also intimated by the fact that the instruction often refers to or echoes his teaching.

But the Jesus of the *Didache* is not only a teacher of morals, nor does the life mediated by him consist only of ethical standards. This is rather but one aspect of the conviction that the Father through Jesus has 'made (his) name dwell (κατασκηνοῦν) in our hearts', which is articulated in his making 'knowledge, faith, and immortality' known (10.2). In other words, Jesus' revelatory work is a divine epiphany, actual and effective in the personal centre of the Christians' life, in a qualified sense of the word.[13] This blessed status was conferred when they became Christians, i.e., underwent the transition we considered above apropos of the Two Ways instruction. Furthermore, this transition, or their conversion, was actually brought about by God, who 'called' those whom 'the Spirit had prepared' (4.10).[14]

This change with its aspects of divine and human activity had a ritual focus, baptism. Baptism marked a boundary, on the other side of which one was a 'sharer of immortality' (4.8) and a person in whom God's 'name' dwelt (10.2). No wonder it was important, indeed so important that provision must be made for several other ways of performing it than the

---

[11] Cf. Mitchell 1995, 232–234.

[12] One may wonder whether 4.8 intimates that this immortality is only regarded as belonging to the future: the Christians are all 'Sharers in the immortality (ἐν τῷ ἀθανάτῳ κοινωνοί)'. But to my mind, the 'sharers' should rather be understood as equal to 'heirs'.

[13] Niederwimmer 1989, 195.

[14] Actually, the passage is somewhat complicated from a linguistic point of view. It says (ὁ θεὸς) οὐ ... ἔρχεται κατὰ πρόσωπον καλέσαι, ἀλλ᾽ ἐφ᾽ οὓς τὸ πνεῦμα ἡτοίμασεν. This can be resolved in two ways, either as ἔρχεται ἐπὶ τούτους οὓς τὸ πνεῦμα ..., or as ἔρχεται καλεῖν τούτους, ἐφ᾽ οὓς ... In the first alternative, the Spirit is the subject of the relative clause, in the latter, God, that is, God has prepared the Spirit (as a gift) for them; Niederwimmer 1989, 143. Without much hesitation, I prefer the first reading, as do Bauer, Harnack, Jacquier, Kleist, Audet, Wengst (see Niederwimmer 1989, ibid.).

norm. This view of baptism's importance is supported by the ruling in 9.5: 'Let no one eat of your eucharist except those who have been baptised into the name of the Lord (εἰς ὄνομα κυρίου). For concerning this also did the Lord say, 'Do not give the holy to the dogs'.' Thus, after baptism one is not a dog. In positive terms, one could be called holy,[15] for this is the epithet of the Christians in 4.2; 10.6, and such are worthy of receiving the holy.

We glimpse another aspect of Jesus' role as a revealer in 4.1, where the convert is summoned to honour him who speaks the word of God, 'for where the Lordship (ἡ κυριότης) is spoken of, there is the Lord'. In other words, the living Lord is present in the activity of the teacher who mediates the Lord's teaching.[16]

The baptismal formula 'into the name of' the Three Persons belongs to the same liturgical tradition as Matt 28.19. Both the somewhat Judeo–Christian background of the *Didache* and, above all, the context indicate that the name-formula has retained the old linguistic function in the *Didache*, suggested above in chapter three, rather than being reduced to empty phrases. Thus, it is meaningful that in the context of the rulings on the eucharist the shorter form is used: 'Let no one eat of your eucharist except those who have been baptised into the name of the Lord'. It is not simply said 'those who have been baptised'. The focus is instead on the Jesus aspects of baptism's fundamental referent, which is reasonable apropos of 'the Lord's supper' (although this expression is not found in the *Didache*). We have already encountered a couple of passages from the eucharistic prayers which contain such Christological associations of the eucharist: they refer to God's servant Jesus through whom the holy ones have received the Father's name in their hearts and acquired knowledge, faith and immortality.

However, in the rite of baptism, the wider *theo*-logical basis is explicit. This is the more natural in a situation where those baptised are mainly non-Jews, as is indicated by the Two Ways instruction. So we can fill in what the baptismal rite (through the recital of the Two Ways instruction) said of the Father and of the Spirit. Thus the Father is the Creator (1.2; cf. also 10.3). We have seen how, in the eucharistic prayers, he stands behind Jesus' revelation of him and of the life and immortality so offered. So he is also the one to love first (1.2) and the one whose will is reflected in the Two Ways, and the one in whom all Christians hope (4.10).

Outside the baptismal formula, except for the references to prophets

---

[15] Niederwimmer 1989, 204.
[16] Niederwimmer 1989, 136.

speaking 'in the Spirit' (11.7–9, 12), the Spirit is mentioned only in 4.10, according to which the Spirit has 'prepared' (ἡτοίμασεν) those who are 'called'. In other words, through the Spirit, God is active in the transition from the old situation of death into newness of life; in other words, the transition the ritual culmination of which is baptism. The mention of prophetic speaking 'in the Spirit' testifies to the existence of some charismatic features in the church, but there is no indication that the Spirit is a gift to the one baptised in the sense that he/she receives extraordinary blessings such as prophecy or glossolalia. (It is a wholly different matter that such attributes as the indwelling of God's name, the gift of knowledge might very well be regarded as a presence of or as activities of the Spirit; but the author does not express himself in these terms.)

I now sum up my deliberations on the *Didache* with an eye to the primitive motifs which we considered in the New Testament baptismal texts. First, we note that baptism stands at the boundary where individuals leave the way of death in order to walk instead on the way of life, revealed as God's will by Jesus. So baptism has a background in *conversion*. The conversion to this life must be followed by a proper way of living. But we have also seen that this life means more than ethics of a certain standard; Christians already have a share in a divine life, and although they are not physically immortal, their life with God – and the divine presence in them (10.2) – is one which surpasses the limits of this world (4.8; 19.2). *Jesus*, being the divine revealer, has mediated this life, as well as the knowledge of God and of his will; he is also present in the community as the 'Lordship' when it is instructed in his teaching. Although baptism is performed with reference to the Trinity, it can also be summarised as one 'into the name of the Lord' (9.5), and so Jesus is still a central figure in the baptismal thinking. However, his death and resurrection are mentioned neither in connection with baptism nor in the passages on the eucharist, and here is a difference vis-à-vis many New Testament authors. It is not advisable to draw any conclusions *e silentio*, but the absence of this motif is noteworthy.

Faith may be indirectly connected with baptism, in so far as the latter so markedly stands as the gate into the new, vital, Christian status. So, in 16.2, 5 'believer' is equal to 'Christian'.

In the *Didache*, the *remission of sins* is not explicitly linked with baptism. But we have encountered the view that after baptism the believer is holy (not a 'dog'; 9.5), and also the circumstance that the way of death, which was left behind at baptism, was lined with sins. When the Sunday eucharist is preceded by a confession of transgressions in order that 'your offering may be pure'(14.1–3), this may be regarded as a renewal of the baptismal purity and holiness which were a prerequisite for communion (9.5: only 'those who are baptised into the name of the Lord').[17] There is a slight possibility that the fasting for two days beforehand pertains to repentance before the cleansing and remission in baptism, but it might be understood as well as an aid to the comprehension of the importance of the rite.[18]

Not least in Paul, we found that baptism has a *church* dimension, which he develops in his own way through his language on the body of Christ. In the *Didache*, the fact that baptism is in such a large measure a rite de passage into the community determined by 'the way of life', the indwelling of God's name, of knowledge, etc., also brings with it a certain church aspect of baptism. It is also visible in the Two Ways instruction daily to seek 'the presence of the saints' and to resist schism (4.1–3).

Thus, notwithstanding that a *rituale* is not always the easiest source of theology, we have surmised a few features in the baptismal thinking behind the *Didache*, which may explain why baptism was considered necessary; in a way it was the gate into life!

14.2. The Shepherd of Hermas

In the *Shepherd of Hermas* (henceforward, *Hermas*) baptism is almost explicitly said to be necessary: in one of the visions the tower, which stands for the church, is said to be built by water 'because your life is saved and will be saved through water' (11.5 = *Vis.* 3.3.5). So, assuming also in this case that we are not confronted by sheer ritualism, what does baptism mean and confer, which makes it so necessary?

The book is a composition which, by different revelations to a certain Hermas, seeks to solve some pastoral problems in the church at Rome.[19] The members of the church are both such as have learnt Christianity at home (cf. 3.2; 7.1 = *Vis.* 1.3.2 and 2.3.1) and new converts from paganism. Some Christians and catechumens tend to be lax in their morals

---

[17] See also 4.14; see further Poschmann 1940; Rordorf, 1973.

[18] Niederwimmer 1989, 164.

[19] One or several redactors have combined 1–24 (= *Vis.* 1–4) with 25–77 (= *Vis.* 5, *Mand.*, and *Sim.* 1–8), and added 78–110 (= *Sim.* 9) and, as a conclusion, 111–114 (= *Sim.* 10). For my purpose it is not necessary to distinguish between the different layers of the text nor to dwell on its literary history. Accordingly these short notes on the situation will have to suffice. Vielhauer 1975, 516f.

and others have even become apostates or renegades. To such people the message is that now there is an opportunity to return, to do *metanoia,* namely, a second *metanoia* after the first which took place when they entered Christianity, or came to faith, and were baptised (31.1f = *Mand.* 4.3.1f). This new possibility is offered only to the Christians of the present time who have sinned or fallen away, not, however, to future converts (6.4f; 45.6–49.5 etc. = *Vis.* 2.2.4f; *Mand.* 12.3.6–6.5 etc.).[20]

The fact that the author is so intent on his main errand makes our task difficult in a somewhat odd way. For baptism is just in the background; now and then we surmise a few contours of the author's thinking about it, but it never really comes to the fore. In addition, the style of the presentation, with numerous elaborate allegories and other pictorial language, is often far from lucid. Furthermore, the book possibly contains allusions to baptismal ideas or to ritual details unknown to us.[21]

I have already mentioned 31.1f (= *Mand.* 4.3.1f) concerning the renewed *metanoia.* Reference is made to some teachers[22] who claim

> that there is no second repentance except the one when we went down into the water and received forgiveness for our former sins. (2) He said to me: 'You have heard correctly, for that is so. For he who has received forgiveness of sins should not sin any more, but live in purity.'

We note how the passage revolves around the remission–*metanoia* problem. The first repentance of sins led to baptism and to the forgiveness bestowed therein. Thus baptism was a ritual focus of the conversion of the past. Pre-Christian life is regarded as being beset by sins and pollution, and when this is the angle from which one sees a person's becoming a Christian, one naturally focuses on conversion from the sins, and on baptism as a rite in which forgiveness of 'the sins of the past' (31.3) is granted.[23] In the immediate context the author also uses other established language to describe this event, 'believe' (31.1) and 'be called' (31.4). The mode of expression in 31.3 ('those who will believe [in the future] have no [opportunity of] *metanoia* of sins, but have forgiveness of their former sins') implies that to the author baptism is the 'sacrament' of faith. For

---

[20] See Windisch 1908, 356–382.
[21] On baptism in *Hermas,* see particularly Benoit 1953, 115–137, and Pernveden 1966, 162–176.
[22] Possibly one such teacher is the author of Hebrews (see Heb 6.4ff).
[23] This indirectly means that baptism acquires a purifying function (differently Pernveden 1966, 164).

having 'gone down into the water and received forgiveness' (31.1) is parallel to 'believe (or: become a believer; the tense is aorist) and have forgiveness of their former sins' (31.3).

Before 31.1ff an earlier reference is made to baptism in 11.5 (= *Vis.* 3.3.5). The context contains a vision of the growth of the church with images from the building of a tower. Stones of different shapes are brought as material, some of which are used for the building, others not. A woman (who also represents the church!) explains the vision and says *inter alia:*

> Hear, then, why the tower is built by the water (ἐπὶ ὑδάτων); because your (ὑμῶν) life was saved and will be saved through (διὰ) water.

Thus baptism is held to be necessary. But in the explanation which follows, the water/baptism is not explicitly mentioned until the interpretation of the last group of stones; they stand for catechumens who do not persevere on their way into the church: they

> fell near the water (τῶν ὑδάτων) and could not be rolled into the water (τὸ ὕδωρ) ... These are they who have heard the word (cf. Mark 4.18; Matt 13.20, 22) and wish to be baptised into the name of the Lord (εἰς τὸ ὄνομα τοῦ κυρίου). Then, when the purity of the truth comes into their remembrance (αὐτοῖς ἔλθῃ εἰς μνείαν), they change their mind (μετανοοῦσιν) and go again after their evil lusts. (15.3 = *Vis.* 3.7.3)

Here evidently baptism stands at the end of the path into the church, which begins at the hearing of the 'word'. We hear of the same thing in 69.2 (= *Sim.* 8.3.2). There the willow tree of vision 8 is said to refer to 'God's law', which is identified with God's Son, who 'has been preached to the ends of the earth' (see also 94.1 = *Sim.* 9.17.1); those who have gathered under the shade of the tree (and whose quality in terms of virtues is tested) are the 'nations who have heard the preaching and believed in him'.[24] Thus baptism is rooted in the mission of the church, which means the proclamation of Christ. This may lead to a preliminary acceptance of the message and to belief and baptism. But the catechumens are also instructed in the strict moral demands of Christianity, and it seems that these demands make some change their mind.

15.3, quoted above, mentions being 'baptised into the name of the

---

[24] See also 94.4 (= *Sim.* 9.17.4). '... the nations which dwell under heaven, when they heard and believed ...'

Lord'. No doubt the old formula 'into the name of Lord Jesus' is the origin of the phrase, but it may have been the object of many reinterpretations in the course of time. Although the usage in *Hermas* is equivocal so that it is not absolutely clear to whom *kurios* refers,[25] the reference is probably to the Son. This, in my opinion, is implied by tradition and, moreover, by the obligatory role of the Son as the gate into the church/the kingdom, which is emphasised in 89.3f (= *Sim.* 9.12.3f). But it is also said that one cannot enter there 'unless he receives (λάβοι) the name of his Son' (89.4), or 'except through the name of his beloved Son' (89.5). It seems to me that Pernveden is right when he maintains that these and similar ὄνομα phrases in *Sim.* 9 refer to baptism.[26] As regards the εἰς τὸ ὄνομα expression, it is impossible to form an opinion about its specific meaning; although it is certainly rooted in the old baptismal formula, this does not tell us anything of its meaning in this context. *Hermas* uses 'name' abundantly but in a rather fluid manner, and the preposition may have lost some of its oddness through traditional use.

11.5, also quoted above, implied that baptism was necessary for salvation. *Hermas* does not explicitly state from what one is saved nor to what or how. But it may be worth while to scrutinise what may be implied.

Let us begin with the question, *from* what is the Christian saved? From 31.5 (= *Mand.* 4.3.5, on the first conversion when the individual went down into the water and was forgiven) it is clear that the baptised person was saved from being a sinner, which in *Hermas* is really a mortal threat. The author's view on the Spirit – the divine powers (of the Son, to which we shall return) – is so optimistic that he maintains that in collaboration with these powers the Christian can shun sin until the final salvation. So he need not fear the devil either (49.2–4 = *Mand.* 12.6.2–4). Moreover, according to the notice on baptism in 11.5 the Christian's life was saved through water. This implies that it was otherwise threatened by death. So, salvation from eschatological death is also explicitly mentioned in several passages, and in some instances indirectly so, through reference to the eternal death which awaits sinners who remain in sin.[27]

To what, then, is the baptised, faithful Christian saved? In 7.2 (= *Vis.* 2.3.2) salvation is almost the same as 'eternal life', and this eschatological reference holds true for the concept throughout *Hermas*. This eschato-

---

[25] See the literature in Pernveden 1966, 165.

[26] Pernveden 1966, 166.

[27] See 62.4; 64.7; 95.1f (= *Sim.* 6.2.4; 4.7; 9.18.1f). Also 93.3 (= *Sim.* 9.16.3).

logical slant explains the expression we have just discussed, that the Christian's life was saved *and will be saved* through baptism (11.5). In other words, salvation in baptism is but preliminary. It is salvation, not least because sins are forgiven there, but it must be retained through fidelity to the moral demands, and the Christian must of course not fall away or become a hypocrite (7.2; 14.1; 72.5; 96.1 = *Vis.* 2.3.2; 3.6.1; *Sim.* 8.6.5; 9.19.1).

So a necessary presupposition of salvation is also faithful observance of the Christian virtues. The following passage from *Sim.* 9 makes this evident. It refers to a 'parable' mentioning some maidens whose garments stand for the principal virtues; in the quotation they are also called the powers of the Son of God. In the immediate continuation, however, the author also refers to them as 'holy spirits' (92.6 = *Sim.* 9.15.6; in 101.2 [= *Sim.* 9.24.2] he even writes 'the holy spirit of these maidens'). Their names too can be these virtues (92.2). The passage also makes use of an expression which is common in *Sim.* 9, viz. to receive or to bear 'the name of the Son of God' (as already mentioned, it seems to refer to some aspect of baptism).

> If you receive (λάβῃς) the name (i.e., of the Son of God) alone, but do not receive the garment from them (i.e. the maidens), you will achieve (ὠφελήσῃ) nothing, for these maidens are the powers (δυνάμεις) of the Son of God. If you bear (φορῇς) the name, but do not bear his power (singular!), you will be bearing his name in vain. (90.2 = *Sim.* 9.13.2)

This moral zeal is a constant feature of *Hermas* and invariably linked with the topic of the renewed *metanoia*.[28] But the Christians are not alone in their struggle to keep the life into which they were saved; this is another part of the answer to the question *to* what the baptised person is saved. The maidens/their garments/their names/their holy spirit are the same as the powers of the Son, indeed of his Spirit (101.4 = Sim. 9.24.4). This is *Hermas'* way of speaking of the Holy Spirit,[29] which is on the Christians' side, indeed 'dwells in' them (33.2 = *Mand.* 5.1.2). But although it is called the powers of the Son, it is very easy to lose it; according to 33.3, if any anger occurs, the Holy Spirit 'being delicate, is distressed and finds the

---

[28] 7.2; 16.3; 31.7; 61.1 (= *Vis.* 2.3.2; 3.8.3; *Mand.* 4.3.7; *Sim.* 6.1.1) the same is the meaning of the motif of the maidens in *Sim.* 9, who stand for/whose names are the main Christian virtues.

[29] Rightly Benoit 1953, 130, finds the author's concept of the Spirit obscure and lacking in unity.

place impure, and so tries to get away from the place'. Thus, the baptised person is saved to a life supported by the Spirit, but nevertheless *Hermas* does not suggest that the Spirit was imparted in baptism.[30]

If we ask *how* salvation is brought about, the salvific function of Jesus in *Hermas* is not easily perceived. In one of the passages on God's merciful salvation, Jesus' role is presented in this manner: 'Those who were *called by the Son* will be saved' (77.1 = *Sim.* 7.11.1). Moreover, according to 89.3 (= *Sim.* 9.12.3) 'in the last days of the end he (the Son of God) was revealed (φανηρός)' and so became the gate into the tower/church through which 'those who are saved enter the kingdom of God'. The meaning of the gate = the Son is further developed in the continuation of 89.3, just quoted. There, entrance through the gate seems to be equal to 'taking his Son's name' (89.4),[31] and in 89.5 it is stated: 'A man cannot otherwise enter the kingdom of God except through the name of his Son, who is beloved (ἠγαπημένου) by him'. In *Sim.* 9 as a whole it is often maintained that receiving or bearing the name of the Son is necessary for salvation. I have already mentioned, and accepted, Pernveden's opinion that these ὄνομα-phrases refer to baptism. Thus, it seems that baptism applies Christ's calling to the person baptised.

We are still asking how people are saved. Above, we noted the place of the word at the beginning of the road to baptism when the preaching is heard, accepted and believed. It is called 'the law of God which was given to all the world'. But the sentence continues: 'and this law is God's Son (who is) preached to the ends of the earth' (69.2 = *Sim.* 8.3.2). What do the missionaries preach when they preach God's Son? Possibly we can grope for an answer by asking what people know when 'knowing the name of the Son', which is necessary for salvation (93.7 = *Sim.* 9.16.7). The phrase is biblical; thus it is typical of the righteous that they know God's name, which means that they have taken to themselves what God has revealed of himself and his will.[32] Similarly, to know the name of the Son of God might mean to know what the church proclaims of him and his will. But nevertheless we are little wiser than before. Although both Paul's Letter to the Romans and The Letter to the Hebrews certainly were to be found in the archives of the community, *Hermas* does not intimate that the kerygma made any mention of a crucified Messiah or of a resurrected Son of God, nor are there any hints that the forgiveness of sins depended on a

[30] See Pernveden 1966, 175. Cf. Benoit 1953, 127ff, 135.
[31] The same in 89.8; in both cases the verb is λαμβάνειν.
[32] See Isa 52.6; Ezek 39.7; Ps 9.11; 91.14.

182

once-for-all sacrifice of Christ. There is no ὑπὲρ ἡμῶν ('for our sake') or 'for our sins' in *Hermas*.[33]

Certainly we should beware of concluding *e silentio,* but the usage of the law terminology as well as the 'knowing the name of' language suggest that Christ is represented as the revealer of God, as God's self-communication, including or implying certain ethical standards;[34] he shows people 'the ways of life' (59.3 = *Sim.* 5.6.3). Accepting this message can be termed 'to be called' (31.4 = *Mand.* 4.3.4), sometimes explicitly by God's Son (77.1; 91.5 = *Sim.* 8.11.1; 9.14.5),[35] or 'to believe' (15.1; 31.3 etc. = *Vis.* 3.7.21; *Mand.* 4.3.3 etc.). So Christ's salvific function is that he is preached and that thereby he calls people, so that the converts know him or bear his name. But, seen with the moral interests of *Hermas* in mind, it is also a saving task which Christ fulfilled when he mediated knowledge of how to live.

It is now time to assess a problematic issue, the meaning of the seal image in *Hermas*. The book is often cited as one of the early Christian texts in which baptism is called a seal.[36] One crucial passage is 93 (= *Sim.* 9.16). In this 'similitude' the righteous dead of earlier times are represented as stones which are brought up from the deep to the building by 'the apostles and teachers who preached the name of the Son of God' (93.5 = *Sim.* 9.16.5). These pre-Christian, righteous souls already possess the virtues necessary for entrance to the kingdom, but nevertheless must 'put away the death (νέκρωσιν) of their former life' (2). This ensues from their acceptance of 'the seal of the Son of God' (3). The following sentence says:

> Before a man gets to bear (φορέσαι) the name of the Son of God, he is dead. But when he receives the seal, he puts death away and takes up life. The seal, then, is the water.

We might understand this as a reference to baptism. Moreover, receiving the seal is equated with receiving the name of the Son of God, an expression which also seems to have something to do with baptism.

But the passage also describes the activity of the apostles and teachers as giving those righteous of earlier times 'the seal of preaching' (5). So it is

[33] There are authors who interpret 59.2 (*Sim.* 5.6.2) in such terms: God's son is charged with God's vineyard. He pulls out the weeds, i.e., cleanses the sins of God's people, 'labouring much and undergoing much toil'. Then (59.3) he shows them the ways of life (which is symbolised by the food which is sent to him by the owner of the vineyard; 58.3). To my mind, Pernveden is right when he doubts that 59.2 refers to Christ's atoning passion and death (1966, 77f).

[34] Cf. Pernveden 1966, 52–57. Cf. Nijendijk 1986, passim.

[35] Cf. 67.1 (= *Sim.* 8.1.1) 'being called by the name of the Lord' (ἐν ὀνόματι τοῦ κυρίου).

[36] See e.g. Lampe 1951, 106.

also said that they 'received the knowledge of the name of the Son of God' (7), which is apparently the same as receiving the seal (8). Thus, in the latter instances being sealed seems to denote acceptance of the message of the Son.

Thus, 93.4 could mean that the pre-Christian righteous had to be baptised in Hades *or* that they had only to listen to the proclamation of God's Son.[37] But in 72.3 (= *Sim.* 8.6.3) we are told of people 'who became believers and have received the seal and broken it and not kept it whole', i.e., they have fallen into sin. When they repent, they receive a new seal and 'praise the Lord because he had mercy on them'. Apparently the mercy shown consists in the possibility of a new repentance. But whatever the seal may signify here, it is not baptism, since the author is no anabaptist.[38]

Thus, either 'seal' stands for the same thing throughout the book and then cannot refer to baptism as such, but possibly to a rite connected with baptism and capable of being repeated, e.g. an anointing or (a sign designating) a confirmation of membership of Christ's community[39] or the imparting of the name of the Son of God in baptism.[40] Or the seal is being used with several meanings, one of which is baptism.[41]

Personally, I cannot find a simple solution to this dilemma. But whichever of the alternatives is chosen, the seal is related to baptism, at least as something which tells or confirms an aspect of what baptism means. So it is meaningful to ask what the imagery stands for.

Without going into details,[42] we may note, first, that it is nothing new when *Hermas* tells us that people are sealed: cf. 2 Cor 1.22; Rev 7.2; 9.4; 14.1. Thus not only things and animals, including sacrifices, but also people are sealed and so it is made evident who is their lord or master.[43] To be sealed also involves the protection of the seal's owner.

Because a seal could very well be inscribed with the owner's name or

---

[37] That 93.4 refers to baptism is assumed by e.g. Quasten, 1950, 101, and Karpp 1969, 64. According to E. Peterson it refers to the preaching (1955, 18).

[38] See e.g. Pernveden 1966, 169. I presuppose, then, that the usage is consistent within 72.3, and thus that the seal does not refer to baptism in the first half of the sentence, nor in its second half to the 'Bussgnade' or to a 'Pass' into the tower (Dibelius 1923, 596). Cf. Windisch 1908, 378.

[39] See Hamman 1961, 287.

[40] Thus Pernveden 1966, 170 – however this may have been performed in the rite.

[41] Thus e.g. Dibelius 1923, 591, 596.

[42] See Fitzer 1966, esp. 940–943 (+ lit.).

[43] I leave aside the usage of a seal for confirmation of legitimacy, for guarding something closed or secret, or as a token of the high value of something.

symbol, it may be worth while to return to the passages in *Sim.* 9 which refer to the necessity of receiving and bearing the name of the Son of God. I have already quoted 93.3, where receiving the name and being sealed seemed to be the same:

> Before a man gets to bear (φορέσαι) the name of the Son of God, he is dead (νεκρός), but when he receives (λάβη) the seal, he puts death away (νέκρωσιν) and takes up life.

I have already mentioned that these name-passages should be connected with baptism.

Thus, whatever the ritual details were, it seems that the rite of baptism was an external confirmation of what the whole process of becoming a Christian (in one word, conversion) meant to the individual. But it also effected that which it confirmed. The sins of the past were forgiven, the one baptised left mortality and received life, and became the property of the Lord, protected and supported by him. The protection was important not least in times of persecution and martyrdom, which were not alien to *Hermas* (cf. 69.6; 105.2–8 = *Sim.* 8.3.6; 9.28.2–8).

Concluding my discussion of the ideas on baptism in *Hermas*, it seems to me that one point is immediately obvious. Baptism is integrated in a whole, i.e. in the process of leaving death for life (72.6; 93.2f = *Sim.* 8.6.6; 9.16.2f), of being saved (11.5; 46.6; 72.1 = *Vis.* 3.3.5; *Mand.* 12.3.6; *Sim.* 8.6.1), and of entering the kingdom of God (89 = *Sim.* 9.12 in 89–106). This all explains why baptism is so necessary.

Returning to the so-called primitive motifs, we could characterise this overall, unifying perspective as *eschatological,* although with a certain accent on the salvation of the individual (but the end is rapidly approaching; 16.9 = *Vis.* 3.8.9). This process has several aspects, of which *repentance/ conversion* is but one. One point of departure is the *preaching* of the word (15.3 = *Vis.* 3.7.3) or of 'God's law', which is said to be the same as God's Son, who 'is preached to the ends of the earth' (69.2 = *Sim.* 8.3.2).

Furthermore, what about *Christ* or, to use the normal title in *Hermas*, the Son of God? Baptism into his (the Lord's) name is necessary for salvation and it seems somehow to apply his call to the person baptised. Knowledge of his name is obligatory, and so is the receiving and bearing of his name; otherwise one is excluded from life and from the kingdom of God. It seems that he reveals God, and it is 'into the name' of this revealer that the believers are baptised as an external sign that they have accepted this divine self-communication. This may explain why the seal in 93 (=

Sim. 9.16) seems to cover both baptism and preaching, and why receiving the seal is equated with receiving the name of the Son or knowledge of him. In this God-revealing function he is of fundamental importance, indeed literally so, as he is pictured as the foundation of the building/the church/God's kingdom, and as the gate through whom everyone who would enter must pass (89.12 = *Sim.* 9.12). This importance of his may also be reflected in the circumstance that his adherents receive and bear his name (89.8; 90.2 etc.). We may even venture the guess that this corresponds to the simple fact that the believer was called a 'Christ'-ian![44]

The life that the believer has acquired when leaving mortality has to be lived. In order to be saved at the last judgment the believer must live in accordance with the powers of the Son of God, i.e., see to it that his *Spirit* bears his life. Actually, once the believer really surrenders himself to these powers, he can also avoid falling into sin (48.2; 49.4; 90.2–8; = *Mand.* 12.5.2; 6.4; *Sim.* 9.13.2–8). But the gift of the Spirit, which belongs to the Christians, is not explicitly linked with baptism.

Finally, in *Hermas* baptism is connected to the *church* in a very characteristic manner. Although the church certainly constitutes a solid, deep unity, not least in an eschatological perspective (95.2–4 = *Sim.* 9.18.2–4), baptism does not seem to play any role in this respect. But it is the absolutely necessary *rite de passage* into the church, presumably because it binds the Christian to the Son of God.

Perhaps this encounter with two early Christian texts from a time only a couple of generations after the apostolic age (vague as this term is) can be a healthy reminder of the presuppositions of our own theological thinking. Apparently some aspects of New Testament theologising on baptism which we have learnt to regard as crucial are hardly represented here. (I think above all of the way in which Christ and his work are described.) But at least it might be a challenge to try to shift for a moment the filters of our Bible reading and of our approach to theology. This challenge would come from early Christians in a culture where the church represented a small minority in a world of many ideologies and shifting ethical standards – a world not so unlike our own.

---

[44] Although it should be noted that neither 'Christ' nor 'Jesus' occur in *Hermas.*

Bibliography

(Abbreviations are according to S. Schwertner, 'Abkürzungsverzeichnis', in *Theologische Realenzyklopädie*, 2nd ed., Berlin, New York 1994.)

Aland, K., 1960, 'Bemerkungen zum Montanismus und zur frühchristlichen Eschatologie', in: *Kirchengeschichtliche Entwürfe 1*, Gütersloh, 105–148.

Attridge, H. W., 1989, *The Epistle to the Hebrews* (Hermeneia), Philadelphia.

Baltzer, K., 1960, *Das Bundesformular* (WMANT 4), Neukirchen–Vluyn.

Bammel, E., 1971/72, 'The Baptist in Early Christian Traditions', *NTS* 18, 95–128.

Barnikol, E., 1956/57, 'Das Fehlen der Taufe in den Quellenschhriften der Apostelgeschichte und in den Urgemeinden der Hebräer und Hellenisten', *WZ* (Halle) 6, 593–610.

Barrett, C. K., 1947, *The Holy Spirit and the Gospel Tradition*, London.

Barrett, C. K., 1962, *A Commentary on the Epistle to the Romans* (BNTC), London.

Barrett, C. K., 1971, *The First Epistle to the Corinthians* (BNTC), London, 2nd ed.

Barrett, C. K., 1978, *The Gospel According to St. John. An Introduction with Commentary and Notes on the Greek Text*, London, 2nd ed.

Barth, G., 1960, 'Das Gesetzesverständnis des Evangelisten Matthäus', in: G. Bornkamm, G. Barth, H. J. Held (ed.), *Überlieferung und Auslegung im Matthäusevangelium* (WMANT), Neukirchen–Vluyn, 54–154.

Barth, G., 1973, 'Zwei vernachlässigte Gesichtspunkte zum Verständnis der Taufe im Neuen Testament', *ZThK* 70, 137–161.

Barth, G., 1981, *Die Taufe in frühchristlicher Zeit* (BThSt 4), Neukirchen–Vluyn.

Barth, G., 1983, 'πίστις κτλ', *EWNT* 3, 216–231.

Barth, K., 1967, *Das christliche Leben (Fragment). Die Taufe als Begründung des christlichen Lebens* (Kirchliche Dogmatik 4/4), Zürich.

Barth, M., 1951, *Die Taufe – ein Sakrament? Ein exegetischer Beitrag zum Gespräch über die kirchliche Taufe*, Zürich.

Barth, M., 1974, *Ephesians. Translation and Commentary* 1–2 (AncB 34A), Doubleday, Garden City, New York.

Beasley-Murray, G. R., 1962, *Baptism in the New Testament*, London.

Becker, J., 1964, *Das Heil Gottes* (StUNT 3) Göttingen.

Becker, J., 1972, *Johannes der Täufer und Jesus von Nazareth* (BSt 63), Neukirchen-Vluyn.

Becker, J., 1976a, *Auferstehung der Toten im Urchristentum* (SBS 82), Stuttgart.

Becker, J., 1976b, 'Der Brief an die Galater', in H. Conzelmann, G. Friedrich, *Die Briefe an die Galater, Epheser, Philipper, Kolosser, Thessalonicher und Philemon* (NTD 8), Göttingen, 1–85.

Becker, J., 1979–81, *Das Evangelium nach Johannes* (ÖTBK 4), Gütersloh, Würzburg.

Behm, J., 1942, 'νοέω', *ThWNT* 4, 947–976, 985–1016.

Benoit, A., 1953, *Le baptême chrétien au second siècle* (EHPhR 43), Paris.

Betz, H. D., 1979, *Galatians. A Commentary on Paul's Letter to the Churches in Galatia* (Hermeneia), Philadelphia.

Betz, H. D., 1995, 'Transferring a Ritual: Paul's Interpretation of Baptism in Romans 6', in T. Engberg-Pedersen (ed.), *Paul in his Hellenistic Context*, Minneapolis, 84–118.

Bietenhard, H., 1954, 'ὄνομα', *ThWNT* 5, 242–283.

Billerbeck, P., *see* Strack H. L., Billerbeck P.

Böcher, O., 1988, 'Johannes der Täufer', TRE 17, 172–181.

Bornkamm, G., 1938, 'Die neutestamentliche Lehre von der Taufe', *ThBl* 17, 42–52.

Bornkamm, G., 1952, 'Taufe und neues Leben bei Paulus', in *Das Ende des Gesetzes. Paulusstudien. Gesammelte Aufsätze 1* (BhEvTh 16), München, 34–50.

Bornkamm, G., 1956, *Jesus von Nazareth* (UB 19), Stuttgart.

Bornkamm, G., 1964, 'Der Auferstandene und der Irdische. Mt 28,16–20', in E. Dinkler (ed.), *Zeit und Geschichte* (FS R. Bultmann), Tübingen, 171–191.

Bornkamm, G., 1971, 'Der Römerbrief als Testament', in *Geschichte und Glaube 2: Gesammelte Aufsätze 4* (BhEvTh 53) München, 120–139.

Bovon, F., 1989, *Das Evangelium nach Lukas 1* (EKK 3/1), Zürich, Neukirchen–Vluyn.

Brandt, A. J. H. W., 1891, 'Onoma en de Doopsformule in het Nieuwe Testament', *ThT* 25, 565–610.

Braumann, G., 1962, *Vorpaulinische christliche Taufverkündigung bei Paulus* (BWANT 5:2), Stuttgart.

Braun, H., 1953, 'Entscheidende Motive in den Berichten über die Taufe Jesu von Markus bis Justin', *ZThK* 50, 39–43.

Braun, H., 1984, *An die Hebräer* (HNT 14), Tübingen.

Brown, R. E., 1966–71, *The Gospel according to John 1–2* (AncB 29, 29 A), Garden City, New York.

Brown, R. E., 1979, *The Community of the Beloved Disciple*, New York, Ramsey, Toronto.

Brown, R. E., 1982, *The Epistles of John* (AncB 30), Garden City, New York.

Brox, N., 1969, *Die Pastoralbriefe* (RNT 7/2), Regensburg.

Brox, N., 1979, *Der erste Petrusbrief* (EKK 21), Zürich, Einsiedeln, Köln, Neukirchen–Vluyn.

Bultmann, R., 1931, *Die Geschichte der synoptischen Tradition* (FRLANT 29), Göttingen, 2nd ed.

Bultmann, R., 1967, 'Bekenntnis- und Liedfragmente im ersten Petrusbrief', in *Exegetica*, Tübingen, 285–297.

Bultmann, R., 1968a, *Theologie des Neuen Testaments*, Tübingen, 4th ed.

Bultmann, R., 1968b, *Das Evangelium des Johannes* (KEK 2.15) Göttingen, 15th ed.

Büchsel, F., 1933, 'παλιγγενεσία', *ThWNT* 1, 685–688.

Campenhausen, H. Frhr. v., 1971, 'Taufen auf den Namen Jesu?', *VigChr* 25, 1–15.

Carlston, C. E., 1992. 'Christology and Church in Matthew', in F. van Segbroeck *et alii* (ed.), *The Four Gospels* (FS F. Neirynck), Leuven, 1283–1304.

Cavallin, H. C. C., 1974, *Life After Death. Paul's Argument for the Resurrection of the Dead in 1 Cor 15. Part I: An Enquiry into the Jewish Background* (CB.NT 7/1), Lund.

Cavallin, H. C. C., 1979, 'Leben nach dem Tode im Spätjudentum und im frühen Christentum: Spätjudentum', in *ANRW* 2:19.1, 240–345.

Chevallier, M. A., 1986, 'L'Apologie du Baptême d'Eau à la Fin du Premier Siècle: Introduction Secondaire de L'Étiologie dans les Récits du Baptême de Jésus', *NTS* 32, 528–543.

Cohen, S. J. D., 1989, 'Crossing the Boundary and Becoming a Jew', *HThR* 82, 13–33.

Cohen, S. J. D., 1990, 'The Rabbinic Conversion Ceremony', *JJS* 41, 177–203.

Conybeare, F. C., 1901, 'The Eusebian Form of the Text Matth. 28,19', *ZNW* 2, 275–288.

Conzelmann, H., 1965/66, 'Paulus und die Weisheit', *NTS* 12, 231–244.

Conzelmann, H., 1967, *Grundriss der Theologie des Neuen Testaments*, München.

Conzelmann, H., 1971, *Geschichte des Urchristentums* (GNT 5), Göttingen.

Conzelmann, H., 1972, *Die Apostelgeschichte* (HNT 7), Tübingen, 2nd ed.

Conzelmann, H., 1981, *Der erste Brief an die Korinther* (KEK 5), Göttingen, 2nd ed.

Cranfield, C. E. B., 1975–79, *A Critical and Exegetical Commentary on the Epistle to the Romans 1–2* (ICC), Edinburgh.

Cullmann, O., 1958, *Die Tauflehre des Neuen Testaments* (AThANT 12), Zürich, 2nd ed.

Cuming, G. J., 1980/81, 'ΕΠΟΤΙΣΘΗΜΕΝ' (1 Corinthians 12.13)', *NTS* 27, 283–285.

Cumont F., 1911, *Die Mysterien des Mithra. Ein Beitrag zur Religionsgeschichte der römischen Kaiserzeit*, Leipzig, 2nd ed.

Dahl, N. A., 1982, 'Dåpsforståelsen i Efeserbrevet', in S. Pedersen (ed.), *Dåben i Ny Testamente* (TeolSt 9), Århus, 141–160.

Dalman, G., 1898, *Die Worte Jesu 1*, Leipzig.

Delling, G., 1961, *Die Zueignung des Heils in der Taufe. Eine Untersuchung zum neutestamentlichen 'Taufen auf den Namen'*, Berlin.

Delling, G., 1963, *Die Taufe im Neuen Testament*, Berlin.

Dibelius, M., 1923, *Der Hirt des Hermas* (HNT, Erg. Bd, Die apost. Väter IV), Tübingen.

Dibelius, M.,1953, *An die Kolosser, Epheser, an Philemon* (HNT 12), rev. by H. Greeven, Tübingen.

Dibelius, M., 1964, *Der Brief des Jakobus* (KEK 15), rev. by H. Greeven, Tübingen.

Dibelius, M., 1966, *Die Pastoralbriefe* (HNT 13), rev. by H. Conzelmann, Tübingen.

Dinkler, E., 1962a, 'Taufe 2', *RGG*, 3rd ed. 6, 627–637.

Dinkler, E., 1962b, 'Die Taufterminologie in 2 Kor 1,21f', in *Neotestamentica et Patristica* (NT.S 6, FS O. Cullmann), Zürich, Tübingen, 173–191.

Dinkler, E., 1974, 'Römer 6,1–14 und das Verhältnis von Taufe und Rechtfertigung bei Paulus', in L. De Lorenzi (ed.), *Battesimo e Giustizia in Rom 6 e 8* (SMBen.BE 2), Rome, 83–126.

Donfried K., 1977, 'False Suppositions in the study of Romans', in K. Donfried (ed.), *The Romans Debate*, Minneapolis, 120–148.

Dunn, J. D. G., 1970, *Baptism in the Holy Spirit* (SBT 2:15), London.

Dunn, J, D. G., 1988, *Romans 1–8* (Word Biblical Commentary 38), Dallas, Texas.

Dunn, J. D. G., 1993, *The Epistle to the Galatians* (BNTC), London.

Dupont, J., 1962, Σὺν χριστῷ, Bruges, Louvain.

Éliade, M., 1949, *Traité d'Histoire des religions*, Paris.

Éliade, M., 1954, *The Myth of the Eternal Return*, New York.

Éliade, M., 1958, *Birth and Rebirth. The Religious Meanings of Initiation in Human Culture*, London.

Éliade, M., 1959, *The Sacred and the Profane*, New York.

Fee, G. D., 1987, *The First Epistle to the Corinthians* (NIC), Grand Rapids.

Felderer, J., 1959, 'Dreifaltigkeit, 5. Systematik', *LThK* 3, 554–560.

Fitzer, G., 1966, 'σφραγίς', *ThWNT* 7, 939–954.

Fitzmyer, J. A., 1981, 'κύριος', *EWNT* 2, 811–820.

Fitzmyer, J. A., 1981–85, *The Gospel according to Luke 1–2. Introduction, Translation, and Notes* (AncB 28), Garden City, New York.

Fitzmyer, J. A., 1993, *Romans. A New Translation with Introduction and Commentary* (AncB 33), New York etc.

Frankemölle, H., 1970, *Das Taufverständnis des Paulus. Taufe, Tod und Auferstehung nach Röm 6* (SBS 47), Stuttgart.

Frid, B., 1986, 'Römer 6,4–5. Εἰς τὸν θάνατον und τῷ ὁμοιώματι τοῦ θανάτου als Schlüssel zu Duktus und Gedankengang in Röm 6,1–11', *BZ* 30, 188–203.

Fuchs, E., 1956, 'Die Frage nach dem historischen Jesus', *ZThK* 53, 210--229.

Furnish, V. P., 1984, *2 Corinthians* (AncB 32 A), Garden City, New York.

Gäumann, N., 1967, *Taufe und Ethik. Studien zu Römer 6* (BEvTh 47), München.

Galling, G., 1956, 'Die Ausrufung des Namens als Rechtsakt in Israel', *ThLZ* 81, 65–70.

Gempf, C., 1993, 'Public Speaking and Published Accounts', in B. W. Winter, A. D. Clarke (ed.), *The Book of Acts in Its Ancient Literary*

Setting (The Book of Acts in Its First Century Setting 1), Grand Rapids, MI, Carlisle, 259–303.

Gennep, A. van, 1909, *Les rites de passage*, Paris.

Gerhardsson, B., 1967/68, 'The Parable of the Sower and its Interpretation', *NTS* 14, 165–193.

Gerhardsson, B., 1973, 'Gottes Sohn als Diener Gottes. Messias, Agape und Himmelsherrschaft nach dem Matthäusevangelium', *StTh* 27, 73–106.

Glasson, T. F., 1945, *The Second Advent*, London.

Gnilka, J., 1971, *Der Epheserbrief* (HThK 10/2), Freiburg, Basel, Wien.

Gnilka, J., 1978–79, *Das Evangelium nach Markus 1–2* (EKK 2), Zürich, Einsiedeln, Köln, Neukirchen–Vluyn.

Gnilka, J., 1980, *Der Kolosserbrief* (HThK 10/1)), Freiburg, Basel, Wien.

Gnilka, J., 1986–88, *Das Matthäusevangelim 1–2* (HThK 1/1–2), Freiburg, Basel, Wien.

Goldammer, K., 1960, *Die Formenwelt des Religiösen. Grundriss der systematischen Religionswissenschaft* (KTA 264), Stuttgart.

Goppelt, L., 1976, *Theologie des Neuen Testaments*, Göttingen.

Goppelt, L., 1978, *Der erste Petrusbrief* (KEK 12/1), Göttingen.

Grässer, E., 1990, *An die Hebräer (Hebr 1–6)* (EKK 17/1), Zürich, Neukirchen-Vluyn.

Graf, F., 1974, *Eleusis und die orphische Dichtung Athens in vorhellenistischer Zeit* (RVV 33), Berlin.

Greenspahn, F. E., 1989, 'Why Prophecy Ceased', *JBL* 108, 37–49.

Grundmann, W., 1971, *Das Evangelium nach Lukas* (ThHK 3), Berlin, 6th ed.

Grundmann, W., 1972, *Das Evangelium nach Matthäus* (ThHK 1), Berlin, 3rd ed.

Haenchen, E., 1968, *Der Weg Jesu. Eine Erklärung des Markus-Evangeliums und der kanonischen Parallelen*, Berlin, 2nd ed.

Haenchen, E., 1977, *Die Apostelgeschichte* (KEK 3), Göttingen, 16th ed.

Haenchen, E., 1980, *Das Johannesevangelium. Ein Kommentar aus den nachgelassenen Manuskripten*, ed. U. Busse, Tübingen.

Hahn, F., 1976, 'Taufe und Rechtfertigung. Ein Beitrag zur paulinischen Theologie in ihrer Vor-und Nachgeschichte', in J. Friedrich, W. Pöhlmann, P. Stuhlmacher (ed.), *Rechtfertigung* (FS E. Käsemann), Tübingen, Göttingen, 95–124.

Halter, H., 1977, *Taufe und Ethos. Eine Untersuchung zu den paulinischen*

Gemeindebriefen im Rahmen des moralphilosophischen Propriumsdiskussion (FThSt 106), Freiburg.

Hamman, A., 1961, La signification de σφραγίς dans le Pasteur d'Hermas, *Stud. Patr.* 4 (TU 79), Berlin, 286–290.

Hartman, L., 1966, *Prophecy Interpreted. The Formation of Some Jewish Apocalyptic Texts and of the Eschatological Discourse Mark 13 par* (CB.NT 1), Lund.

Hartman, L., 1973/74, '"Into the Name of Jesus". A Suggestion concerning the Earliest Meaning of the Phrase', *NTS* 20, 432–440.

Hartman, L., 1974, 'Baptism "Into the Name of Jesus" and Early Christology. Some Tentative Considerations', *StTh* 28, 21–48.

Hartman, L., 1976, 'Taufe, Geist und Sohnschaft. Traditionsgeschichtliche Erwägungen zu Mk 1,9–11 par', in A. Fuchs (ed.), *Jesus in der Verkündigung der Kirche* (StNT), Linz, 89–109.

Hartman, L., 1979, *Asking for a Meaning. A Study of 1 Enoch 1–5* (CB.NT 12), Lund.

Hartman, L., 1980, 'Bundesideologie in und hinter einigen paulinischen Texten', in S. Pedersen (ed.), *Die Paulinische Literatur und Theologie* (TeolSt 7), Århus, Göttingen, 103–118.

Hartman, L., 1985, 'La formule baptismale dans les Actes des Apôtres: quelques observations relatives au style de Luc', in *À cause de l'Évangile* (FS J. Dupont; LeDiv 123), Paris, 727–738.

Hartman, L., 1993, 'Galatians 3:15–4:11 as Part of a Theological Argument on a Practical Issue', in J. Lambrecht (ed.), *The Truth of the Gospel (Galatians 1:1–4:11)* (SMBen.BE 12), Rome, 127–158.

Hartman, L., 1994, 'Obligatory Baptism – but Why? On Baptism in the Didache and in the Shepherd of Hermas', *SEÅ* 59, 127–143.

Hasler, V., 1978, *Die Briefe an Timotheus und Titus (Pastoralbriefe)* (ZBK 12), Zürich.

Haufe, G., 1976, 'Taufe und Heiliger Geist im Urchristentum', *ThLZ* 101, 561–566.

Hay, D. M., 1973, *Glory at the Right Hand. Psalm 110 in Early Christianity* (SBL.MS 18), Nashville, New York.

Hegermann, H., 1988, *Der Brief an die Hebräer* (ThHK 16), Berlin.

Heitmüller, W., 1903, *'Im Namen Jesu'. Eine Sprach- und religionsgeschichtliche Untersuchung zum Neuen Testament, speziell zur altchristlichen Taufe* (FRLANT I:2), Göttingen.

Hellholm, D., 'Enthymemic Argumentation in Paul', in T. Engberg-Pedersen (ed.), *Paul in his Hellenistic Context*, Minneapolis, 119–179.

Hemer, C. J., 1989, *The Book of Acts in the Setting of Hellenistic History* (WUNT 49), Tübingen.

Hengel, M., 1979, *Zur urchristlichen Geschichtsschreibung*, Stuttgart.

Hengel, M., 1989, *The Johannine Question*, London, Philadelphia.

Hoffmann, P., 1966, *Die Toten in Christus. Eine religionsgeschichtliche und exegetische Untersuchung zur paulinischen Eschatologie* (NTA 2), Münster.

Hoffmann, P., 1972, *Studien zur Theologie der Logienquelle* (NTA 8), München.

Hollenbach, P., 1979, 'Social Aspects of John the Baptizer's Preaching Mission in the Context of Palestinian Judaism', *ANRW* 2.19.1, 850–875.

Holtz, G., 1972, *Die Pastoralbriefe* (ThHK 13), Berlin, 3rd ed.

Holtz, T., 1979, *Jesus aus Nazareth*, Berlin.

Horn, F. W., 1992, *Das Angeld des Geistes. Studien zur paulinischen Pneumatologie* (FRLANT 154), Göttingen.

Hughes, J. H., 1972, 'John the Baptist: the Forerunner of God Himself', *NT* 14, 191–218.

Jeremias, J., 1958, *Die Kindertaufe in den ersten vier Jahrhunderten*, Göttingen.

Jeremias, J., 1962, *Nochmals: Die Anfänge der Kindertaufe. Eine Replik auf Kurt Alands Schrift: 'Die Säuglingstaufe im Neuen Testament und in der alten Kirche'* (TEH 101), München.

Jeremias, J., 1966, 'Das tägliche Gebet im Leben Jesu und in der ältesten Kirche', in *Abba. Studien zur neutestamentlichen Theologie und Zeitgeschichte*, Göttingen, 67–80.

Jeremias, J., 1981, 'Die Briefe an Timotheus und Titus', in J. Jeremias, A. Strobel, *Die Briefe an Timotheus und Titus. Der Brief an die Hebräer* (NTD 9), Göttingen, 2nd ed., 1–77.

Jervell, J., 1971, 'Der Brief an Jerusalem. Über Veranlassung und Adresse des Römerbriefs', *StTh* 25, 61–73.

Jervell, J., 1972. *Luke and the People of God. A New Look at Luke-Acts*, Minneapolis.

Käsemann, E., 1960a, 'Eine urchristliche Taufliturgie', in *Exegetische Versuche und Besinnungen 1*, Göttingen, 34–51.

Käsemann E., 1960b, 'Kritische Analyse von Phil 2,5–11', in *Exegetische Versuche und Besinnungen 1*, Göttingen, 51–95.

Käsemann, E., 1964, 'Die Johannesjünger in Ephesus', in *Exegetische Versuche und Besinnungen 2*, Göttingen, 158–168.

Käsemann, E., 1973, *An die Römer* (HNT 8a), Tübingen.

Karpp, H., 1969 (ed.), *Die Busse. Quellen zur Entstehung des altkirchlichen Busswesens*, Zürich.

Karris, R., 1977a, 'Romans 14:1–15:13 and the Occasion of Romans', in K. Donfried (ed.), *The Romans Debate*, Minneapolis, 75–99.

Karris, R., 1977b, 'The Occasion of Romans: A Response to Professor Donfried', in K. Donfried (ed.), *The Romans Debate*, Minneapolis, 149–151.

Kasting, H., 1969, *Die Anfänge der urchristlichen Mission* (BEvTh 55), München.

Kingsbury, J. D., 1974, 'The Composition and Christology of Matt 28:16–20', *JBL* 93, 573–584.

Klos, H., 1970, *Die Sakramente im Johannesvangelium. Vorkommen und Bedeutung von Taufe, Eucharistie und Busse im vierten Evangelium* (SBS 46), Stuttgart.

Knoch, O., 1990, *Der Erste und Zweite Petrusbrief. Der Judasbrief* (RNT), Regensburg.

Koester, H., 1982, *Introduction to the New Testament*, Philadelphia, Berlin, New York.

Kosala, K. Ch. P., 1985, *Taufverständnis und Theologie im ersten Petrusbrief* (Diss. Kiel), Kiel.

Kraeling, C. H., 1951, *John the Baptist*, New York, London.

Kramer, W., 1963, *Christus, Kyrios, Gottessohn. Untersuchungen zu Gebrauch und Bedeutung der christologischen Bezeichnungen bei Paulus und den vorpaulinischen Gemeinden* (AThANT 44), Zürich.

Kretschmar, G., 1970, 'Die Geschichte des Taufgottesdienstes in der alten Kirche', in K. F. Müller, W. Blankenberg (ed.), *Leiturgia 5: Der Taufgottesdienst*, Kassel, 1–348.

Kümmel, W. G., 1969, *Die Theologie des Neuen Testaments nach seinen Hauptzeugen* (GNT 39), Göttingen.

Kuhn, K. G., 1931, 'Rm 6,7', *ZNW* 30, 305–310.

Kuhn, K. G., 1959, 'προσήλυτος', *ThWNT* 6, 727–745.

Kuhn, K. G., Stegemann H., 1963, 'Proselyten', in *PRE Suppl. 9*, 1248–1283.

Kuss, O., 1957–78, *Der Römerbrief 1–3*, Regensburg.

Kuss, O., 1963a, 'Zur vorpaulinischen Tauflehre im Neuen Testament', in *Auslegung und Verkündung 1*, Regensburg, 98–120.

Kuss, O., 1963b, 'Zur Frage einer vorpaulinischen Todestaufe', in *Auslegung und Verkündung 1*, Regensburg,

Lagrange, M.-J., 1929, *Évangile selon saint Marc* (EtB), Paris, 4th ed.

Lamarche, Ch., Le Dû, 1980, *Épître aux Romains 5–8. Structure littéraire et sens*, Paris.

Lampe, G. W. H., 1951, *The Seal of the Spirit. A Study in the Doctrine of Baptism and Confirmation in the New Testament and the Fathers*, London.

Lang, F., 1959, 'πῦρ', *ThWNT* 6, 927–953.

Lang, F., 1986, *Die Briefe an die Korinther* (NTD 7), Göttingen, Zürich.

Lange, J., 1973, *Das Erscheinen des Auferstandenen im Evangelium nach Matthäus. Eine traditions- und redaktionsgeschichtliche Untersuchung zu Mt 28,16–20* (FzB 11), Würzburg.

Larsson, E., 1962, *Christus als Vorbild. Eine Untersuchung zu den paulinischen Tauf- und Eikontexten* (ASNU 22), Lund, Copenhagen.

Leaney, A. R. C., 1966, *A Commentary on the Gospel according to St Luke* (BNTC), London, 2nd ed.

Leenhardt, F. J., 1944, *Le baptême chrétien* (CThAP 4), Neuchâtel, Paris.

Leeuw, G. van der, 1956, *Phänomenologie der Religion*, Tübingen, 2nd ed.

Legasse, S., 1993, *Naissance du baptême* (LeDiv 153), Paris.

Leipoldt, J., 1928, *Die urchristliche Taufe im Lichte der Religionsgeschichte*, Leipzig.

Lentzen-Deis, F., 1970, *Die Taufe Jesu nach den Synoptikern* (FTS 4), Frankfurt a. M.

Leroy, H., 1978, *Jesus. Überlieferung und Deutung* (EdF 95), Darmstadt (repr. 1989).

Lindars, B., 1961, *New Testament Apologetic. The Doctrinal Significance of Old Testament Quotations*, London.

Lindeskog, G., 1983, 'Johannes der Täufer. Einige Randbemerkungen zum heutigen Stand der Forschung', *ASTI* 12, 55–83.

Lohfink, G., 1976, 'Der ursprung der christlichen Taufe', *ThQ* 156, 35–54.

Lohse, E., 1973, 'Taufe und Rechtfertigung bei Paulus', in *Die Einheit des Neuen Testaments. Exegetische Studien zur Theologie des Neuen Testaments*, Göttingen, 228–244.

Lohse, E., 1977, *Die Briefe an die Kolosser und an Philemon* (KEK 9:2), Göttingen, 2nd ed.

Lüdemann, G., 1989, *Early Christianity according to the Traditions in Acts. A Commentary*, London.

Luz, U., 1985–90, *Das Evangelium nach Matthäus 1–2* (EKK 1), Zürich, Einsiedeln, Köln, Neukirchen–Vluyn.

Maddox, R., 1982, *The Purpose of Luke–Acts* (Stud. of the NT and its world), Edinburgh.

Marcus, J., 1995, 'Jesus' Baptismal Vision', *NTS* 41, 512–521.

Marxsen, W., 1964, 'Erwägungen zur neutestamentlichen Begründung der Taufe', in *Apophoreta* (FS E. Haenchen, BZNW 30), Berlin, 169–177.

Meeks, W. A., 1983, *The First Urban Christians. The Social World of the Apostle Paul*, New York, London.

Meier, J. P., 1994, *A Marginal Jew. Rethinking the Historical Jesus 2* (AncB Reference Library), New York, London etc.

Merklein, H., 1981a, 'Paulinische Theologie in der Rezeption des Kolosser- und Epheserbriefes', in K. Kertelge (ed.), *Paulus in den neutestamentlichen Spätschriften. Zur Paulusrezeption im Neuen Testament* (QD 89), Freiburg, Basel, Vienna, 25–69.

Merklein, H., 1981b, 'μετάνοια', *EWNT* 2, 1022–1031.

Merklein, H., 1990, 'Gericht und Heil. Zur heilsamen Funktion des Gerichts bei Johannes dem Täufer, Jesus und Paulus', *JBTh* 5, 71–92.

Michel, O., 1963, *Der Brief an die Römer* (KEK 4), Göttingen, 12th ed.

Michel, O., 1966, *Der Brief an die Hebräer* (KEK 13), Göttingen, 6th ed.

Mitchell, N., 1995, 'Baptism in the *Didache*', in C. N. Jefford (ed.), *The Didache in Context. Essays on Its Text, History and Transmission*, Leiden, New York, Köln, 226–255.

Müller, P., 1988, *Anfänge der Paulusschule. Dargestellt am zweiten Thessalonicherbrief und am Kolosserbrief* (AThANT 74), Zürich.

Müller, P.-G., 'Die jüdische Entscheidung gegen Jesus nach der Apostelgeschichte', in J. Kremer (ed.), *Les Actes des Apôtres. Traditions, rédaction, théologie* (BEThL 48), Paris, Gembloux, Louvain, 523–531.

Murphy-O'Connor, J., 1981, 'Baptized for the Dead (1 Cor XV, 29), a Corinthian Slogan?', *RB* 88, 532–543.

Mussner, F., 1964, *Der Jakobusbrief* (HThK 13/1), Freiburg, Basel, Vienna.

Mussner, F., 1974, *Der Brief an die Galater* (HThK 9), Freiburg, Basel, Vienna.

Mussner, F., 1982, *Der Brief an die Epheser* (ÖTBK 10), Gütersloh, Würzburg.

Nepper-Christensen, P., 1985, 'Die Taufe im Matthäusevangelium', *NTS* 31, 189–207.

Neugebauer, F., 1974/75, 'Die Davidssohnfrage (Mark xii.35–37 parr.) und der Menschensohn', *NTS* 21, 81–108.

Niederwimmer, K., 1989, *Die Didache* (Kommentar zu den apostolischen Vätern 1), Göttingen 1989

Nijendijk, L. W., 1986, *Die Christologie des Hirten des Hermas, exegetisch, religions- und dogmengeschichtlich untersucht*, Utrecht.

Nissilä K., 1979, *Das Hohepriestermotiv im Hebräerbrief. Eine exegetische Untersuchung* (SESJ 33), Helsinki.

Noack, B., 1982, 'Dåben i Didake', in S. Pedersen (ed.), *Dåben i Ny Testamente* (TeolSt 9), Århus, 246–265.

Nolland, J., 1989, *Luke 1–9:20* (Word Biblical Commentary 35A), Dallas, Texas.

Oepke, A., 1933, 'βάπτω' *ThWNT* 1, 527–544.

Olsson, B., 1987, 'The History of the Johannine Movement', in L. Hartman, B. Olsson (ed.), *Aspects on the Johannine Literature. Papers Presented at a Conference of Scandinavian New Testament Exegetes at Uppsala, June 16–19, 1986* (CB.NT 18) Uppsala, 27–43.

O'Toole, R. F., 1993, 'Reflections on Luke's Treatment of the Jews in Luke–Acts', *Bib* 74, 529–555.

Perlitt, L., 1969, *Bundestheologie im Alten Testament* (WMANT 36), Neukirchen–Vluyn.

Pernveden, L., 1966, *The Concept of the Church in the Shepherd of Hermas* (STL 27), Lund.

Perrin, N., 1967, *Rediscovering the Teaching of Jesus*, London.

Pesch, R., 1970, 'Anfang des Evangeliums Jesu Christi. Eine Studie zum Prolog des Markusevangeliums (Mk 1,1–15)', in G. Bornkamm, K. Rahner (ed.), *Die Zeit Jesu* (FS H. Schlier), Freiburg, Basel, Vienna, 108–144.

Pesch, R., 1976–77, *Das Markusevangelium 1–2* (HThK 2), Freiburg, Basel, Vienna.

Pesch, R., 1986, *Die Apostelgeschichte 1–2* (EKK 5), Zürich, Einsiedeln, Köln, Neukirchen–Vluyn.

Peterson, D., 1993, 'The Motif of Fulfilment and the Purpose of Luke-Acts', in B. W. Winter, A. D. Clarke (eds.), *The Book of Acts in Its Ancient Literary Setting (The Book of Acts in Its First Century Setting 1)*, Grand Rapids, Carlisle, 83–104.

Peterson, E., 1955, 'Die Taufe im acherusischen See', *VigChr* 9, 1–20.

Plümacher, E., 1972, *Lukas als hellenistischer Schriftsteller. Studien zur Apostelgeschichte* (StUNT 9), Göttingen.

Pokorný, P., 1980/81, 'Christologie et Baptême à l'Époque du Christianisme Primitif', *NTS* 27, 368–380.

Pokorný, P., 1984, *Die Entstehung der Christologie. Voraussetzungen einer Theologie des Neuen Testaments*, Stuttgart.

Pokorný, P., 1987, *Der Brief des Paulus an die Kolosser* (ThHK X/1), Berlin.

Poschmann, B., 1940, *Paenitentia secunda* (Theoph. 1), Bonn.

Quasten, J., 1950, *Patrology 1*, Utrecht, Brussels.

Quesnel, M., 1985, *Baptisés dans l'Esprit. Baptême et Esprit Saint dans les Actes des Apôtres* (LeDiv 120), Paris.

Ratschow, C. H., 1962, 'Waschungen', *RGG*, 3rd ed. 6, 1549.

Reitzenstein, R., 1927, *Die hellenistischen Mysterienreligionen nach den Grundgedanken und Wirkungen*, Berlin, 3rd ed.

Reitzenstein, R., 1929, *Die Vorgeschichte der christlichen Taufe*, Leipzig.

Rissi, M., 1962, *Die Taufe für die Toten* (AThANT 42), Zürich.

Robinson, J. A. T., 1957, *Jesus and His Coming. The Emergence of a Doctrine*, London.

Rogers, E., R., 1983, 'ΕΠΟΤΙΣΘΗΜΕΝ Again', *NTS* 29, 139–142.

Roloff, J., 1981, *Die Apostelgeschichte* (NTD 5), Göttingen.

Roloff, J., 1988, *Der erste Brief an Timotheos* (EKK 15), Zürich, Neukirchen–Vluyn.

Rordorf, W., 1973, 'La rémission des péchés selon la Didachè', *Irén.* 46, 283–297.

Rordorf, W., 1972, 'Le baptême selon la Didachè', in *Mélanges liturgiques . . . B. Botte*, Louvain, 499–509.

Rudolph, K., 1981, *Antike Baptisten* (SSAW Phil.–hist. Kl. 121/4), Berlin.

Rusam, D., 1992, 'Neue Belege zu den στοιχεῖα τοῦ κόσμου (Gal 4,3.9; Kol 2,8.20)', *ZNW* 83, 119–125.

Sabbe, M., 1967, 'Le baptême de Jésus', in I. de la Potterie (ed.), *De Jésus aux Évangiles* (FS J. Coppens; BEThL 25), Gembloux, Paris, 184–211.

Sampley, J. P., 1971, *'And the Two Shall Become One Flesh': A Study of Traditions in Ephesians 5:21–33* (MSSNTS 16), Cambridge.

Sanders, E. P., 1966, 'Literary Dependence in Colossians', *JBL* 85, 28–45.

Sanders, E. P., 1977, *Paul and Palestinian Judaism. A Comparison of Patterns of Religion*, London.

Sanders, J. T., 1987, *The Jews in Luke-Acts*, London, Philadelphia.

Schelkle, K. H., 1961, *Die Petrusbriefe. Der Judasbrief* (HThK 13/2), Freiburg, Basel, Vienna.

Schenk, W., 1990, *Lima-Ökumene als Gegenaufklärung und Gegenreformation* (FThL 19), Bonn.

Schenke, H.-M., 1974/75, 'Das Weiterwirken des Paulus und die Pflege seines Erbes durch die Paulus-Schule', *NTS* 21, 505–518.

Schille, G., 1960, 'Katechese und Taufliturgie', *ZNW* 51, 112–131.

Schille, G., 1965, *Frühchristliche Hymnen*, Berlin.

Schlier, H., 1963, *Der Brief an die Epheser. Ein Kommentar*, Düsseldorf, 4th ed.

Schlier, H., 1977, *Der Römerbrief* (HThK 6), Freiburg, Basel, Vienna.

Schnackenburg, R., 1950, *Das Heilsgeschehen bei der Taufe nach dem Apostel Paulus. Eine Studie zur paulinischen Theologie* (MThS 1), München.

Schnackenburg, R., 1965–84, *Das Johannesevangelium 1–4* (HThK 4), Freiburg, Basel, Vienna.

Schnackenburg, R., 1971, 'Todes- und Leidensgemeinschaft mit Christus. Neue Studien zu Röm 6,1–11', in *Schriften zum Neuen Testament*, Münster, 361–391.

Schnackenburg, R., 1982, *Der Brief an die Epheser* (EKK 10), Zürich, Einsiedeln, Köln, Neukirchen–Vluyn.

Schneider, G., 1977, *Das Evangelium nach Lukas* (ÖTBK 3), Gütersloh, Würzburg.

Schneider, G., 1981, 'μαρανα θα', *EWNT* 2, 947–948.

Schneider, G., 1980–82, *Die Apostelgeschichte 1–2* (HThK 5), Freiburg, Basel, Vienna.

Schneider, J., 1952, *Die Taufe im Neuen Testament*, Stuttgart.

Schneider, J., 1960, 'Der historische Jesus und die urchristliche Taufe', in H. Ristow, K. Matthiae (ed.), *Der historische Jesus und der kerygmatische Christus*, Berlin, 530–542.

Schnelle, U., 1983, *Gerechtigkeit und Christusgegenwart. Vorpaulinische und paulinische Tauftheologie* (GTA 24), Göttingen.

Schnelle, U., 1987, *Antidoketische Christologie im Johannesevangelium. Eine Untersuchung zur Stellung des vierten Evangeliums in der johanneischen Schule* (FRLANT 144), Göttingen.

Schrage, W., 1980, 'Ist die Kirche das "Abbild seines Todes"? Zu Röm 6.5', in D. Lührmann, G. Strecker (ed.), *Kirche* (FS G. Bornkamm), Tübingen, 205–220.

Schrage, W., 1991, *Der erste Brief an die Korinther 1* (EKK 7/1), Zürich, Neukirchen-Vluyn.

Schürer E., 1973–87, *The History of the Jewish People in the Age of Jesus Christ (175 B.C.–A.D. 135). A New English Version Revised and Edited by G. Vermes, F. Miller, M. Black 1–3*, Edinburgh.

Schürmann, H., 1969, *Das Lukasevangelium 1* (HThK 3/1), Freiburg, Basel, Vienna.

Schweizer, E., 1959, 'πνεῦμα', *ThWNT* 6, 387–453.

Schweizer, E., 1970, 'Die "Mystik" des Sterbens und Auferstehens mit Christus bei Paulus', *Beiträge zur Theologie des Neuen Testaments. Neutestamentliche Aufsätze (1955–1970)*, Zürich, 183–203.

Schweizer, E., 1973, *Das Evangelium nach Matthäus* (NTD 2), Göttingen.

Schweizer, E., 1976, *Der Brief an die Kolosser* (EKK 12), Zürich, Einsiedeln, Köln, Neukirchen–Vluyn.

Schweizer, E., 1982, *Das Evangelium nach Lukas* (NTD 3), Göttingen.

Schweizer, E., 1988, 'Slaves of the Elements and Worshippers of Angels: Gal 4:3, 9 and Col 2:8, 18, 20', *JBL* 107, 455–468.

Segelberg, E., 1982., 'Masbuta. Studien zum Ritual der mandäischen Taufe', in G. Widengren (ed.), *Der Mandäismus* (WdF 167), Darmstadt, 115–24.

Siber, P., 1971, *Mit Christus leben. Eine Studie zur paulinischen Auferstehungshoffnung* (AThANT 61), Zürich.

Sint, A., 1964, 'Die Eschatologie des Täufers, die Täufergruppen und die Polemik der Evangelisten', in K. Schubert (ed.), *Vom Messias zu Christus*, Freiburg, Vienna, Basel, 55–163.

Sjöberg, E., 1938, *Gott und die Sünder im palästinischen Judentum nach dem Zeugnis der Tannaiten und der apokalyptisch-pseudepigraphischen Literatur* (BWANT 4,27), Stuttgart.

Stanton, G. N., 1989, *The Gospels and Jesus* (Oxford Bible Series), Oxford.

Stegemann, H., 1993, *Die Essener, Qumran, Johannes der Täufer und Jesus. Ein Sachbuch*, Freiburg, Basel, Vienna.

Stendahl, K., 1976, *Paul Among Jews and Christians*, Philadelphia.

Stommel, E., 1959, 'Christliche Taufriten und antike Baderiten', *JAC* 2, 5–14.

Stowasser, M., 1992, *Johannes der Täufer im Vierten Evangelium. Eine Untersuchung zu seiner Bedeutung für die johanneische Gemeinde* (ÖBS 12), Klosterneuburg.

Strack, H. L., Billerbeck, P., 1922–28, *Kommentar zum Neuen Testament aus Talmud und Midrasch 1–4*, München.

Strecker, G., 1966, *Der Weg der Gerechtigkeit. Untersuchungen zur Theologie des Matthäus* (FRLANT 82), Göttingen, 2nd ed.

Tannehill, R. C., 1967, *Dying and Rising with Christ. A Study in Pauline Theology* (BZNW 32), Berlin.

Taylor, V., 1966, *The Gospel according to St Mark*, Melbourne, Toronto.

Thiering, B. E., 1979/80, 'Inner and Outer Cleansing at Qumran as a Background to New Testament Baptism', *NTS* 26, 266–277.

Thiering, B. E., 1980/81, 'Qumran Initiation and New Testament Baptism', *NTS* 27, 615–631.

Thomas, J., 1935, *Le mouvement baptiste en Palestine et Syrie*, Louvain.

Thüsing, W., 1967–68, 'Erhöhungsvorstellung und Parusievorstellung in der ältesten nachösterlichen Christologie', *BZ* 11, 95–108, 205–222; 12, 54–80, 223–240.

Thyen, H., 1964, 'βάπτισμα μετανοίας εἰς ἄφεσιν ἁμαρτιῶν', in E. Dinkler (ed.), *Zeit und Geschichte* (FS R. Bultmann), Tübingen, 97–125.

Thyen, H., 1970, *Studien zur Sündenvergebung im Neuen Testament und seinen alttestamentlichen und jüdischen Voraussetzungen* (FRLANT 96), Göttingen.

Towner, P. H., 1986, 'The Present Age in the Eschatology of the Pastoral Epistles', *NTS* 32, 427–448.

Trilling, W., 1959, 'Die Täufertradition bei Matthäus', *BZ* 3, 271–289.

Trilling, W., 1964, *Das wahre Israel. Studien zur Theologie des Matthäus-Evangeliums* (StANT 10), München, 3rd ed.

Trummer, P., 1978, *Die Paulustradition der Pastoralbriefe* (BET 8), Frankfurt, Bern, Las Vegas.

Übelacker, W., 1989, *Der Hebräerbrief als Appell. Untersuchungen zu exordium, narratio und postscriptum (Hebr 1–2 und 13,22–25)* (CB.NT 21), Stockholm.

Unnik, W. C. van, 1979, 'Luke's Second Book and the Rules of Hellenistic Historiography', in J. Kremer (ed.), *Les Actes des Apôtres. Traditions, rédaction, théologie* (BEThL 48), Paris, Gembloux, Louvain, 37–60.

Vielhauer Ph., 1959, 'Johannes der Täufer', *RGG*, 3rd ed., 804–808.

Vielhauer, Ph., 1975, *Geschichte der urchristlichen Literatur. Einleitung in das Neue Testament, die Apokryphen und die Apostolischen Väter*, Berlin, New York.

Vögtle, A., 1936, *Die Tugend- und Lasterkataloge im Neuen Testament* (NTA 16/4,5), Münster.

Wagner, G., 1962, *Das religionsgeschichtliche Problem von Römer 6,1–11* (AThANT 39), Zürich, Stuttgart.

Wedderburn, A. J. M., 1983, 'Hellenistic Christian Traditions in Romans 6?', *NTS* 29, 337–355.

Wedderburn, A. J. M., 1987, *Baptism and Resurrection. Studies in Pauline Theology against Its Graeco-Roman Background* (WUNT 44), Tübingen.

Weiser, A., 1981–85, *Die Apostelgeschichte* (ÖTBK 5,1–2), Gütersloh, Würzburg.

Weiss, H.-F., 1973, 'Taufe und neues Leben im deuteropaulinschen Schrifttum', in E. Schott (ed.), *Taufe und neue Existenz*, Berlin, 53–70.

Weiss, H.-F., 1991, *Der Brief an die Hebräer* (KEK 13), Göttingen.

Wibbing, S., 1959, *Die Tugend- und Lasterkataloge im Neuen Testament und ihre Traditionsgeschichte* (BZNW 25), Berlin.

Widengren G., 1969, *Religionsphänomenologie*, Berlin.

Widengren G., 1982, 'Einleitung', in G. Widengren (ed.), *Der Mandäismus* (WdF 169), Darmstadt, 1–17.

Wilckens, U., 1974, *Die Missionsreden der Apostelgeschichte* (WMANT 5), Neukirchen–Vluyn, 3rd ed.

Wilckens, U., 1978–82, *Der Brief an die Römer 1–3* (EKK 6,1–3), Zürich, Einsiedeln, Köln.

Windisch, H., 1908, *Taufe und Sünde im ältesten Urchristentum bis auf Origenes*, Tübingen.

Wink, W., 1968, *John the Baptist in the Gospel Tradition* (MSSNTS 7), Cambridge.

Wolff, C., 1982, *Der erste Brief des Paulus an die Korinther 2* (ThHK 7/2), Berlin, 2nd ed.

Wolff, H. W., 1951, 'Das Thema "Umkehr" in der alttestamentlichen Prophetie', *ZThK* 48, 121–148.

Wolff, H. W., 1961, 'Das Kerygma des deuteronomistischen Geschichtswerks', *ZAW* 73, 171–186.

Index of ancient references

Other Early Christian Writings

Other Authors from Antiquity

Index of modern authors